HOUSING, HOME OWNERSHIP AND SOCIAL CHANGE IN HONG KONG

For Angela & Lyndon

Housing, Home Ownership and Social Change in Hong Kong

JAMES LEE

Ashgate

Aldershot • Brookfield USA • Singapore • Sydney

Published by
Ashgate Publishing Ltd
Gower House
Croft Road
Aldershot
Hants GU11 3HR
England

Ashgate Publishing Company
Old Post Road
Brookfield
Vermont 05036
USA

Ashgate website: http://www.ashgate.com

British Library Cataloguing in Publication Data
Lee, James Z., 1952-
    Housing, home ownership and social change in Hong Kong. -
    (Social & political studies from Hong Kong)
    1. Home ownership - China - Hong Kong
    I. Title
    363.5'83

Library of Congress Catalog Card Number: 99-76349

ISBN 1 84014 562 5

Printed in Great Britain by
Antony Rowe Ltd, Chippenham, Wiltshire

Contents

Figures and Tables

Acknowledgements

This book is an outgrowth of my doctoral studies in the then School for Advanced Urban Studies (SAUS) in the University of Bristol. As a post-graduate student, it was probably one of the best intellectual environments I have ever come across. Some of the themes I developed in this book benefited enormously from those seminars I was fortunate enough to attend in the early 1990s at SAUS.

There are a number of people to whom I feel particularly indebted. Professor Ray Forrest is my mentor and a close friend who patiently guided me through the maze of urban policy and housing research. Professor Alan Murie, whose incisive criticisms as my external examiner and my subsequent engagements with him in the City University of Hong Kong provided me with tremendous insights into the relationship between state, society and housing. Professor James Midgley of Berkeley, University of California, my former teacher in LSE, who has never failed to encourage me to publish.

Special thanks must go to a few best friends who helped me enormously in one way or the other in coming to terms with publishing this book. K.W. Chan, whose knowledge in housing sociology and information technology has encouraged me to take on the challenge of submitting a manuscript. T.K. Lee provided me with constructive comments on my early manuscript. There are a number of best friends, Hans Meusen, Paul Burton, Chris Lambert and Tricia Kennet, whose friendship has enabled me to suffer less from those 'doctoral diseases'.

I am extremely grateful for editorial help from my friend Margaret Yau, and Yau Man Siu who kindly volunteered to edit my earlier drafts.

Finally, I am deeply indebted to my family for their support. Without them, this project would have been impossible.

Exchange Rate

Unless otherwise specified, all currency referred to in the book is in Hong
  Kong dollars (HK$)
1 British Pound = approximately HK$12.5 in 1999
1 US dollar = approximately HK$7.75 in 1999

Part One

THEORY AND METHOD

1 Introduction

This study starts with three simple observations of the housing scene in Hong Kong in the recent two decades. First, house price inflation in Hong Kong has been extremely phenomenal. At the peak in mid-1997, average house price of a 500 square feet flat was 15 times of the price in 1980. Even after the Asian economic crisis, house price in mid-1999 is still twice as much as houses in the Silicon Valley, the most expensive house price regime in USA. Why is there such phenomenal growth in house prices? Second, while housing is not affordable for many, Hong Kong sees many middle class people craving for home buying, mobilizing all kinds of financial resources they can lay their hands on, including hard earned money from their parents. Third, buying and selling of homes has become an extremely important part of middle class life in Hong Kong. Many people have made substantial capital gains through home purchase. There are claims that in Hong Kong everyone is addicted to a home buying culture. To what extent are these observations true and what are their social implications?

These initial observations on the Hong Kong housing system form the basis of the current study. However, the rationale of the study emanates from a fundamental concern with the way housing studies have hitherto been developed. Over the last three decades, housing sociologists have developed keen interest in identifying social processes underlying housing development. Their interests have largely been concerned with the way growth in home ownership has affected consumption and social divisions. One of the key theoretical arguments put forth is that mass home ownership represents a new social division. While this theoretical debate has somehow subsided in recent years, its influence on home ownership studies could not be neglected. This book argues that contemporary housing research has adopted a rather narrow and confining focus, to the extent that it has effectively neglected a number of important social processes, for example, the role of the family, cultural values, and their relation to home ownership. Housing studies rarely confront the question of *place-boundedness*, which implies that the housing system represents the result of a complex system of interactions between the individual, the family, the state, the housing market and the society over time. Housing theories were often applied uncritically across national boundaries, to the extent that they hindered the development of a fuller body of research – one that is more sensitive to local culture and specificity (Williams, 1983; Ball, Harloe & Martens, 1988). Although some researchers have sought to remedy this deficiency at some point, development to this end has remained relatively weak (Dickens, Duncan, Goodwin & Gray, 1985, Forrest & Murie 1995).

One purpose of this study is to bring back the discussion of the role of family and culture into the main stream discussion of home ownership and social change. In this respect, Hong Kong is taken to be a case analysis since the city offers a good example of cultural and institutional diversity between the East and the West. This then leads us back to the primary focus of this book - home ownership and social change. The transformation of Hong Kong from a predominantly public rental tenure to burgeoning home ownership represents the most dramatic post-war social change. The shifting tenure and the vibrant housing market have profoundly transformed Hong Kong's urban structure and the political economy. Anyone walking around the Eastern District, Hong Kong Island, or strolling along the promenade of Tsim Sha Tsui, Kowloon Peninsula, could easily notice the massive urban transformation of the built environment. This book explores how the growth of owner-occupation in recent decades have been affected by both societal and policy shifts. How owner-occupation as an emerging tenure has impacted upon social life and opportunities? How individual housing experiences have come to be shaped by societal forces? In sum, it is about the complex relationship between a shifting housing sector within a rapidly changing society.

This study also arises out of a discontent with the current state of local housing research. For two decades, housing studies have been largely dominated by economic geography and traditional social policy analysis focusing largely on the public housing sector. Little research has been devoted to home ownership. In addition, traditional local housing policy analyses have been largely confined to the housing sector itself and rarely situate the housing question in a wider social context. It is argued that Hong Kong needs a radically new focus on housing research by re-instituting home ownership studies into local housing studies.

Organization of the Book

Following the Introduction, Chapter two provides a general mapping of the social, economic, and political restructuring processes that have taken place in Hong Kong over the past two decades and examines in detail how they bear upon the main focus of this book. The chapter revolves around three issues: (1) the loss of legitimacy in governance by the receding colonial government before 1997; (2) the economic restructuring of Hong Kong from a manufacturing-centred economy to a service-based economy since the 1980s; and (3) the emergence of the middle class as a major contender for housing resources. The chapter concludes by posing the housing question as having both an economic as well as a social root. It is suggested that local housing research has thus far been largely dominated by economics and related studies based on rationality to the extent that social explanations of the housing question are often undermined or trivialized by economic explanations.

Chapter three describes the structure of housing research in Hong Kong as well as the social organization of housing and home ownership. The aim of the chapter is to provide a socio-spatial mapping of the housing situation. Given the fact that owner-occupation is a relatively recent phenomenon, it is argued that the middle class is facing the greatest challenge in meeting their housing needs. The chapter also demonstrates that housing research thus far has been much biased towards a uni-focus orientation and needs to be properly expanded to cover home ownership. The lack of local home ownership research means more than just a research gap. It is a form of structural hegemony in research tradition aiming at legitimizing the role of the government in housing intervention. As a concluding remark, the chapter briefly introduces the methodological basis of this study and explains why a housing history approach is a preferred method.

Chapter four outlines the contours of contemporary theoretical debates in home ownership in Western literature. I would argue that deeply embedded in the rhetoric of Western housing studies is a social relation of housing that is highly ethnocentric. It is, therefore, necessary to carefully examine the ideological underpinnings of these debates when they are applied to societies with a different cultural background. The chapter examines two broad debates in home ownership: the consumption sector cleavage debate and the meaning of home. Using the work of Bourdieu, the chapter tries to develop a cultural perspective as an alternative theoretical framework.

Chapters one to four together form the backbone of Part One of the book, which attempts to deal with issues surrounding housing policy, home ownership and housing theories as against the socio-political context of Hong Kong in the post-war era. From Chapter five onwards, the book turns to the main body of this study. Empirical results have been organized around three themes: (1) housing history and social values; (2) family and its impact on housing choices and home ownership; and (3) capital gains from home ownership and their impact on the formation of middle class. The purpose of Part Two is to delineate the relationship between home ownership, family and class formation.

To illustrate the importance of an individual's early housing experience and its impact on housing consumption, Chapter five provides a qualitative description of individual housing histories for the period from the 1950s to the 1970s. It goes from inner-city old tenements, squatter huts, to the first resettlement housing estates built by the government. It reveals a housing picture of extreme spatial deprivation. This carries deep impacts on an individual's desire for home ownership.

Chapter six focuses on the relationship between home ownership and the Chinese family. The broad theoretical question being addressed is how important is inter-generation family support in home financing contributes to the development of home ownership. The chapter concludes by challenging some of the traditional assumptions in Western home ownership studies which tend to take family relationships as given and fail to take into account the impact of the family on the desire for home ownership.

Chapter seven takes on board one of the most salient themes of Western home ownership studies - capital accumulation through home ownership. It examines the relationship between middle class formation and wealth accumulation through house price inflation. The findings of this study reveal that, while the wealth accumulation effect of home ownership fragments the middle class, on the whole, it is fair to say that positive wealth accumulation effect of home ownership far outweighs the burden of home financing. It is also argued that the enormous wealth accumulation opportunities of home ownership in the past two decades have exacerbated an already divided middle class. This poses a tremendous threat to the balance of power between various sectors of an already politically fragmented society.

Chapter eight is divided into two sections. The first section re-examines the major findings and debates advanced in this book by linking it to a broader context - housing policy in a small high-growth Asian city.

Based on the discussions surrounding the following four factors: (1) extreme geographical constraints; (2) impact of an individual's housing history, (3) the influence of the Chinese family, and (4) the wealth accumulation effect of home ownership, the chapter examines the social consequences of a home ownership policy in a congested and high-growth city. The second section of the chapter tries to make a preliminary evaluation of the impact of the recent Asian economic crisis on home ownership. It is argued that for a high-growth, export-oriented city like Hong Kong, home ownership has both a stabilizing and destabilizing effect. A housing system so much dependent on home ownership could be highly risky for both the individual and the economy. Hence, the state must take great caution not to adopt any policy measures which, intended or unintended, increase the vulnerability of the housing system. As far as Hong Kong is concerned, the problem lies in the social construction of home ownership as a preferred tenure. It is argued that, within an inherently constrained environment like Hong Kong, housing policy choices are extremely limited. Therefore, it is more a question of what modes of state intervention in housing rather than what is the best tenure choice. The chapter concludes by calling for a thorough re-examination of role of the state in housing.

2 Socio-Political Change, Economic Restructuring and the Housing Question

By Western standard, Hong Kong is not a democracy. Until 1 July 1997, when sovereignty was returned to the People's Republic of China under the Sino-British Agreement, Hong Kong was still very much a British colony in the legal and political sense. The last British-appointed governor, Chris Pattern, reiterated this point all the more clearly during his first two years of governorship in 1994. However, Hong Kong society had undergone tremendous changes in the last two decades. Such changes were unprecedented and had profound impact on social development. While the British government still exercised considerable control in its daily administration of Hong Kong during the transition period, the British colonial legacy was fast fading. In many ways, Hong Kong was already well advanced into Chinese rule before 1997. Major public works projects, such as highway construction, new container terminals and the new airport construction, had to seek the consensus of the Chinese government before they could be effectively implemented. For the ordinary people, the hard fact to swallow was that they must look North instead of West for solutions to their problems. In the decade prior to 1997, political groups were travelling much more frequently to Beijing for consultation on major policy issues rather than looking up to the colonial government for support. In this chapter, I shall demonstrate that ahead of the 1984 Sino-British Agreement, Hong Kong had already set in motion a number of social processes that eventually brought important bearings on the housing market. The combined effects of these processes provided the necessary social conditions in predisposing Hong Kong for an impending housing crisis. In particular, this chapter will examine three processes, namely: (1) political restructuring; (2) economic restructuring; and (3) the emerging middle class. The main argument is that rapid socio-political transformation in the last two decades has greatly affected housing development and home ownership. To unravel the complexity of the Hong Kong housing question, it is necessary to first make explicit these social processes.

The Crisis of Legitimacy: Political Restructuring and the 1997 Question

Hong Kong had never had an elected political leader. Before 1997, the colonial governor, who was appointed by the Queen through the recommendation of the Foreign and Commonwealth Office of the British government, was the Chief Executive of Hong Kong. He was assisted by two councils: the Executive Council and the Legislative Council. The Executive Council, which was composed of appointed members including important heads of government departments and community leaders, claimed to represent important factions of social and economic interests and acted as the central decision-making body of the government. The Legislative Council, which enacts legislation and approves the government budget through its Finance Committee, was composed largely of appointed members from a very exclusive group of business and community leaders. Through a public appointment system, a unique blend of politics called *the politics of administrative absorption*, where the government skillfully screened and absorbed indigenous political leaders into the central decision-making council to ensure political acquiescence, had successfully come to dominate the Hong Kong political arena for the past hundred years (King, 1975).

Indeed, this political structure was what happened before the 1980s. To a great extent, this constituted the backbone of legitimacy for the colonial government before that period. Nonetheless, when the Sino-British Agreement was reached in 1984, both the Chinese and the British governments were well aware that legitimacy was no longer a matter of *administrative absorption* politics. For the Agreement to be widely accepted, there must be new political devices to ensure the continuation of the much needed legitimacy and political stability for a smooth transition in 1997. To achieve this, the first White Paper: *The Future Development of Representative Government in Hong Kong*, was published in 1984. The major recommendation in the White Paper was the introduction of a minimal representative element to the legislature through the introduction of the *functional constituencies*, members of which were indirectly elected through various occupational sectors (e.g., business, banking, engineering, legal and medical professions, etc.). This particular constitutional change was meant to kill two birds with one stone. First, it aimed at achieving political consensus through the introduction of corporatist strategies, but without conceding any diminution of government's authority (Scott, 1989). Second, for a highly sensitive period of Sino-British relations in the post-agreement era, it was thought that minimal changes to the legislature would be welcomed by the Chinese government. Despite all the good intentions, the plan failed to work. The 1984 proposal unintentionally triggered a time bomb in 1987.

The Touchstone of Post-agreement Politics: The 1987 Review on Direct Elections

One of the recommendations of the 1984 White Paper suggested that direct elections on a geographical constituency base might be considered in the 1987 Review. This created both political obligations for the government as well as high hopes amongst emerging liberal political groups. In 1987, the government published a Green Paper to seek the views of the community on how a system of representative government should be further developed. This marked the climax of three years of fervent political debates, where liberal political groups seized the opportunity to advance the ideas of direct elections to the legislature. A White Paper was finally published in February 1988, outlining the political development up to 1991. The essence of the paper as it stood, with absolutely no elements of direct elections until 1991, was considered highly conservative. It met with strong opposition from liberal political groups. At the same time, the Chinese government had consistently made clear its distaste for a Western style democracy and did not support any form of direct elections before 1991. Meanwhile, social unrest, mainly in the form of student protests, began to rise in China, which finally led to the 'June 4th Event' in Beijing in 1989. Political movements in China during that period invariably carried immense significance for officials of the Chinese government in Hong Kong. By and large they responded negatively to local political development. Political onslaughts through the media by Chinese officials in Hong Kong began to target liberal political leaders with smear tactics.[1]

The social effects of political debates up to the 1987 Review can be summarized in three points: (1) it became clear to the Hong Kong government that her sure-footed legitimacy of ruling through a long established elitist model of politics was beginning to crumble; (2) it also became clear that, to maintain stability of the system, direct elections to the legislature must be hastened in order to depressurize pent-up political demands from emerging political groups; and (3) in the transitional period, Hong Kong must be able to maintain her political integrity by not yielding to undue pressure from the Chinese government. Hence, the government must act swiftly. However, the Hong Kong government's maiden political venture into democratic elections in the 1990s turned out to be a highly tricky business. Subsequent events proved that the Chinese government was extremely annoyed and displeased with the ambivalent stand which the British and the Hong Kong governments adopted on direct elections. In April 1987, Deng Xiaoping made a major speech to the Basic Law Drafting Committee, setting out clearly a baseline to the meaning of democracy and the meaning of *Hong Kong self rule* as perceived by the Chinese government, and hoping also to put an end to growing discontent amongst local liberal groups. Deng said:

> If some problems arise in Hong Kong someday which cannot be solved without the central authorities taking the matter up, we shall take that up. When something happened in the past, Britain also took the matter up! There are certain things that can hardly be solved without the central authorities taking the matter up. The central authorities will not infringe upon Hong Kong's interests with their policies and hope that things infringing upon the interests of Hong Kong will not happen. Therefore, I ask you to give consideration to these aspects in the Basic Law. After 1997, if there are certain people in Hong Kong who curse the Chinese Communist Party and China, we shall allow them to do so. However, it is not allowed to turn curses into actions and turn Hong Kong into a base for opposing the mainland under the cloak of democracy. If that ever happens, we shall have to interfere. We do not necessarily have to call out the People's Liberation Army. Only when great turmoil happens will the garrison troops be summoned (Wen Hui Bao Daily, 17 April 1987).

Nonetheless, what happened from 1987 to 1989 in both Hong Kong and China marked a further departure from consensus and confidence as enshrined in Deng's words. Indeed, what happened in June 1989 in Beijing had almost eradicated those efforts of political assurance made by the British and Chinese governments since 1984 to produce an acceptable blue print in the form of a Basic Law for the people of Hong Kong. Tripartite interventions between Britain, China and Hong Kong to appease the public only resulted in more intensified political quibbles. Results from public opinion polls conducted in 1988-90 indicated a profound distrust of the Chinese government's intention to honour the promise of self-government as spelt out in the Basic Law, as well as Britain's moral integrity in the handling of the matter.[2] The upshot of all this was a sustained increase in emigration by professionals and small businessmen, culminating to a hysterical apex during the aftermath of the 'June 4th Event', with people swarming to the consulate offices of Canada, Australia, New Zealand and Singapore. The Basic Law, released as draft in 1988 and in its final version in 1990, marking five years of political propaganda on the sincerity, determination and generosity of the Chinese government's intention after 1997, received very little attention from the public. Public sentiments towards such an important document at best reflected a period of prolonged remorse after the 'June 4th Event'. At worst it revealed a state of complete distrust or apathy towards their future.

Political Consensus, Social Policies and the Middle Class

The middle class has traditionally been the most neglected group in Hong Kong. It has been amongst the first group to emigrate since the early 1970s. Political uncertainties in the 1980s have aggravated the problem, with an average of 50,000 professional and managerial personnel leaving annually. This section will discuss a series of social policy measures implemented in the latter part of the 1980s, aiming at keeping the middle class to stay on in Hong Kong.

Apart from the political impasse and gradual erosion of legitimacy, the result of the heightened political interventions by the government was an unprecedented interest by emerging liberal political parties on the allocation of welfare resources (Scott, 1989). The well being of the middle class suddenly topped the political agenda. Why? The government's post-Sino-British Agreement objectives were meant to achieve political stability by containing possible dissent within the legislature as well as to obtain wider support in the community by increasing the supply of social goods. Although the first wave of representative politics seemed to benefit the working class, it had apparently failed to attract the middle class. The middle class in Hong Kong had always been self-reliant, hard working, and seldom blamed the government. This had somehow changed since the Sino-British negotiations began in the early 1980s. While some sectors of the middle class, such as engineers, lawyers and physicians were represented in the legislature, it was obvious that the majority of the non-professional middle class (small businessmen and white collar workers) still had little say in the political arena. It was considered that the only alternative to contain middle class sentiments was to give concessions in social policy that traditionally draws middle class support. The main concern of the middle class in Hong Kong invariably centres on issues such as more university places, improvement of the medical services, better care for the elderly and expansion of home ownership. Social policy improvements in higher education and housing were taken on board.

Social demand for the expansion of higher education has been high since the early 1980s. But it was never given such high priority as the establishment of the City Polytechnic (now City University) in 1987 and the Hong Kong University of Science and Technology in 1989 (Director of Audit, 1993).[3] As rightly pointed out by Scott (1989), the decision to build the university was made before any substantial planning had been made for the future needs of higher education in Hong Kong. The announcement of the decision to build the university as well as to quickly achieve an across-the-board increase in first degree places was seen as a political gesture to woo the middle income groups, since there were constant complaints on the high costs of sending their children abroad for university education.[4]

Since the 1980s, the government has been seeking ways to trim the public rental sector by promoting home ownership, mainly in the form of subsidized sale flats and home loans. This policy has sustained itself throughout the 1980s and 1990s and has been consistently reaffirmed by the Housing Bureau under the new regime.

The housing system is broadly divided into the public sector and the private sector. Half of the population live in the public sector that takes up 46% of the housing stock (34% public rental housing plus 12% subsidized sale flats). Generally it takes 6-7 years before a working class household could be allocated a public rental unit. For the subsidized sale flats or the Home Ownership Scheme, there is no waiting list system. Applicants largely come from the lower middle income brackets or public housing tenants who are willing to give up their tenancy. The demand for home ownership has always been extremely keen since sale prices are set at 50% of the market price. New houses for sale are generally over-subscribed by more than ten times. For a short period after 1998, the demand for these subsidized flats dropped slightly as a consequence of the economic downturn. However, sale of flats in April 1999 still indicated four times over-subscription. Despite incidents of defective construction and poor maintenance over the past few years, there are still repeated demands from housing pressure groups urging the government to expand the public home ownership sector.

Over the past two decades, a number of pressure groups have been developed to pursue issues related to the well being of public rental tenants. One notable example is the Hong Kong People's Council on Public Housing Policy. In the 1970s, the Council was able to exert considerable pressure on rent and allocation policy for the public rental sector, as well as the rehousing policy for people living in temporary housing areas. In contrast, the home ownership sector is much less organized and its

14

concerns are less likely to be expressed through pressure groups. This might be the result of the existence of a rather fragmented and politically apathetic middle class. Nonetheless, in view of the wave of middle class emigration in the mid-1980s, the government decided that something ought to be done to keep the middle class (Scott, 1989).

This resulted in the 1987 Long Term Housing Strategy policy paper, where the government emanated a clear policy shift towards home ownership. It started with the introduction of a Home Purchase Loan Scheme, providing interest free loans to eligible households to buy flats in the private market, as well as the increased production of subsidized sale flats. Subsequently, the government introduced the pilot scheme in the 1990s, where sitting tenants of public rental units were given an option to buy their own flats. While the policy implications of these changes will be examined in detail in later chapters, it is important to reiterate here that there was a clear intention by the government to woo the middle class through the promotion of home ownership in the 1980s, with a view to slowing down the outflow of professionals and managerial classes.

Economic Restructuring

In the past two decades, Hong Kong has come to be known as one of the *four little tigers* (together with Taiwan, Korea and Singapore) that has been able to sustain high economic growth even when major Western economies were either in recession or slow growth in the early 1980s. In a comparative survey of economic performance in Pacific Rim countries, it was shown that even in the face of social and political uncertainties, Hong Kong's economic performance was still estimated to be better off than countries like Australia and New Zealand (Asianmoney Survey, 1991). The estimated growth rate for 1991 was 4.7%, while Australia was 1.8% and New Zealand only 0.8%. Even in the first quarter of 1998, Hong Kong still recorded a 2.7% growth rate, although in the first quarter of 1999, a negative 7.1% was recorded. Nonetheless, even during such difficult times (1997-98), Hong Kong still enjoyed a per capita income of US$24,455, well surpassing UK and Australia. This explains why even in the face of political and economic uncertainties, Hong Kong still manages to attract foreign investments. An expected high rate of return and a freer and more competitive economic environment still contribute to sustaining international confidence. Hong Kong also had one of the lowest unemployment rates in the 1980s and 1990s (see Table 2.1), although this full-employment regime is being slowly eroded in the face of the recent Asian economic crisis.

Table 2.1   Unemployment Rates in Hong Kong (%)

1976	5.1
1977	4.2
1978	2.8
1979	2.9
1980	3.8
1981	3.9
1982	3.6
1983	4.5
1984	3.9
1985	3.2
1986	2.8
1987	1.7
1988	1.4
1989	1.1
1990	1.3
1991	1.8
1992	2.0
1993	2.0
1994	1.9
1995	3.2
1996	2.8
1997	2.2
1998	4.7

Source: Hong Kong Annual Report(s) 1976-98.
         Hong Kong Monthly Digest of Statistics.

Hong Kong's economic performance has been remarkable by world standards. Over the last three decades, there was an average GDP growth rate of 8% (see Table 2.2). The economy started to pick up since the late 1960s. Chen (1988) suggested this as the first stage of development in an export-oriented economy. Unlike many other developing economies, the uniqueness of the Hong Kong economy lies in the fact that it did not have to go through a period of import substitution in her early stage of growth. In this way, Hong Kong was able to shorten her development process and reap the gains from economic growth at a much earlier stage. Nonetheless,

Table 2.2   Hong Kong's Gross Domestic Product

Year	(HK$ million)	Year-on-year % change	Per Capita GDP (HK$)
At constant 1980 market price			
1969	51,046	11.8	13,211
1970	55,844	9.4	14,106
1971	59,921	7.3	14,812
1972	66,512	11.0	16,161
1973	74,959	12.7	17,194
1974	76,608	2.2	17,735
1975	76,761	0.2	17,462
1976	89,887	17.1	19,895
1977	101,124	12.5	22,062
1978	110,725	9.5	23,723
1979	123,624	11.7	25,081
1980	137,081	10.9	27,075
1981	149,987	9.4	28,936
1982	154,512	3.0	29,350
1983	164,550	6.5	30,785
1984	180,149	9.5	33,374
1985	181,200	0.6	33,210
1986	196,984	11.2	35,604
1987	214,365	13.6	38,450
1988	247,501	7.9	43,564
1989	253,223	2.3	43,952
1990	259,352	2.4	44,711
1991	273,434	5.4	47,514
At constant 1990 market prices			
1992	650,347	6.3	112,119
1993	690,223	6.1	116,967
1994	727,506	5.4	120,540
1995	755,832	3.9	122,778
1996	789,753	4.5	125,139
1997	831,319	5.3	127,854
1998	788,677	-5.1	117,938

Source: Hong Kong Annual Report(s) 1969-98.

Hong Kong's economic performance is highly susceptible to events in the world economy. 1973 was a unique point in history. The collapse of the world stock market in mid-1973, followed by the rise in oil prices and slowing-down in world trade, triggered off a world economic recession. The effect on Hong Kong could be seen in the GDP growth rate of 1974 and 1975. It dropped from 12.7% in 1973 to 2.2% and 0.2% in the following two years. From 1977 to 1981, the economy was fortunately fuelled by an emerging growth in domestic demand. This was compounded by a revised Defense Cost Agreement with the UK government, with Hong Kong having to pay more for defense, hence pushing up government expenditure by 2.5%. This increased expenditure triggered an inflationary process which eventually led to the devaluation of Hong Kong dollar and the 1982 collapse of the property market. It resulted in a slackened export market, an overheated domestic economy, a high interest rate (the highest mortgage interest rate was 23%), double-digit inflation and rising labour costs. All these factors contributed to a rather disheartening start to the 1980s. The recovery of the US economy in 1983 helped the Hong Kong economy to improve somewhat, but then there were a series of bank failures, coupled with the political clouds hanging over the beleaguered Sino-British negotiations. The net effect on the economy was disastrous. GDP grew at only 0.6% in 1985. However, the turning point of the economy came in the post-agreement era. In 1986-89, Hong Kong experienced three years of consecutive growth, partly as a result of the new air of confidence brought by the Sino-British Agreement, and partly the result of continued strong domestic demand, particularly by the revival of intense speculations in the property market. While the Hong Kong economy began to revive, the world economy entered one of the longest recessions in the post-war period. Commencing in late 1988, there was a gradual slackening of exports and manufacturing, coupled with stringent internal supply constraints such as labour shortage. GDP plummeted to 2.3% in 1989 and 2.4% in 1990. The outbreak of the Gulf War and the sudden upsurge in oil prices should have sent the growth barometer further down, if not for the emergence of one of the most speculative and bizarre periods beginning in the second quarter of 1991 in the real estate and stock markets.

For the rest of 1991, prices in the real estate market increased in the range of 35%-100%, while the Hang Seng Index passed the 4,000 bench mark. It was considered unprecedented in the stock market history. The anomaly was the result of pure demand-pull inflation and growth resulting from domestic demand in consumption and investment. The net result was that, even in the face of a world recession and a dwindling industrial economy, GDP climbed back to 5% and was stabilized at this level until 1996 when the government started to introduce administrative measures to cool down the overheated housing market. A report on the *Task Force on Land Supply and Property Prices* was released in June 1994 where administrative measures were introduced to cool off the highly speculative housing market (Planning, Environment and Lands Branch, 1994). The market cooled slightly in the beginning, but no sooner the temporary price equilibrium was eclipsed by even more speculations in March 1997.

A cursory glance at the Hong Kong growth pattern unveils three interesting phenomena. First, the economy is highly susceptible to external forces such as oil prices or trade embargoes. Second, it is also highly resilient. This was evidenced by the quick bounce back of the economy after the 1973 oil crisis and the world economic recession during the early 1980s. Third, increase in domestic demand, particularly in the housing and stock markets, is invariably a source of growth. While I do not attempt to answer all questions arising from these phenomena, it is sufficient to say here that while the working of any economy is always a key to understanding the development of the housing sector, the reverse is also true. The housing market, more than anywhere else in the world, is always instrumental to the Hong Kong economy.

As shown in Table 2.2, growth rate since 1991 has been stabilized at around 5%. The Hang Seng Index surged to 9,000 at the beginning of 1994, apparently fuelled by an increase in capital investments such as the new airport construction. The slow recovery of the world economy, particularly the US economy, and the increase in real interest rate in US did not seem to hamper growth in the property-sensitive economy. The Hang Seng Index hit its record high at 16,000 during the handover in July 1997, and plummeted to a dramatic low of 8,000 in 1998. While heralding the Hong Kong's economic vibrancy, these indicators tend to paint an overly rosy picture. In fact, many of the traditional macro economic problems were deliberately played down or concealed. To name a few: high inflation, a weakening industrial base, a highly volatile Chinese economy and a colonial government whose only concern was to effect a graceful, if not glorious, retreat. Hong Kong, consciously or unconsciously, was slowly being dragged into an illusory growth path fuelled by a desire for home ownership, housing speculation and a 1997 *handover fever*.

Table 2.3   Private Domestic Housing Stock by Vacancy and Class

	Size Range M²	Stock (at December 1997)		Vacancy	% Vacant
A	<20	12,578			
	20-29.9	117,647	347,926	8,186	2.4
	30-39.9	217,701			
B	40-49.9	188,460			
	50-59.9	136,271	428,911	18,934	4.4
	60-69.9	104,180			
C	70-79.9	44,904			
	80-89.9	28,531	93,496	5,477	5.9
	90-99.9	20,061			
D	100-119.9	23,962			
	120-139.9	14,877	47,646	2,296	4.8
	140-159.9	8,807			
E	160-199.9	10,362			
	200-239.9	7,394	22,149	1,090	4.9
	240-279.9	2,249			
	>279.9	2,144			
	All Class	940,128	940,128	35,983	3.8

Source: Rating and Valuation Department, *Property Review 1998*.

Economic Growth and Restructuring in the 1980s

To fully appreciate Hong Kong's growth path, this section maps out changes that have taken place in the economy since the late 1970s. The Hong Kong economy has been undergoing profound structural changes that carry an immense impact on both the socio-economic structure as well as the housing market. I shall describe some of these problems before embarking on their relationship with the housing question.

Since 1980, Hong Kong has entered an inflationary period which is largely demand pull in origin (Shea, 1989). As a result of the economic boom and buoyant stock and property markets, the inflation rate reached 15.5% in 1980. It dropped to 8.1% in 1984 as a result of political uncertainties and a dwindling demand in the consumption and property markets. Inflation rate hit its lowest point in 1986 at 2.8% as world commodity prices remained soft. It then emerged from the trough as a result of a recovering US economy as well as a reviving property market. It was 9% in 1988, 12% in 1990 and reached 12.9% in March 1991 (Rating and Valuation Department, 1992). The contradiction was that even with extremely low social and political confidence and an escalating emigration rate of professionals and small businessmen, the property market performed extremely well. While the complex relationship between the economy, the growth of per capita income, inflation and housing demand is yet to be elaborated, at least two factors contribute to the continual buoyancy of the property market. First, with a private housing stock of approximately 1.1 million units and an annual output of around 16,000 units in 1997, Hong Kong maintains a rather stable low vacancy rate of 3.8% (Rating and Valuation Department, 1998). This indicates that the level of private residential housing stock is carefully maintained by developers and is always at a rather healthy short-term equilibrium of supply and demand (see Table 2.3). Second, the mortgage interest rates, with the exception of the early part of the 1980s, have been kept at a stable level (8%-12%), hence providing a relatively secure environment for home financing.

Structural Changes in Economy: From Manufacturing to Service

One of the most profound changes of the economy in the last two decades has been a gradual shift from a manufacturing and industrial-based economy to one characterized by a growing service sector and a burgeoning international finance sector. The working population increased from 2.4 million in 1981 to 3 million in 1996. However, the change in the distribution of the workforce between and within sectors was more significant than the growth in numbers. The most noticeable decline in the workforce was in the manufacturing industry: the number dropped from 990,365 in 1981 to 768,121 in 1991, and further to 574,867 in 1996, with the most acute decline in the clothing and textile industry, where in 1977 comprised 60% of the manufacturing workforce. On the contrary, the service sector saw a phenomenal growth. In the wholesale, retail, import and export trading, restaurants and hotel industry sector, the increase was from 19.2% in 1981 to 24.9% in 1996. Indeed, the increase in the hotel industry should be much greater if not due to one of the most acute labour shortages in recent years. While the transport, storage and communication sector saw encouraging growth, the most substantial increase in workforce

Table 2.4 The Changing Industrial Distribution of the Working Population

Industry	1981		1986		1991		1996	
	No.	%	No.	%	No.	%	No.	%
Manufacturing	990,365	41.3	946,653	35.8	768,121	28.2	574,867	18.9
Construction	185,999	7.7	164,268	6.2	187,851	6.9	245,440	8.1
Wholesale, retail, import/ export, restaurants, hotel	461,489	19.2	589,918	22.3	611,386	22.5	757,239	24.9
Transport, storage and communication	181,368	7.5	210,367	8.0	265,685	9.8	330,974	10.9
Financing, insurance, real estate and business services	115,870	4.8	169,967	6.4	287,168	10.6	408,686	13.4
Community, social and personal service	375,703	15.6	486,167	18.4	539,123	19.9	680,048	22.3
Others*	93,273	3.9	75,933	2.9	55,768	2.1	46,444	1.5
Total	2,404,067	100	2,643,273	100	2,715,102	100	3,043,698	100

* Others include industries such as agriculture & fisheries, mining & quarrying, electricity, gas & water, and other unclassifiable industries.

was in the financing, insurance, real estate and business services sector: from 4.8% in 1981 to 13.4% in 1996. One of the less noticeable increases was in the community, social and personal service sector, which also indicated considerable increases, reflecting to some extent the development of an expanded welfare sector as a support to the expanding service economy (see Table 2.4).

In the face of such massive labour restructuring over the last two decades, three economic questions could be raised. First, how would these structural changes affect the industrial base? Second, how these structural changes affect the labour force? Third, what should be the role of the government in the light of these changes?

To attempt a full answer to the first question obviously goes beyond the scope of this study. From what we see in the GDP growth pattern up till 1993, it seems that economic performance of Hong Kong is very much a function of the international economic climate and domestic demand. In a very broad sense, we can say that an economy largely based on domestic consumption and heavily biased towards the service sector could be dangerous. By slowly drifting away from export orientation, Hong Kong may end up having an even more inflationary and volatile economy. However, it may also be the case that we are in the middle of an economic transformation. In his maiden budget speech in 1992, the then Financial Secretary, Hamish MacCleod, summed up Hong Kong's then economic position:

> A wide spread view among Hong Kong's economists, which I accepted, is that inflation has mainly been generated by the strains and distortions involved in the restructuring of our economy. We are switching from an industrial to a mixed manufacturing/service economy (Budget Speech, 1992).

It has also been keenly argued elsewhere that in order to compete with the other three tigers (Singapore, Korea and Taiwan), Hong Kong should embark on a second industrial revolution. We should enter into the second stage of export-orientation economy, whereby Hong Kong should have a high technology manufacturing base, supported by a strong service sector, especially financial services, with growth much more supply-oriented rather than demand-oriented. In the words of Chen:

> In the new stage of development, a different type of neo-classical interventionism is necessary for the acquisition of an economy's dynamic comparative advantage; a class of entrepreneurs of a different calibre is

23

called for to face the problems imposed by a type of economic growth which is based on the supplier's ability to direct the market. Confucianism may be too soft a cultural system to effect transformation; the autocratic political institution may be too closed a system to formulate and implement policies for the emergence of a complex industrial structure (Chen, 1988, p.30).

The statement of Chen goes some way in answering the first two questions: Hong Kong needs a more proactive industrial base and a new breed of entrepreneurs - one which is supply-oriented rather than market-driven. The colonial government might be blamed for her inertia to advance Hong Kong into the new stage of industrial development. What is even more disturbing is that a dangling housing question and an ever-buoyant property-driven economy actually prevent Hong Kong from moving towards that direction. The Asian economic meltdown of 1998, like it or not, might provide the best catalyst for Hong Kong's economic transformation. Recent establishment of a high level consultative committee on new technology, led by Professor Tien, the ex-President of the University of California at Berkeley, to explore the development of information technology and the subsequent proposal to set up a cyberport could be seen as a belated effort by the government to transform Hong Kong's industrial base. I shall turn to another pertinent economic restructuring issue, that is, the new economic policy of China.

China's New Economic Policy and its Relationship with Hong Kong

In the 1960s and early 1970s, China's economic involvement in Hong Kong was negligible. Apart from being one of the major food suppliers as well as operating a few large retail outlets for low quality consumer goods, China's involvement in Hong Kong's economy was very low. Owing to political and economic instabilities during the Chinese Cultural Revolution in 1966-76, there was little attraction for Hong Kong businessmen to invest or to sell consumer goods in China, not to mention overcoming the many daunting bureaucratic controls on China's external trade. Nonetheless, when Deng Xiaoping resumed power in 1977, one of the national objectives was to attract foreign investments and to set up *Special Economic Zones* along the Chinese coastline. The Shenzhen Special Economic Zone was established in 1979 at the northern border of Hong Kong. It turned the barren border town into a thriving industrial economy with over one million population and an annual growth rate of over 10%.

24

By 1982, US$1.5 billion had been invested in Shenzhen, of which 90% came from Hong Kong. Total outputs and exports from the Zone accounted for US$3 billion in 1988. The upshot of the new open door economic policy is the successful attraction of investments from Hong Kong as well as from overseas, which sees Hong Kong as a stepping stone for trading with China. As shown in Table 2.5, although the value of trade is still very much weighted towards China, there is a discernible trend of increase in the volume of trade, particularly for re-exports.

Table 2.5   Value of Trade between Hong Kong and China, 1977-1997 (In Hong Kong $ million)

	HK imports from China	HK exports to China	Re-exports to China	Trade Balance
1977	8,082	31	175	-7,876
1978	10,550	81	214	-10,255
1979	15,130	603	1,315	-13,212
1980	21,948	1,065	4,642	-16,241
1981	29,510	2,924	8,044	-18,542
1982	32,935	3,806	7,992	-21,137
1983	42,821	6,223	12,183	-24,415
1984	55,753	11,283	28,064	-16,406
1985	58,963	15,189	46,023	2,249
1986	81,633	18,022	40,894	-22,717
1987	117,357	27,871	60,170	-29,316
1988	155,634	38,043	94,895	-22,696
1989	196,676	43,272	103,492	-49,912
1990	236,134	47,470	110,908	-77,756
1991	293,356	54,404	153,318	-85,634
1992	354,348	61,959	212,105	-80,284
1993	402,161	63,367	274,561	-64,233
1994	470,867	61,009	322,835	-87,023
1995	539,480	63,555	384,043	-91,882
1996	570,442	61,620	417,752	-91,070
1997	608,372	63,867	443,878	-100,627

Source: Hong Kong Monthly Digest of Statistics (1977-98).
         Hong Kong Government Annual Report(s) (1977-98).

Hong Kong and China are now each other's largest trading partners. In 1997, the total value of visible trade between Hong Kong and China amounted to $608 billion. Apart from being the largest market for Hong Kong's domestic exports ($63.9 billion) and the largest supplier of imports into Hong Kong, China is particularly important in Hong Kong's re-export trade ($443.9 billion). China is the largest market for, and the largest supplier of, Hong Kong's re-exports. Hong Kong is also the most important source of foreign investment in China, amounting to two-thirds of her total foreign investments in the 1990s. These investments take the form of light industries, hotel and tourist-related industries and infrastructure construction. Light industrial manufacturing is at present largely concentrated in the Pearl River Delta Region which, together with the Shenzhen Special Economic Zone, forms a cap-shaped light industrial belt to the north of the Hong Kong border (or more precisely, the southern part of the Guangdong Province). It has been estimated that in the Province alone, more than 1.5 million people are working for Hong Kong, either through joint ventures or in tasks commissioned by Hong Kong companies in the form of outward processing arrangements. Besides constituting an important source of demand for goods and services produced by Hong Kong, China is equally important as a source of productive capacity to manufacturers based in Hong Kong. While it has been suggested elsewhere that the road to the construction of this new socialist economic order in the South is nothing short of a rough ride (Sklair, 1991; Henderson, 1991; Smart, 1991), what we have seen in this major economic transformation for the last two decades is a successful blurring of the economic border of Hong Kong and China. Although the successful economic relationship between Hong Kong and China may have been overstated as a result of political propaganda (Chai, 1989), the fact that there exists a great potential for mutual economic cooperation is undoubted. Put simply, while political integration of the two places commenced on 1 July 1997, economic integration had taken place much earlier. Moreover, as Chinese interests in Hong Kong were concentrated more on import/export, wholesale/retail, transportation and warehousing, the mid-1980s also saw a new wave of economic endeavour in banking, financial services, and more recently real estate development. Chinese interests in construction, distribution and management of real estates were definitely a new force to be reckoned with in the property market in the last decade. In addition, increasing financial links between Hong Kong and China were reflected in the rapid growth in financial transactions with China. The Bank of China group is now the second largest banking group in Hong Kong, second only to the Hong Kong and Shanghai Banking group. Hence, within the context of growing economic interdependence between Hong Kong and China, the net effect is that the Hong Kong GDP is no longer a good indicator of growth because a major portion of the production process is now done in the Mainland, eventually going through Hong Kong as exports.

The impact of all these developments on the Hong Kong economy has yet to be seen. On the positive side, Hong Kong undoubtedly witnesses re-surging importance of re-export trade that is growth inducing. Escalating economic activities on both sides of the border mean more earnings and eventual accelerated economic activities. On the negative side, the existence of a huge and vastly untapped cheap labour resource just at the doorstep of Hong Kong would amount to a regional restructuring of the division of labour between the two economies. To maintain product competitiveness, many small and medium-sized manufacturers have, over the years, moved their production lines to Shenzhen and other parts of the Mainland. The reason is apparent: to avoid the soaring labour costs in Hong Kong and to reap the benefits of extraordinary low production costs in the early period of China's economic modernization. While it has been argued generally that the essence of doing business in the region is still *GuanXi* - meaning human relationship rather than rules, it has also been suggested that once the chaotic early years are over, regulations in the form of a complex tax structure would eventually increase production costs (Smart, 1991). By then, the Hong Kong economy will be fully integrated with the Mainland.

The Role of the State in the Hong Kong Economy: Laissez-Faire versus Interventionism

The economic success of Hong Kong drew much international attention in the 1970s in both the academic and business circles. The question was: why the success? Explanations of Hong Kong's success story could broadly be divided into two schools of thought. First, the *natural resource school*, where the qualities of the Chinese, a strong work ethic, perseverance and thriftiness, were emphasized (Lethbridge, 1980). Second, the *institutional school*, where the existence of the free-market economy and the absence of government intervention were emphasized (Friedman, 1981; Rabushka, 1976; Woronoff, 1980). While these two schools of thought were valuable to explain the Hong Kong story, it has been stated elsewhere that they are at best inadequate, and at worst misleading (Schiffer, 1983).

One of the most important studies was by Schiffer (1983), who argued that the economic success of Hong Kong was very much the result of discrete government intervention. Basing on a study of the expenditure pattern of local households, he discovered that Hong Kong's dependency on relatively cheap food supplies from China and the low rent in public housing effectively lowered household budgets by approximately 25%. Public housing therefore constituted a major welfare subsidy for the low-income families. He further argued that through absolute control of land ownership, the government was able to finance a huge public rental housing sector. Schiffer has stimulated other studies on the role of government interventions in the *four little tigers*. A study by Castells et al. (Castells, Goh, & Kwok, 1990) in the late 1980s was along the same strand. Amongst other things, Castells argued that continual economic success in Hong Kong and Singapore was largely the result of deliberate intervention by the government in the public housing sector. While Castells' argument was criticized for being over-generalized and lacked empirical support, the suggestion that economic development and state intervention in public housing being positively related is considered important (Lee, 1993).

Besides theory, what happened in real economics in the last decade did demonstrate a successive record of active economic interventions, especially in the financial sector and the housing market. Two salient examples can be cited here: the rescue of the banking crisis in 1983 and the restructuring of the Hong Kong stock market.

As a result of the world recession in 1982, the unveiling of the Sino-British political discussions and the property market slum at the end of 1982, the economic climate in 1983 was more than gloomy. Partly the result of over-lending and partly due to the devaluation of Hong Kong dollar, several local banks went into bankruptcy in the early 1980s. In order to stabilize the banking sector and to avoid an adverse chain-effect on panicky bank-runs, the government acquired ownership of the Hang Lung Bank and the Overseas Trust Bank, and rescued the Ka Wah Bank. The government acted as a public guarantor for failing banks - a role that contradicted the long-established policy of *positive non-interventionism*.

The intervention in the stock market was even more dramatic. At the height of the stock market crash in September 1987, the Hong Kong Stock Exchange, without much consultation with the government, suspended trading for two days. The act drew severe criticisms from the international financial markets, as it had obviously threatened investment confidence.

The situation came to a turn when a group of senior management personnel were arrested for alleged corruption and insider trading. Subsequent revelations indicated that over the years laissez-faire policy had encouraged the development of paternalism and oligopolistic practices amongst big stock brokers. The Stock Exchange management was completely revamped in 1988 with new legislation introduced to bring better protection of investment interests and prevention of insider trading.

Intervention in the Housing Market

Before August 1988, the housing market, like any markets in Hong Kong, was not subject to any restrictions or regulations. Buying and selling of properties were largely governed by the sales and purchases agreement subject, of course, to the payment of relevant taxes and stamp duties. Nonetheless, what happened in the housing market after March 1991 was unprecedented. House prices soared sharply after the Gulf War as well as the signing of the Memorandum of Understanding in Beijing on the construction of the new Hong Kong airport by John Major, the then British Prime Minister. House prices doubled within half a year. In order to cool off the overheated housing market, a series of measures which aimed at controlling sales and purchases of houses were introduced in August, 1994. A high-level government committee was set up to recommend measures to cool off the market. What were later proposed in the *Report of the Task Force on Land Supply and Property Prices* (Planning, Environment and Lands Branch, 1994) amounted to completely shifting Hong Kong's long-cherished philosophy of positive non-interventionism. These measures included: (1) levying tax on sales and purchases of flats under construction; (2) increasing initial deposit from 1.5% to 10% of purchase price; (3) setting the mortgage ceiling at 70% of the price of domestic dwellings; (4) replacing queuing by computer randomization as a method of allocation of new flats to prevent organized gangsters from using illegal means to control queues; and (5) limiting the number of new flats that might be reserved by developers for internal sales (purchase by staff members). These measures were unheard of in the history of the Hong Kong housing market, as they represented a clear tampering with the free market. In the first six months following the implementation of the measures, the market cooled off slightly. This was attributed not so much to the measures of sales control, because the triads could obviously find better ways to monopolize access to buying new flats. Rather, it was the new 70% mortgage ceiling which created a real hindrance for the genuine first-time buyers.

What is really behind this frantic chase for properties? The following observations may yield some clues. In Figure 2.1, we can see that except for the period from 1982-84 when there was a brief property market slump as a result of the unsettling political negotiations on Hong Kong's future, house prices have been on the rise since 1985 and, with some minor fluctuations, have grown robustly, and there is a strong indication that it is demand-led. House prices rose extremely rapidly after 1991 and continued all the way until the first two quarters of 1997. Why?

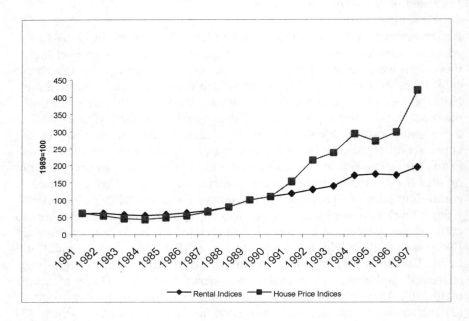

Figure 2.1 Comparing House Prices and Rental Indices

Source: Rating and Valuation Department, *Hong Kong Property Review 1991 and 1998*.

To sum up, three factors have accounted for the phenomenal house price increase in the 1980s and the 1990s. First, a robust economy had produced a reservoir of savings for consumption and investment. Second, there was a genuine need and demand for dwellings. It was estimated by the Housing Authority in the 1987 Long Term Housing Strategy that there would be 550,000 net households formation, and a total of 960,000 new housing units required to satisfy the demand by 2001. That did boost up property demand. The figures later turned out to be grossly underestimated as they omitted estimates for legal and illegal immigrants from Mainland China for family reunion. After 1997, it is expected that cross-border marriages will bring even more pressure on housing with increasing number of Mainland immigrants seeking abode in Hong Kong on the basis of blood relationship. In fact a Court of Final Appeal ruling in January 1999 has gone further to give legal rights even to children not born out of marriage. In April 1999, it was estimated that 1.6 million people might eventually obtain the right of abode in Hong Kong (South China Morning Post, 29 April 1999). This will certainly add enormous pressure on the housing market in the first decade of the twenty-first century. Third, a condition of *tenure neutrality* existed where people inclined towards buying rather than renting. From Figure 2.1, we can see that for the period 1981-90, the rental indices curve almost collapsed with the house price indices curve. This enabled an economic condition where any rational consumer would have a natural tendency to buy rather than to rent as the cost of buying and renting was roughly the same. There were of course other economic factors that were instrumental in the home buying process, such as the low interest rate. But as far as economic explanation is concerned, a condition of tenure neutrality provided the best incentive for owning rather than renting. However, from 1990 onwards, the cost of owning became more expensive relative to renting. Under such condition, the motivation to buy homes was more likely to be affected by investment motive and speculative activities.

Whilst economic causes for home purchase offer the necessary condition for the growth of home ownership, they do not sufficiently explain the social roots of home ownership. In other words, economic decisions such as home buying, when explained in terms of economic concept such as *tenure neutrality*, cover up a network of social relationships. In fact, an individual's economic decision is deeply *embedded* in a network of social relationships (Granovetter, 1985). It is only through the unraveling of such relationships that we could be able to fully account for the genesis of mass home ownership. This theoretical orientation will be more fully expounded in Chapter four.

The Long Term Housing Strategy 1987 and 1997: A Panacea or a Time Bomb?

The previous discussion impinged upon two distinct but related social processes. First, the process of political restructuring arising from the 1997 question has resulted in a legitimacy crisis, to which the colonial government before 1997 responded by desperately re-positioning herself. This has been clearly analyzed by Scott (1989). However, to the surprise of many political analysts, the first two years after the handover were also marked by a different form of legitimacy problem. The new Special Administrative Region government under the leadership of Tung Chee-hua fought fiercely in 1997-98 to maintain continuity in policy, apparently for the fear that a quick departure from the colonial order would create instability. One salient example is that home ownership policy was reiterated in the second Long Term Housing Strategy policy paper (Housing Bureau, 1998). Second, the process of economic restructuring has resulted in the creation of an economy characterized by a large service sector composing of professional and managerial personnel. Rapid expansion in management and business-related courses in local tertiary institutions in the last two decades is a good indicator. The convergence of these two processes, however, is the social construction of a new middle class largely composed of white-collar workers in the import and export, tourist and real estate industries, middle-management in the financial sector and various kinds of professionals such as lawyers, accountants and computer personnel. As shown in Table 2.6, a longitudinal increase in middle income groups of the population over the last two decades also confirms this development. People in income brackets E, F, G and H all have across-the-board increase from 1981 to 1996. These four income brackets that comprise 63.7% of the three million plus working population roughly constitute the middle mass. They form an extremely powerful force in consumption. Indeed, it also partially explains why the demand for home buying has been so keen since 1981.

If these figures do provide some light to the burgeoning middle mass, it seems right for the government to herald two important objectives: (1) to ensure adequate housing supply at an affordable price or rent; and (2) to take the lead to promote home ownership.

In order to achieve the above policy objectives, the government implemented two major policy instruments in 1988: (1) introducing an interest free Home Purchase Loan Scheme in the form of down payment loans to those who meet the income criteria for government Home

Ownership Scheme but who have not been able to buy a government flat or a flat from the private market; and (2) providing opportunity for sitting tenants in newer public rental units (six years old or less) to purchase their own flats.

Table 2.6 Monthly Income from Main Employment of the Labour Force

	1981		1986		1991		1996	
	No.	%	No.	%	No.	%	No.	%
A	442,503	18.7	165,219	6.4	91,184	3.4	31,447	1.0
B	1,170,899	49.6	564,612	21.8	91,431	3.4	26,154	0.9
C	587,968	24.8	1,248,648	48.1	557,366	20.8	242,429	8.0
D	94,637	4.0	336,662	13.0	794,962	29.6	316,331	10.5
E	25,638	1.1	113,535	4.4	461,003	17.2	478,408	15.9
F	12,950	0.5	55,332	2.1	221,526	8.3	476,114	15.8
G	18,164	0.8	57,075	2.2	242,996	9.1	668,722	22.2
H	5,456	0.2	21,240	0.8	84,154	3.1	295,968	9.8
I	8,263	0.3	31,860	1.2	136,961	5.1	480,891	15.9
	2,366,478	100	2,594,183	100	2,681,583	100	3,016,464	100

*Income Group: A=<$1,000   B=$1,000-$1,999   C=$2,000-$3,999
                  D=$4,000-$5,999   E=$6,000-$7,999   F=$8,000-$9,999
                  G=$10,000-$14,999   H=$15,000-$19,999   I=>$20,000

Source: Census and Statistics Department, *Hong Kong 1991 Population Census Summary Results.*
             Census and Statistics Department, *Hong Kong 1996 Population By-census Summary Results.*

It is a fact that these two policy instruments have failed to achieve their objectives. The market has failed to produce affordable houses throughout the decade since 1987. Why? In the early days of the Loan Scheme, the loan was set at 10% of the flat price or a maximum of $50,000. Although the amount had been revised a few times since 1988 and ended up at $130,000 in 1990, it was never really able to catch up with the spiraling house prices in the private sector. The Scheme was poorly received by potential applicants because middle class people could not manage to buy their desirable home with the amount of loan provided. Subsequently, the government also introduced the first Tenant Purchase Scheme where sitting tenants were allowed to buy their own rented unit at a discounted price. In the first round of the Scheme when 5,000 units were offered for sale in 1991, only 6% of the potential buyers indicated an interest to buy. Two major reasons could be adduced for the failure of the Scheme. First, tenants considered the price, set at 70% of the market value, far too high.   Second, tenants generally considered the built quality of public rental housing poor, and they were also worried about possible high maintenance costs in the future. After being stalled for five years, the Scheme was again proposed and re-packaged in 1997. This time the price was hugely reduced to as low as 12% of the market price (Housing Bureau, 1998).   Although public housing tenants are still somewhat ambivalent about whether or not to buy, many incline to consider buying for fear that future rent increases would eventually make public rental housing unaffordable.

However, for those middle income families who are not eligible to public housing at all, home financing puts a heavy burden on their shoulders. Mortgage repayment for a median income family could easily fetch more than 50% of the total family income. Taking the median household income of 1996 as an example ($17,500), for a small 2-room flat (500 square feet) in an ordinary urban location, a household has to pay $2 million for the flat. With a down payment of 30% and a 25-year mortgage of an annual interest rate of 8%, a household has to spend practically everything for the mortgage every month, unless they have additional income from a second job. Even for some who can afford to own, a heavy mortgage burden is likely to cause distortions to their consumption pattern.

Since the publishing of the first Long Term Housing Strategy in 1987, what happened to the Hong Kong housing system? There is still a long waiting list for public rental housing (150,000), a keenly demanded and a largely unsatisfied subsidized home ownership sector and a growing private home ownership sector with seemingly unaffordable prices.

There are two major policy assumptions of the Long Term Housing Strategy which are quite unwarranted. First, it is the assumption that there is homogeneity of desire in the society to move towards owner-occupation to the effect that government should stop producing public rental units. I shall demonstrate in later chapters that the desire for home ownership or the broader question of tenure preference is much less homogenous than is usually thought of. The fact that a considerable number of people flock to

34

buy houses does not necessarily indicate an innate desire for home ownership. Second, the supposition that housing needs could be effectively and efficiently met in the private market is fallacious. It has already been demonstrated by a Consumer Council study in 1996 that the housing market behaved in a less than competitive manner and housing prices were not at the efficient level (Consumer Council, 1996). Among other things, this reflects that a home ownership policy advocated by the state but provided by the market is both idealistic and reckless. What we shall look into carefully is the delicate balance between the public and private housing sectors, as well as the whole concept of state intervention in housing in the Hong Kong context.

Conclusion

This chapter has examined two distinct and yet related social processes in Hong Kong during the last two decades, that is, the socio-political changes as a result of the 1997 handover and the economic restructuring process. I have pointed out that such processes have created profound social impacts in terms of the creation of a new middle class with higher income and a strong desire for home ownership. Furthermore, such changes in the social structure heavily impinge upon the demand for housing. It has been revealed that the policy assumptions that the desire for home ownership is both rational and universal, and that it could best be met in the private market, might be unfounded. Rational explanations in housing could only provide a short-term circumstantial picture of the housing question and thus fail to fully explain the social genesis of home ownership. To explore the housing question adequately we need first to look at the whole question of the role of state intervention in housing in a small city-state like Hong Kong. Second, it is argued that deeply embedded in an individual's housing decision is an array of social relationships that shape housing choices. Three factors which may affect the growth of home ownership would be explored: (1) an individual's early housing experiences and social change; (2) intra-familial support for home finance; and (3) the social implications of capital gains through home ownership. The underlying argument is that each society has an evolving consumption culture of housing. This affects the choice of tenure, the housing market and ultimately the whole social relationship of housing. It may be erroneous to assume that the development of home ownership necessarily reflects the same type of social processes arising from the same set of social relationships in every society. These processes and relationships may vary over time and space. Before going into details of why such a theoretical framework on home ownership is adopted, I shall examine in the next chapter some key perspectives on housing research and the social organization of housing and home ownership. While this chapter aims to provide the broad brush of the social context leading to the growth of home ownership as well as challenging the limitations of rational explanations, the next chapter will provide the actual housing context as it has developed in the last two decades. The implications of a general neglect of studies on home ownership as well as an unprecedented rise in owner-occupation in the last two decades provide an uneasy and yet interesting start for this study.

Notes

1. The most severe criticisms were launched against a liberal political group headed by Martin LEE and SZETO Wah, who later founded the United Democrats (now Democratic Party) and who won a clear majority mandate in the 1991 and subsequent elections to the Legislative Council.

2. A public opinion poll conducted in 1990 indicated that after the 'June 4th Event', 37% of the respondents said that they were actively preparing to emigrate. The same poll also indicated that one-third of the 1.55 million families in Hong Kong were planning to emigrate. Among executives, professionals and entrepreneurs, 64% planned to leave Hong Kong (Centre for Hong Kong Studies, University of Hong Kong).

3. The Hong Kong University of Science and Technology triggered one of the most fervent political rows in January 1991 when the efficiency and equity of the building programmes were questioned by legislators, because of its massive cost-overrun.

4. Address by the late Governor Sir Edward Youde, at the opening of the Legislative Council on 30 October 1985, Hong Kong: Government Printer, p. 19.

3 Housing Studies, the Social Organization of Housing and Home Ownership

Any Western housing researchers coming to Hong Kong will be surprised to find that home ownership as a stream of housing study is almost non-existent prior to 1994.[1] Despite the fact that frantic home-buying and house price speculation have been so conspicuous over the last two decades, home ownership as a focus of academic enquiry has failed to attract the attention of researchers in both the academia and government. Thus far, academic papers or books have been largely concentrated on the study of public housing. Most of them could be grouped into two main categories: (1) those that focus on the production and distribution of public housing (Dwyer, 1971; Chan, 1982; Drakakis-Smith, 1979; Fong & Yeh, 1984; Lau, 1984); and (2) those that approach housing from an urban geography and planning perspective (Drakakis-Smith, 1971; Dwyer, 1970 & 1971; Choi & Chan, 1979; Bristow, 1989; Chiu & Fong, 1989) or a social policy perspective (Ho, 1986; Lau, 1991). There are two possible reasons for this lacuna. First, owing to a general dearth of materials regarding home ownership, researchers are inclined to work on the more conspicuous public housing sector that abounds with government statistics and documents. Second, housing studies have been largely dominated by state sector analyses to the extent that the owner-occupier sector is considered relatively unimportant as a policy focus.

This chapter attempts to do three things. First, to briefly introduce the evolution of local housing studies. Second, to provide an overview of the current socio-spatial organization of home ownership. It is my contention that home ownership studies should be more robust in local housing research, not simply because we need to strike for an academic balance. More important, it is argued that a uni-dimensional mode of housing research would lead to gross misunderstanding in the working of the housing system and the possibility of oversights in policy formulation. Evidence from my study suggests that Hong Kong's current middle class housing crisis is partly the result of such a misunderstanding. Third, to introduce briefly the methodological orientation of this study and to briefly state why a housing history approach will better capture the dynamics of housing and social change. It is suggested that the public rental sector has a lower tendency to be marginalized since public housing tenants do occupy a stable position within the housing ladder. However, it is the new middle class - young professionals in the service sector - who find most difficulties in affording home ownership.

Housing Research in Hong Kong: From Third World Geography to the Political Economy of Housing

Housing Research as Third World Urbanization

No one today would regard Hong Kong a third world developing country. But when a group of geographers began to teach at the University of Hong Kong in the early 1960s, their major concern was about the development process of developing countries in Southeast Asia, such as Singapore, Malaysia, Indonesia, Philippines and Hong Kong. They considered that theories of development in the West were irrelevant in explaining urban development in the East, and that it was necessary to discern a unique theory applicable for urban analysis in the third world.

One attempt was made by McGee, a geographer of the 1960s genre. He was amongst several others who were interested in developing a theoretical link between the increase in urban population, the traditional employment sector and economic development. He argued that with rapid increase in urban population, third world cities were faced with a plethora of urban problems such as housing, transportation, sanitation, and unemployment. The underdevelopment in the third world was due largely to the persistence of a labour intensive traditional economic system. To quote his argument:

> It is our preliminary contention that a basic reason for the slowness of revolutionary change is the persistence of labour intensive economic system which, while characterized by low productivity and underemployment, serve a vitally important function of providing a sense of employment to many Third World city population (McGee, 1971, p.65).

The way McGee approached the urban question was seen as an effort to unravel a structural explanation of the process of urban growth in a muddy conceptualization of the third world. His study could be criticized

38

on at least three counts, namely: (1) the assumption that there is a homogeneity of urban development processes within the developing countries is questionable; (2) his study has failed to take into account the diverse social, cultural, political and geographical environment of these countries; and finally (3) the whole conceptualization of *under-development* is problematic. It represents both a theoretical and ideological hegemony with the first and second world dominance of the *underdeveloped* world. While it is true that Hong Kong had a large traditional labour intensive economic sector and that there was a high level of rural-urban migration in the post-war years, these conditions had in fact provided a favourable environment for the development of a competitive manufacturing economy in the 1960s. These factors alone were insufficient to explain the urbanization process. Cuthbert (1991) was right to suggest that extra precaution was necessary in studying the relationship between the state and society in Hong Kong. His study on Hong Kong's urban planning process revealed that there was a powerful connection between ideology and social formation. What appears to be an undue emphasis on economic explanation of Hong Kong is in fact part and parcel of the whole process of legitimization by the state acting on behalf of the capitalists.

Other students of urban geography, perhaps less ambitious than McGee, reflected the same ideological underpinnings, only to a lesser extent. The common thread that went through them is the endeavour to explain Hong Kong's public housing programme as a success story (Dwyer, 1971; Pryor, 1973; Drakakis-Smith, 1971, 1979; Wong, 1976; Fong & Yeh, 1984). They questioned that, given the enormous growth of resettlement housing and subsequent low-cost housing programmes, what were the justifications for the government to intervene if Hong Kong worked so well under a free market economy? Three explanations were advanced. The first explanation saw public housing as an inevitable response in which the government was reluctantly forced to intervene, since the private sector was incapable of responding to the needs of the huge influx of Chinese migrants in the post-war years (Fong, 1986). The government was seen to be left with little choices when, in a short span of time at the turn of the 1950s, the population had increased threefold. The second explanation suggested that government intervention was not directed at the welfare of the citizens as such. Rather, it was directed at the welfare of property developers who badly needed the land provided by slum clearance for industrial development (Drakakis-Smith, 1979). The two explanations, although essentially disagreed with each other, were nonetheless of the same genesis. As described by Nientied and Jan van der

Linden (1985), they only managed to touch on the *social appearance* of the massive public housing programme in Hong Kong, without really addressing the issue of *social reality* (Gugler, 1988). The third explanation was neo-Marxist in flavour. The public housing programme is seen as the product of the need for the state to intervene in order to reproduce labour power for the capitalist economic system. Such an approach, though seemingly more powerful than the previous two, has nonetheless been shrugged off by critics as partial and unsubstantiated. In his analysis of the political economy of the squatter market operation in Hong Kong, Smart concluded that even without the welfare benefits of public housing provisions, illegal squatting could also reproduce labour power. To quote Smart:

> A structuralist explanation, though, runs into the difficulty that Hong Kong's squatters manage to survive and to reproduce their labour power just as in public housing, there is little evidence that concern for the reproduction of labour power was a powerful motivation of government officials...there is little historical evidence for the instrumentalist view that the state intentionally adopted the Resettlement Programme as the ideal one for achieving the general needs of capital (Smart, 1989, pp. 183-184).

Housing Research as Studies of Political Economy

It is with this general dissatisfaction of the structuralist explanations that housing research in Hong Kong took yet another trajectory in the last decade. Other than the simplistic notion of state intervention as the reproduction of labour power (Castells, Goh & Kwok, 1990),[2] a number of more recent research projects, utilizing theoretical tools from contemporary debates in state theories (Skocpol, 1985; Block, 1980; Offe, 1984; Evans, 1987), embarked on more detailed analyses of the role of the Hong Kong government in public housing policy (Law, 1988; Smart, 1989; Ho, 1990). All of them concentrated on the *relative autonomy* thesis of the state as the major explanatory tool to account for the heavy involvement of the government in public housing provision since 1954. The main tenet of the explanation is that the ruling class does not always rule, especially after 1972. Law (1988) argued that during the period when the government transcended from a colonial state to a capitalist state, the state must achieve autonomy to survive. In order to maintain law and order, as well as to develop Hong Kong into a competitive state, the government must devise social plans which, in the short-run, might stand against the interests of the ruling capitalists. In fact, British colonial bureaucrats, following the well-established traditions of Whitehall politics of incrementalism and a separation of politics and administration (Miner, 1986), were able to provide an efficient administrative framework and enjoy a high degree of governability and legitimacy. In examining the squatter clearance policy of the 1950s, Smart (1986) concluded that although government enjoyed a high degree of autonomy in land development, it still opted for a policy of public housing. One explanation was that squatter clearance without proper rehousing would earn political credits for the then newly formed Communist regime. It would be extremely risky for the colonial government to bear such policy consequences.

Ho (1990), not agreeing entirely with Smart's thesis, went on to explain the development of public housing from the relative autonomy framework. His findings suggested that the autonomous role of government in sustaining a policy of massive public housing was somewhat checked by a declining economy in the early 1970s. As a consequence, the Housing Authority was reorganized, not merely for efficiency, but as a necessary way out in order to preserve government resources aiming at maintaining the capital accumulation process. Put simply, the autonomy of the government was checked by differences in economic and political situations during different periods of development history.

More recent research have again highlighted the role of the state in housing provision. La Grange and Lee (1999) argue that the Asian economic crisis of 1997-98 and the continual failure of the housing market to reflect competitiveness have successfully prompted the government to adopt a more regulatory and hard-line approach. Public housing policy and land supply are now gradually being seen as agents of intervention to stabilize house prices. In a recent comparative work, Doling (1999) even goes as far as to suggest that housing policy in the four little tigers are essentially corporatist in nature. Such generalization, while useful to some extent, fails to capture the unique socio-political background which gave rise to housing policy. To some extent, Singapore practises *state corporatism* for a clear political goal. But a close examination of the structure of the Housing Authority will easily manifest that Hong Kong is far from *corporatist*.

Housing Research as Social Policy Analysis

That housing as a crucial part of social policy analysis seems indisputable. Since the early 1960s, significant research has been carried out in areas of rent control and the allocation process of public housing by prominent academics in the social administration field (Nevitt, 1968; Donnison, 1967; Townsend, 1979; Cullingworth, 1963). The concern is about the production and distribution of social services, and housing invariably forms one of its crucial components. Titmuss (1974) defined social policy as choices amongst competing government policies to distribute social service resources, suggesting that the prime concern of social policy research is about ways in which scarce social resources are distributed.

Hong Kong is no stranger to this mode of research. A study into the brief history of social administration and the development of social work education is self-explanatory. Most teachers and researchers in social policy administration were trained in British universities with a long tradition of social administration and Fabianism, notably London School of Economics (LSE), Bedford College, Essex, Birmingham and York Universities. In the early 1970s, the Chair of Social Administration and Social Work of the University of Hong Kong - Professor Peter Hodge - was a veteran of LSE. In his inaugural lecture, Hodge (1974) suggested that the training of students in applied social studies had two important purposes: (1) to ascertain the state of living of people in the low income strata, their needs and predicaments; and (2) to influence government policies through the study of social situations and government decision-making process. The first major piece of empirical work in housing studies was completed by a sociologist of the University of Hong Kong. Hopkins (1969) was the first academic in the 1960s to carry out an empirical research (with a sample size of 1,650 households) to discern the effect of the public housing programme on poor people's livelihood in Hong Kong. His research made significant impact on housing policy. He suggested that government should not concentrate entirely on resettling people from squatter areas. Instead, it should progressively shift housing improvement from resettlement estates to old inner-city tenement, because over-concentration on resettlement would lead to marginalization of poor people living in the inner-city decaying areas, where the extent of dilapidation of old houses was most severe. Interestingly, in a more recent study by a practising town planner (Keung, 1985), the same conclusion was drawn. The failure of government housing policies in the 1970s was characterized by a neglect on the rehabilitation of inner-city old tenement blocks. Housing policy was somehow skewed towards squatter resettlements and new towns.

Since the establishment of the Housing Authority in 1974 and the subsequent launching of the Ten Year Public Housing Programme by one of Hong Kong's most ambitious and social-minded governors, the study of social policy for housing took a new turn. Arriving in Hong Kong in the early 1970s, MacLehose was struck by the appalling sights of a fast decaying inner-city and an unprecedented increase in the number of squatters at the city periphery. He tried to effect two fundamental changes in housing policy: (1) to relieve inner-city congestion by building new towns in suburban areas; and (2) to improve the quality of living in resettlement estates and low-cost housing estates (an improved version of public rental housing with independent toilet facilities). In order to implement these changes, the Housing Authority was established to consolidate the out-dated structure of the then Resettlement Department, the old Housing Board and the Housing Department under one umbrella. This was considered more conducive to efficiency in planning and operations. To many people's dismay, the Ten Year Housing Programme failed eventually, and the government was only able to meet half of the rehousing target (the original target was to build houses for 1.8 million people or 400,000 housing units). Housing research along the social policy trend in this period was characterized by a strong engagement in criticizing the government for the policy failure. One prominent project was completed by a community worker who founded one of the few early housing pressure groups, the Ecumenical Social Service of Kwai Chung (Chan, 1982). In her findings, Chan suggested two main reasons for government's failure in the Ten Year Housing Programme: (1) failure to provide sufficient funding for the building programme; and (2) unwillingness to provide more land for public housing for fear that this would entail adverse price effects on land sales. She urged the government to devise a more coherent policy towards public housing provision, and argued that housing for the lower class must be treated as an integral part of the social welfare system. As a result of these findings and other community actions, particularly those organized by the Hong Kong People's Council on Public Housing Policy (Lui, 1983), the governor openly admitted the failure of the Ten Year Housing Programme in a speech delivered in the Legislative Council in October 1981. As a policy remedy, the Housing Department managed to catch up with the building programme in the following five years.

In the mid-1980s, housing policy research took a slightly different course. Research aiming at understanding the production side of public housing began to gain popularity. The focus was on the efficiency of public housing production. One example was Yu and Li (1985). Based on statistics from the Census and Statistics Department for the period 1977-79, their study concluded that the production efficiency of public housing was higher than that of private housing. This was contrary to the belief that public sector production usually carried a lower efficiency. The major reasons cited were largely the result of the existence of economy of scale and a good relationship network with local building contractors. In another study, Yu and Li sought to address the question of distributive justice of the public housing programme to see if housing provision had any effect on the general income distribution of households. Using the 1986 by-census statistics on household income and income distribution data from the Department of Economics of the University of Hong Kong, they arrived at the conclusion that although the distribution of housing benefits amongst the population was not equitable, there was evidence of a redistribution of income from the rich to the poor (Yu & Li, 1990).

In 1985, public housing policy took a new turn. The government introduced a rent review on public housing (Hong Kong Housing Authority, 1985). The idea was to induce public housing tenants, who had achieved an increased income level while in residence, to pay double rent. Implicit behind the policy was the introduction of a *housing filtering system* whereby rich tenants are encouraged to leave the public rental sector and to take up government Home Ownership Scheme flats. This would vacate rental units for applicants on the long waiting list. Since the release of the proposal, there were heated debates amongst grassroot housing organizations and pressure groups. Housing research was largely aimed at deciphering the real financial burden of the Housing Authority and arguing that the government should not adopt a differential rent system for public housing tenants. A typical debate was succinctly advanced by Lau (1984a) whose research revealed that government's injection of funds into the public housing sector was largely composed of land prices, whereas funding for building programmes was heavily dependent on rents from tenants. Lau suggested that government should consider public housing as part of the social welfare system and that to allow the Housing Authority to stand on its feet prematurely would amount to a real cut in the already thin welfare cake. The research pointed to two salient features of welfare arguments: (1) the question of adequacy - whether or not housing provision has met people's needs; and (2) whether policy change means a reduction in social welfare. It can easily be discerned that housing research is generally critical towards government policy. It is reactive rather than proactive. Researchers seem to have implicitly assumed that people have already attained a certain set of agreed principles in housing policy. What is left behind is to find out whether or not the government is still on the right track.

The above outlined a historical sketch of housing research in Hong Kong since the 1960s with a few observations coming to light. Firstly, early housing research bears a definite influence from urban geographers. The concern was more about description of the spatial structure and the tension within. They portrayed a socio-economic spatial mapping of Hong Kong's urbanization process very much following the ecological tradition of the Chicago School (Park, 1952). The assumption is that, given certain socio-geographical constraints, people as a conglomerate would respond in a certain set of relationships and manners within the social and physical environment. The task of geographers is to discern this unique socio-spatial form. Hence, the focus of concern is a structural or functional view of people's relationship with the housing environment. Secondly, in the 1970s and thereafter, housing research has been influenced more by social policy analyses as manifested in various studies reacting to failures in housing policies. These studies are invariably concerned with whether or not the state has performed its duty and whether social justice is maintained. The focus of analysis is thus the relationship between housing policy and the deprived sector of the community, a locality or sometimes even a particular group. The shift towards the role of the state in recent research has pushed the focus of analysis towards the society, and away from the group and the individual.

One generalization emanates from this brief survey. The focus of housing research in Hong Kong has been largely confined to the macro/social policy level. This reflects an apparent neglect of the role of the individual and family in the development of home ownership. Second, the emphasis of housing research on the state housing sector as well as the apparent neglect of the home ownership sector points to a hegemonic tradition in housing research. The much-glorified intervention in the state housing sector of the 1960s and 1970s, as reflected in the social administration tradition in local research, has successfully obscured an unbalanced development of the state and the private housing sector. Such research has painted a housing picture suggesting that the state has successfully met most housing needs of the working class through public rental housing while middle class housing demand could be largely satisfied through the market. Such an approach conceals the real demand for housing and problems associated with middle class housing affordability. The 1987 Long Term Housing Strategy has reiterated this misleading point by suggesting that Hong Kong will be able to achieve by

2001 a home ownership rate of 60% (subsequently increased to 70% by the new Special Administrative Region Government after 1997). Even in a report by a high level government crisis management task force to investigate into house price speculations in June 1994, the government still claimed that house price speculations and the affordability problem were overstated (Planning, Environment and Lands Branch, 1994). What is surprising here is that hegemony in housing research has systematically over-rated government's role in housing provision and trivialized housing problems in the private home ownership sector.

The Hong Kong Housing Environment

Sheer Over-crowdedness

Looking northeast from the Victoria Peak on a clear summer evening in Hong Kong, one is stunned by the sprawling mixture of lights and colours of the harbour and waterfront. These are the Central District, Wan Chai, Causeway Bay and the northern tip of the Kowloon Peninsula, where one would find the best eating and shopping places in the world. Lying beyond the Lion Rock to the north is the New Territories where all the glittering new towns are located. Further north is the border, then the Shenzhen Special Economic Zone, and then Mainland China - Hong Kong's motherland.

While admiring the sheer beauty of this Pearl of the Orient in the evening lights, one is always tempted to overlook the fact that what lies beneath is one of the world's most congested human settlements. While the average population density in Hong Kong was 6,160 per square kilometre in 1997, the density in some residential cum industrial areas such as Kwun Tong and Mong Kok in Kowloon was 9 to 10 times higher. Other than Ginza, Tokyo, Hong Kong is perhaps the most crowded place on earth.

With a size of 1,096 square kilometres, Hong Kong is roughly two-thirds the area of Greater London. Over 80% of the territory consists of uninhabitable hilly land. The total built-up area for residential use in the urban and suburban districts is 58 square kilometres, comprising a mere 5.3% of total land use. Roughly half of these are in the urban areas, comprising the Hong Kong Island and the area south of the Lion Rock in Kowloon (which includes Kowloon and New Kowloon), and half in the New Territories, which comprises all the new towns and outlying islands.

Table 3.1 Household Number by Type of Tenure 1996

Type of Housing	Hong Kong Island	Kowloon	New Territories	Total
				Number of housing units
Public Rental Housing	76,289	246,452	344,995	667,736 (36%)
Owner-occupier in Public Sector (Subsidized Sale Flats)	23,915	43,886	123,721	191,522 (10.2%)
Owner-occupier in Private Sector	191,813	198,534	242,315	632,662 (34%)
Private Rental Housing	76,976	100,755	97,131	274,862 (14.8%)
Others	34,202	23,435	28,829	86,466 (5%)
Total	403,195 (21.8%)	613,062 (33%)	836,991 (45.2%)	1,853248 (100%)

Source: Census and Statistics Department, *1996 By-census data.*

It must be noted that 6.6 million people live in only a space the size of any European city with half a million population. Table 3.1 sets out the distribution of the population in Hong Kong. Throughout the last two decades, there had been significant internal migration from Kowloon and New Kowloon to the New Territories. Today, the New Territories has the highest number of public housing estates, and houses almost half of the population.

Very few people in Hong Kong live in houses. The concept of a 3-bedroom terraced or semi-detached town house is quite alien to most people, and also unattainable. Only the very rich and the senior civil servants are found living in something similar to that genre around the Peak area, the Mid-Level or some secluded parts of Island South. Most people live in small flats in high-rise buildings (average 20-30 storeys high), either in public housing estates or in huge private developments. These self-contained flatlets range from studio flats of 250 square feet to 2 or 3-room flats of about 800 square feet. The average room size is 50-80 square feet, usually without built-in wardrobes. The typical population size of a housing estate, whether public or private, is about 20,000. It usually contains about 6,000 households in 10-15 high-rise blocks with a shopping and parking complex in the middle. Any flats of 1,000 square feet or above would belong to the upper-range of the market and are normally found in private housing estates. Space and green plots between buildings are rare while parks or 'commons' are extremely uncommon. The present day Hong Kong solution to the craze for something green and communal, a place to sit, stroll or jog, would be found usually on a *podium* floor of the high-rise. It is usually the floor above the car park and could only be found in new estates. A 'concrete jungle', though a slightly clinched term, is nonetheless an appropriate description of the urban scene in Hong Kong.

Table 3.2   Housing Supply in the Public Sector 1988-1998

Year	Public Rental Housing	Subsidized Public Sale Flat	Total Public Sector Housing
1988-89	40,368	11,872	52,240
1989-90	34,915	19,600	54,515
1990-91	34,773	15,612	50,385
1991-92	22,307	15,026	37,333
1992-93	22,424	15,960	38,384
1993-94	20,274	25,143	45,417
1994-95	24,440	4,004	28,444
1995-96	14,828	20,456	35,284
1996-97	15,917	16,878	32,795
1997-98	18,295	15,318	33,613

Source: Housing Authority, *Annual Report(s) 1988-98.*

Table 3.3   Comparison of Housing Stock

	1986	1988	1993	1998
Public Rental Housing	544,950 (41%)	596,000 (38%)	673,000 (38%)	706,000 (35%)
Subsidized Sale Flats	57,134 (4%)	84,000 (10%)	162,000 (9%)	242,000 (12%)
Private Housing	743,974 (55%)	804,000 (52%)	946,000 (53%)	1,056,000 (53%)
Total Housing Stock	1,346,058 (100%)	1,484,000 (100%)	1,781,000 (100%)	2,004,000 (100%)

Source: Housing Authority, *Housing in Figures 1998.*

Housing Supply and Tenure Distribution

In 1998, Hong Kong had approximately 2 million housing units against a population of 6.6 million. As shown in Table 3.3, while public rental housing stood at 41% of the housing stock in 1986, it has decreased to 35% in 1998. In other words, although public rental housing increased in absolute terms, it has in fact decreased relative to other tenure. On the other hand, subsidized sale flat has increased from 4% in 1986 to 12% in 1998. Although the size of the tenure is still relatively small, this clearly indicates that the government is slowing down the production of public rental housing to pave way for more home ownership. Private renting is continually losing its importance as a form of tenure. In 1996, it stood at 14.8%, with the majority falling in either Kowloon or the New Territories. From Table 3.1, it could be seen that geographically speaking, Hong Kong Island is dominated by owner-occupation, with roughly half of its inhabitants being owner-occupiers. Kowloon and New Kowloon have a more mixed tenure, with owner-occupiers taking up one third of the tenure. New Territories and all the new towns are undoubtedly dominated by public housing tenants, with owner-occupation taking up slightly more than a quarter. However, it should be noted that many new subsidized sale flats and private housing estates are being built in the New Territories. Because of the land scarcity problem in Hong Kong and Kowloon, New Territories

Table 3.4 Housing Supply in the Private Sector and Inflation (CPI-A)

Year	Housing Supply No. of Units	Consumer Price Index A (CPI-A)*
1980	24,995	15.5
1981	34,475	15.4
1982	23,900	10.5
1983	32,620	9.9
1984	22,270	8.1
1985	29,875	3.2
1986	34,105	2.8
1987	34,375	5.5
1988	34,470	7.5
1989	36,485	10.1
1990	29,400	9.8
1991	33,380	12.0
1992	26,222	9.4
1993	27,673	8.5
1994	34,173	8.1
1995	22,621	8.7
1996	19,875	6.0
1997	18,200	5.8

* *CPI(A) denotes the expenditure pattern of households in the lower and middle income strata.*

Source: Census and Statistics Department, *Monthly Digest of Statistics (various issues)*.
Rating and Valuation Department, *Hong Kong Property Review (various years)*.

will clearly be moving towards more owner-occupation as more land will be developed. On the supply side, a comparison of Tables 3.2 and 3.4 suggests that annual production of both private housing and public rental housing has been clearly slowed down in the 1990s. While we note in Table 3.3 that the percentage distribution of both public and private has been rather stable, the annual housing supply has been decreased towards the second half of the 1990s. The only substantial change in housing stock distribution is within the subsidized sale flat sector, or the *Home Ownership Scheme*. The government has tried to encourage the development of owner-occupation through promoting the Home Ownership Scheme and controlling the production of public rental housing. Notwithstanding these policy initiatives, we still do not see substantial increase in the overall percentage of private housing. The supply of private flats has been rather stable throughout the 1980s averaging to about 30,000 units per annum and as suggested, slowly decreasing in second half of the 1990s (see Table 3.4). Why? Two tentative reasons may be adduced. First, the policy instruments have clearly failed to regulate the private housing market. This then encourages private developers to respond more actively to market demand signals through pricing and supply strategies, and hence partially explains why profit margins of developers have remained extremely high. Second, the deliberate control and slowing down of public rental housing production has upset the delicate balance between the public and the private sectors, hence trivializing the role of public housing as a market stabilizer. The promotion of home ownership through the market, coupled with enormous effective demand, and with very little intervention from the government, have given the developers the best market signals to begin non-competitive practices. Continual and consistent housing price inflation could be seen in Table 3.4 throughout the 1980s and 1990s. This set the scene for the eventual bubble economy.

Keen Competition for Space

The keen competition for space could perhaps be reflected by the average household size. It was 3.4 in 1991 and gradually decreased to 3.3 in 1996, while the average UK household size was 2.5 for the same period. Two-person household has increased from 33% of the population to 38% in 1996. The desire for more family space has always remained keen. Contrary to government policy statements, both the actual and percentage increases in public rental housing for the last decade were minimal. The number of people on the waiting list for public rental housing in March 1991 was 135,000 and has increased to 150,000 in 1998. The competition for public housing and subsidized sale flats has always been keen. In the late 1960s and early 1970s, to secure a public housing unit was like winning a lottery. Interestingly, the same psychological phenomenon still applies today, with the additional dimension that one would be equally happy for being given the chance to purchase a government Home

Ownership Scheme flat. Sadly, after 40 years of state intervention in housing, Hong Kong people are still in dire shortage of affordable housing!

Who Lives Where?

Geographically, Hong Kong can be divided into three main regions: Hong Kong Island, Kowloon and New Kowloon, and the New Territories. The main urban built-up areas lie along the coast of the Hong Kong Island and the Kowloon Peninsula. The suburban areas, largely villages and new towns, are in the New Territories. From an aerial view, Hong Kong is surrounded on all sides by water (even along the northern border where the Shenzhen River divides Hong Kong and Mainland China), and hence it is natural to find settlements along the coastline. The size of the population has not changed much for the Island since the 1980s. The major change lies perhaps in a process of gradual urban-suburban migration where the population of Kowloon and New Kowloon dropped from 43.8% in 1985 to 32% in 1996, while the population of the New Territories increased from 33.6% in 1985 to 46.8% in 1996. The increase of population in the New Territories is the result of the development of new towns in the early 1970s and more recently, the phenomenal rise in urban house prices, creating a push factor for urban-suburban migration. The following sections provide a socio-spatial introduction to people and place of the three major regions of Hong Kong.

The Hong Kong Island

For a first time visitor to Hong Kong, locating the city centre could be daunting because there is none. The whole urban area could be regarded as one big city centre. The major business district is located on the southern side of the Victoria Harbour, called the Central District, where most banks, embassies and the central government offices are situated. To the east of Central District lies a mixture of commercial and private residential areas, stretching eastward to Wan Chai, Causeway Bay, North Point and gradually into huge private residential developments in places such as Tai Koo Shing and Kornhill Estates in the Eastern District, where most new middle class people now reside. In terms of the distribution of home ownership, the Eastern corridor finds the highest concentration of owner-occupation in the territory. Wan Chai has the highest home ownership rate (93%) because it is one of the oldest inner-city areas where there is no public housing. Owner-occupation is rather fragmented in areas near the waterfront, having more a mixture of old tenement blocks and high-rise commercial buildings, and hence, comparatively less concentrated in home ownership when compared to the hill side area to the immediate north of Wan Chai where many middle class private residential developments are located. To the northern Mid-level area approaching Kennedy Road, the Wan Chai settlement turns middle class. Professionals and expatriates live along Kennedy Road leading up to the Mid-level of the Central District. Spatially, the altitude of one's dwelling represents one's social class and hence its worth. This is not just true of buying property, where the highest flat in a high-rise block is normally the highest priced. In Central and Wan Chai District, it is always the middle class and professionals who live in the Mid-level. Then it is the upper class and the *taipans* who live on the Peak either in luxurious condominiums or maisonettes. Western District is again a mixture of old tenement blocks and post-war high-rise. Demographically, Western District has the highest concentration of elderly people in Hong Kong. Hence the lower end of the district is a typical settlement of non-skilled manual workers while the middle class clusters around Bonham Road near the University of Hong Kong. Southern District on the Island is a vast geographical area and has a fair mix of tenure (30% owner-occupiers, 49% public rental). Upper class dwellings cluster around the famous beaches such as Repulse Bay, Deep Bay and Stanley. Middle class dwellings can be found along the northern fringe of Southern District in Chi Fu Estate, Baguio Villa and Aberdeen Centre, while some working class public housing estates are found in Wah Fu and Wong Chuk Hang.

Hong Kong Island as a whole has a fairly stable population (21%) and one of the highest home ownership rates in the territory. This is seen as the result of an acute shortage of available land for new development. The centrality of its location and the history of its development also enable the area to reap enormous strategic benefits both as a choice of residence and a place to do business. As a consequence, Hong Kong Island marks the highest concentration of middle and upper class interests in comparison to working class domination in public rental housing estates in New Kowloon.

Kowloon and New Kowloon

For an urban populace as concentrated, condensed and well served by public transport, it is difficult to imagine any substantial spatial differences in terms of home-buying and residential choices, particularly between Hong Kong Island and Kowloon. However, the fact remains that it is easy to find people spending their entire life in Kowloon without ever thinking of crossing the harbour (or vice versa). The subtle distinction between Hongkongers and Kowlooners, however, does not apply to intra-regional mobility. People do move frequently between districts within a region, but seldom crossing the harbour in a normal range of life activities. The real inter-regional migration over recent years, nevertheless, is between Kowloon and the New Territories. The division between Kowloon and New Kowloon is the Boundary Street. South of it lies the peninsula, representing the old residential and commercial districts of Yau Ma Tei, Tsim Sha Tsui and Mong Kok. The rate of home ownership is extremely high here, with 91%, 90% and 96% for the three districts respectively. This could be explained by the fact that a substantial percentage of residential ownership is being used for commercial purposes, such as offices or 'second-floor shops'. This is a common practice in Hong Kong due to scarcity of land and high rent of street level shop space. Typical owner-occupation in this area would be small high-rise blocks of 10-15 storeys built in the 1960s. Each floor has two flats of 600 square feet and is usually serviced by one small lift. It usually has larger space but no permanently fitted rooms. A typical owner would be a middle-age shop owner who bought his place for as little as $50,000 in the 1960s. Knowing the difficulties of selling a flat built some 30 years ago, he has very low motivation to move. After all, his place is so conveniently located and so close to the subway.

Northwest of Boundary Street lies Sham Shui Po and Cheung Sha Wan, together they form the 'backyard' of Kowloon. The area is characterized by post-war old tenement blocks and early public housing estates. The private housing blocks are usually below 10 storeys high and are seldom serviced by lifts. Homeowners in Sham Shui Po are typically retired elderly people who bought their places in the late 1950s at very low prices. The buildings are of much less residential value compared to their potential for redevelopment. In fact, many small developers are keenly interested in luring these owners to sell their flats. There are real estate agents who specialize in the business of trying to round up a plot of land comprising several of these old tenement blocks which offers development potential. Because of the lucrative nature of the business, it is not uncommon to find the underworld (the triad society) involved in the solicitation process, occasionally playing dirty tricks against innocent homeowners.

Northeast of Boundary Street lies the middle class district of Kowloon City (a rather deceptive name because it is only a district of Kowloon and New Kowloon). It is one of the best locations in the district, with low-rise townhouses (4-5 storeys high) of middle and upper class dwellers, largely composed of retired businessmen and expatriates. The best international schools for English, American and Japanese are found in the vicinity along Waterloo Road and Kowloon Tong (an adjacent sub-district). The district also boasts one of the most sought after catchment areas for the best primary and secondary schools. Professionals and white-collar workers are seldom found in Kowloon Tong. Instead they cluster around the fringe areas of Kowloon City, particularly north of Grampian Road.

Further to the northeast of Boundary Street lie the two huge districts of Wong Tai Sin and Kwun Tong, which house most of the old public housing estates, standing side by side with the oldest industrial establishments in Hong Kong. It is not surprising to find the percentage of home ownership in these two districts comparatively low (12% for Wong Tai Sin, 21% for Kwun Tong). The typical homeowner of Kwun Tong and Wong Tai Sin is either a skilled labourer whose income slightly exceeds the public housing eligibility limit and hence not eligible for public rental housing, or someone who chooses to live near his workplace and who bought his house in the late 1960s at an affordable price.

New Territories

South of the Lo Wu border and north of the Lion Rock lies the hilly suburban backyard of Hong Kong. Although known as the 'New' Territories, it contains some of the oldest rural settlements (e.g. Kam Tin) in the Territory. Nowadays, the New Territories houses most of Hong Kong's new towns: Tsuen Wan, Kwai Tsing, Sha Tin, Tuen Mun, Tai Po, Fanling, Sheung Shui and Yuen Long. To call it suburban is in fact rather misleading. The joint districts of Kwai Tsing and Tsuen Wan now boast a population of 700,000 which is comparable to any major city in Europe in terms of population size. Sha Tin, with half a million population, is now the fastest growing modern city-within-a-city, with a vibrant industrial and commercial sector. It has the highest concentration of middle class homeowners (44%).

The broad image of home ownership in the New Territories, hence, is one of fragmentation. In Kwai Tsing and Tsuen Wan, it is more of a blue-collar, skilled labour or service sector home ownership. It is more often linked up with the public rental sector. The typical situation is that the second generation of families in the public rental sector move out to the nearby private housing developments after they have left school or got married. In Yuen Long or Sheung Shui, the northern-most districts of a more rural nature, the home ownership pattern is one of the offspring of rural families, wishing to improve their living standards and moving to more urban living in new developments within the new town centres. However, in the case of Tuen Mun, Tai Po and Sha Tin, where original rural settlements are relatively small, the pattern of home ownership is largely the result of a deliberate policy of urban-suburban migration since the early 1960s. The early households moving there were largely white-collar workers who could no longer afford to live in urban Kowloon. In recent years, it is more the young urban professionals seeking a better housing alternative on the not-so-urban fringe areas. While there is not a general pattern of home ownership distribution in the New Territories, one can safely discern that the further north you move, the cheaper the house price and the greater the connection of home ownership with the indigenous rural population.

Taking the north bound Kowloon-Canton Railway, one is often amazed to find the regulated and orderly nature of Sha Tin, Tai Po and Fanling new towns. But as suggested by Bristow (1989) in his study of Hong Kong's new town development, there has always been a certain degree of reluctance and uneasiness in the development of the New Territories, since thus far the early experiences of Hong Kong in new town development has been fraught with more problems than success.

The Social Organization of Home Ownership

An Ideal Home Owner

The ideal image of a homeowner (e.g. the Ho family) in Hong Kong is a couple in their early thirties with two kids living either in Kornhill Estate on Island East or Whampoa Estate in Central Kowloon. They bought a 3-bedroom flat of 700 square feet in 1990. They have a total of five persons in the house, two adults, two kids and a Filipino helper. The couple occupy the en-suite master bedroom. There would be an all-purpose study room and a room where the two children share with the maid. The price they paid for their flat depends on where and when they bought the flat. In 1990, it would be roughly $1.5 million. They should have paid 10% down payment and taken out a mortgage of $1.3 million, or 30% down payment for properties bought after 1991. Since the couple are middle class professionals, the husband working in the civil service and the wife working as a nurse, they should have no problem in obtaining a 90%

mortgage from the bank. For middle class flats in Island East or Central Kowloon, there is always an active second-hand market. These districts abound with large and small real estate agents and the couple took great trouble to identify a reliable one. Prior to 1997, real estate agents were minimally regulated and they were notorious for unethical practices. Both the buyer and the seller are required to pay about 1% of the purchase price as the agent fee. Depending on the competitiveness of the prevailing market, a lower percentage is sometimes acceptable. With 2% stamp duty and also a sizeable solicitor's fees for conveyancing, they paid about $50,000 for the whole transaction. Adding on the costs for fitting-out and new furniture, they would be paying about $250,000, which they considered to be quite reasonable in the early 1990s. If they were wise enough to sell their flat before October 1997, the flat would fetch $4.5 million, tripling the value in seven years, with an average 20% annual appreciation. They would have never dreamt of saving that much in their lifetime. With that money, even if they had decided to emigrate because of the 1997 question, they would be able to buy a reasonable-sized family home anywhere in the UK, Canada and Australia, and still managed to have a secured early retirement. The case of the Ho family sets the stage of why an economy so much dependent on house price appreciation would finally become problematic.

Socio-Economic Groupings and Housing Tenure

So much for the ideal construction of a middle class homeowner. Even after the Asian economic downturn, it is still a dream for many in Hong Kong to be able to afford their home. For those who entered the market before 1991, many have become homeowners with an asset having at least 100% appreciation. Using a modified Goldthrope classification, Table 3.5 suggests that there has been a substantial increase in owner-occupation for the middle class, increasing from 33.8% in 1976 to 68% in 1991. While many people consider clerical workers and low-grade service professionals (such as real estate agents and salesmen) as being less able to buy, the figures show that their representation in the owner-occupier market has been rising steadily. While there is an across-the-board increase in the level of owner-occupation for all occupational categories, two interesting observations could be made: first, both technician and routine-manual workers show an increase in home ownership, although the increase is comparatively slower than the middle class. Second, other than the capitalist class being the traditional stronghold of owner-occupation, it is

Table 3.5   Socio-economic Groupings and Housing Tenure in Hong Kong (in percentage) 1976, 1986 and 1991

Tenure	Year	Capitalist	Middle Class	Routine Non-manual Worker	Petite Bourgeoisie	Supervisor Technician	Routine Manual Worker
Owner-Occupier	1991	74.8	68.0	49.8	47.1	45.1	30.4
	1986	66.4	54.3	41.8	43.1	36.9	25.5
	1976	47.7	33.8	24.1	37.0	9.1	13.4
Public Rental	1991	22.3	20.5	37.4	40.2	32.8	50.8
	1986	26.6	23.2	42.3	43.8	37.1	49.8
	1976	36.0	39.0	44.7	36.3	72.7	47.5
Private Renting	1991	1.8	3.8	8.2	9.0	5.8	17.2
	1986	3.7	4.2	10.6	9.1	6.1	20.1
	1976	11.5	11.6	25.5	21.6	18.2	32.6
Rent Free	1991	1.0	0.8	1.5	2.8	0.3	1.2
	1986	1.0	1.0	1.6	3.1	0.6	2.2
	1976	4.0	1.5	3.5	4.2	0.0	3.8
Employer Provided	1991	1.1	6.9	6.9	0.9	16.0	0.4
	1986	2.3	17.4	3.6	0.9	19.4	2.5
	1976	0.8	14.2	2.2	0.9	0.0	2.7

Note: Estimate based on a 1% random sample of the 1976, 1986, and 1991 Census and By-census data.

quite clear that professionals and managers are the emerging homeowners in the last two decades. These two points are confirmed in a follow-up study by using 1996 By-census figures. As far as private home ownership tenure is concerned, it can be seen from Table 3.6 that professionals, managers and associate professionals, together take up more than 40% of the total tenure. And then, clerks and service workers are the emerging new homeowners of the 1990s, occupying some 27% of the tenure. It is interesting to note that machine operators and workers in the elementary occupations also take up 22% of the tenure. This may be explained by the fact that working class people bought their houses in the 1960s and 1970s in poor inner city areas like Sham Shui Po, Yau Ma Tei and Mong Kok where house prices were generally affordable. However, as a result of a continuous property boom in the last two decades and the shortage of low-grade inner city houses, even these people are no longer able to buy. The other observation in Table 3.5 is the general decrease in private renting across all classes. The figures reflect a rather large-scale social mobility between tenures. People originally belonging to the public rental sector have moved up to home ownership. This confirms one of the earlier claims that there was implicit government policy to control the size of the public rental sector. This policy orientation has been effectively conceived even in as early as the 1970s. It was never the intention of the government to expand the public rental sector.

One more interesting observation concerns the comparatively slower decrease in private renting for the working class. Over the last two decades, private renting has ceased to an alternative for most middle class people. However, it still constituted 17% in 1991 for the routine manual worker, suggesting that working class people still need to turn to the private renting market when they are on the long waiting list for public rental housing. In fact, private renting dominates the two far ends of the housing ladder. It is either the very poor or the senior civil servants or senior executives of the private sector who are likely to rent. This phenomenon is further confirmed by a follow-up census study (see Table 3.6) in 1996 that working class people still take up half of private renting as a tenure. On the other hand, professionals and administrators take up only 36%. After the Asian economic crisis in 1998, it is expected that more middle class people would turn to private renting, as the tenure becomes relatively cheaper and less risky than owner-occupation. Private renting in 1998 is estimated to be around 17.5% of the total tenure. Table 3.6 also suggests that amongst homeowners in the public sector, the associate professionals, clerks, service

Table 3.6   Housing Tenure and Occupational Class 1996

Occupation	Type of Tenure				
	Public Tenant	Public Homeowner	Private Homeowner	Private Renting	Others
Skilled worker	4,872 (0.46%)	826 (0.24%)	7,495 (0.69%)	2,766 (0.72%)	7,519 (4.98%)
Manager, administrator	37,527 (3.50%)	35,396 (10.27%)	207,828 (19.07%)	63,991 (16.60%)	24,581 (16.29%)
Professional	21,483 (2.00%)	12,025 (3.49%)	74923 (6.87%)	29,612 (7.68%)	13,548 (8.98%)
Associate professional	89,401 (8.34%)	50,297 (14.61%)	166368 (15.26%)	44,470 (11.54%)	18,596 (12.33%)
Clerk	194,062 (18.09%)	72,786 (21.12%)	182,927 (16.78%)	49,137 (12.75%)	13,807 (9.15%)
Service worker, sales worker	171,481 (15.99%)	46,827 (13.59%)	116,589 (10.69%)	56,890 (14.76%)	27,934 (18.52%)
Craft worker	183,233 (17.08%)	45,556 (13.22%)	93,294 (8.56%)	41,590 (10.79%)	9,470 (6.28%)
Machine operator	131,657 (12.27%)	35,081 (10.18%)	64,083 (5.88%)	23,711 (6.15%)	5,377 (3.56%)
Elementary occupation	238,868 (22.27%)	45,775 (13.28%)	176,662 (16.20%)	73,346 (19.01%)	30,031 (19.91%)
Total	1,072,584 (100%)	344,569 (100%)	1,090,169 (100%)	385,513 (100%)	150,863 (100%)

Source: Census and Statistics Department, *1996 By-Census data.*

workers and craft workers have come to dominate the picture. They form the primary target group of homeowners for the subsidized government Home Ownership Scheme. Together with their counterparts in private home ownership, they now form the core of the new middle class homeowners. Under the existing policy to promote home ownership, both the Housing Authority and private developers will be competing with each other in the future for this potential owner-occupation market. Taking a broad view of Table 3.6, we are definitely witnessing a transition towards a tenure dominated by continual rising home ownership in the next millennium.

Housing Finance, House Price Inflation and Speculation

Unlike the UK, Hong Kong does not have such institutions as building societies. Almost 95% of all mortgages emanate from 28 major local and international banks. These are the licensed banks, e.g. Hong Kong and Shanghai Bank, Hang Seng Bank, Standard Chartered Bank, Bank of East Asia and Bank of China. Other international banks quite active in mortgage lending are Citicorp, Bank of America and Barclays Bank. The other two groups of banks are the Restricted Licence Banks and the deposit-taking companies (Jao, 1990). Banks in Hong Kong are renowned for their competitiveness in the mortgage business. The last two decades saw an enormous growth of mortgage loans for residential property, increasing almost 10-fold from $15.4 billion in 1981 to $145.8 billion in 1990, with an annual growth rate of 31.4%. It is approximately $590 billion in 1998, increasing again fourfold since 1990. Bank loans for residential mortgages take up 30% of all loans. Including loans for building and construction, housing related loans take up 52% of the total loan portfolio. The health of the banking sector in Hong Kong is certainly highly dependent on the performance of the property sector. Although the banking sector is reputed internationally to be very conservative, such portfolio weight on the housing sector begs a lot of questions. Heavy housing investment could be attributed to two factors. First, there was substantial growth in the economy during the 1980s, giving rise to a boom in the total level of wealth and hence investment. Second, owing to the high profitability of the capital market, Hong Kong successfully attracted a huge amount of 'hot money' from the international money market throughout the last two decades, resulting in a substantial growth of the

Table 3.7   Distribution of Bank Loans (In Hong Kong $ million)

Economic sector	1990	1998
Manufacturing	49,315	94,452
Agriculture and fisheries	585	1,617
Transport	41,232	105,630
Electricity, gas and telephone	8,074	25,654
Building, construction, property development and investment	108,112	419,101
Property development and investment		
Industrial	*10,735*	*9,518*
Residential	*22,158*	*179,462*
Commercial	*43,474*	*112,064*
Other properties	*23,064*	*98,423*
Others	*8,681*	*19,635*
Mortgage loans	145,830	590,036
Wholesale and retail trade	74,641	178,122
Mining and quarrying	1,185	2,050
Miscellaneous	260,394	541,153
Total Loans and advances for use in Hong Kong	689,368	1,957,815

Source: Census and Statistics Department, *Annual Digest of Statistics 1998.*

total money supply. Total money supply increased from $138.8 billion in 1981 to $1,288 billion in 1990, and to $2,611 billion in 1996, a 19-fold increase in less than two decades. In addition, the decades also witnessed one of the most important post-war era in the growth of the construction and building business. The increase in loan activities in mortgage and construction since 1991 has sent tremendous warning signals to the banking system that has triggered a series of interventionist activities in the housing as well as mortgage loan markets. In August 1991, the government issued a number of directives to regulate the sales and purchases of new flats. Such clear tampering with the operation of the housing market stems from strong outcries in the community over the manner in which the sales of new flats were controlled by the underworld (*the triad society*), to the extent that genuine buyers were effectively prevented from buying any new flats. It would be difficult for any one from a Western society to imagine that all new flats in a private development would be snapped up within hours of their release, with price going up 5%-10% on the same day.

One of the intervention directives aiming at curbing speculations was the requirement that developers must conduct secret ballots for all new flats to be sold after August 1991, so that there would be no more long queues outside the developer's office, hence preventing the triad society from tampering with the queues. Another directive was to set down rules to make it more risky for buyers to buy new flats under construction and as a result to prevent frequent exchanges of these flats. Buyers were not allowed to change the title of the ownership of a flat before its completion. In the heyday of property speculation, it was not uncommon that a flat might have undergone more than five exchanges within a year. This situation was more common in those much sought after middle class private housing estates such as Kornhill and Tai Koo Shing.

In November 1991, the Commissioner for Banking and Securities issued an unprecedented directive in Hong Kong's banking history: asking all mortgage lending banks to lower the mortgage ceiling from the long established 90% to 70%. Most banks followed the directive and as a result the mortgage business for the first quarter of 1992 dropped by 20%. However, in a study commissioned in June 1992 by the Secretary for Planning, Environment and Lands to look into the price effect of the new mortgage ceiling amongst six major housing estates, e.g. Tai Koo Shing, in Island East, Laguna City in Kowloon East, the result was extremely discouraging. During the period June 1991 to April 1992, there was an overall increase of 40% in house prices. In other words, the policy instruments of putting a mortgage ceiling only managed to cool off the market in terms of sales volume, but failed to lower house prices. Prices kept soaring.

Affordability

Since the 1983 property slump, house prices have been constantly on the rise. Prices for flats in the urban areas increased from $600 per square foot in 1983 to about $6,000 in 1992. While many critics concluded that house

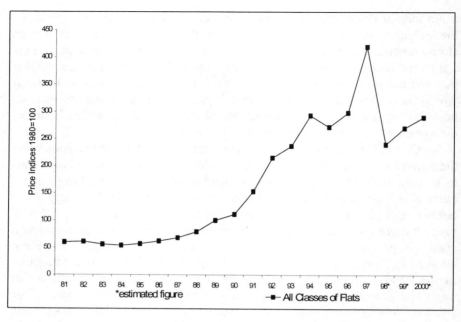

Figure 3.1   House Price Inflation – Price Indices by Class

Source: Rating and Valuation Department, *Property Review 1998.*

price inflation was very much the result of widespread speculation, it should not be overlooked that the housing market was basically fuelled by an economy which guaranteed much-inflated wage income and a market characterized by keen demand and absolute scarcity of housing. In Figure 3.1 we can see that since 1986, housing price has been on steady rise. It fell slightly in 1995 when government sought regulatory practices. However, it began to rise again after a year and reached its peak in March 1997. In 1997, an average-sized flat anywhere in town could easily fetch $3 million. A 70% mortgage ceiling means that the family had to fetch $900,000 as down payment and a 25-year mortgage of $2.1 million. At a 9% interest rate, the family had to pay a monthly mortgage of approximately $25,000. Given a median household monthly income of $17,500 in 1997, no one could afford to buy one's own home. A family must come up with twice as much before they could consider ownership. Even if a family could manage to buy, they would easily run into financial troubles if some contingencies happened in the family. The cost of home ownership was thus extremely high. Any increase in interest rates would have serious consequences on the family budget. Figure 3.2 gives some idea of the problem of affordability. It uses a price-income ratio basing on the ratio between median house price and median annual income. We can see that housing affordability has been a problem since early 1980. Political uncertainties in the early 1980s may have helped reduce the affordability problem. Nonetheless, at no time the ratio fell below 6. According to a crude international comparison (see Table 3.8), the affordability ratio in Hong Kong probably tops the world, particularly in 1997, when the ratio reached an all-time high of 15.

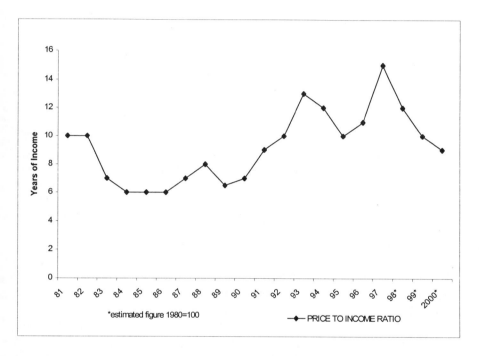

Figure 3.2   Housing Affordability

Source: Rating and Valuation Department, *Property Review 1998*.
Census and Statistics Department, *General Household Survey*.

Table 3.8   Housing Affordability Ratio – An International Comparison

Country	Year	Affordability Ratio (Price-Income Ratio)
Australia	1988	4.0
Canada	1986	4.8
France	1982	2.8
Germany	1988	3.8
United Kingdom	1988	3.7
	1995	4.5
United States	1988	2.8
	1996	3.0
Hong Kong	1988	6.0
	1997	15.0

Source: Renaud (1989), *Affordable Housing and Housing Sector Performance: The Housing Price-to-Income Ratio as Summary Indicator*, Working Paper, Centre for Urban Planning and Urban Studies, University of Hong Kong.

Wright, J W (1998) *New York Times 1998 Almanac*, New York: Penguin.

According to the 1996 census, about 630,000 households in Hong Kong (34% of the total population) fell within the monthly income range of $10,000-$30,000. They constituted the majority of the lower middle class. Economically, they are the most vibrant group, with their earning power more likely to increase in the coming years. Studies elsewhere (Lee, 1990) have indicated that people in Hong Kong are barely satisfied with their current living conditions, and many genuinely desire for an improvement. Certainly this group creates the greatest pressure on housing. For, on the one hand, they are barred from the state housing system because they are well above the income limit, and certainly most of them are not eligible for the government Home Ownership Scheme. Put simply, they are in the state's view, self-sufficient in housing. However, as I explained above, they can hardly afford home ownership. Or even if they could, they have to put up with a heavy mortgage burden and a very stringent life.

Unfortunately many did buy in 1997 and the consequence is disastrous. Many of them have already found themselves in negative equity. The risk of home ownership is thus fully realized for those who bought in 1997. The cruel reality of life in Hong Kong is that: if you are not in the public rental sector or government Home Ownership Scheme, you are not receiving any form of state subsidy in housing. Until 1998, there is absolutely no tax allowance for mortgage financing and home ownership. Once you are in the private sector, you are entirely on your own. So either you are enjoying cheap rent in public rental housing where your social entitlement enables you to what Castells et al. (1990) refers to as a *social wage* or you must be rich enough to buy a house and be able to afford the mortgage repayment.

There is no doubt that the middle income groups are experiencing the most severe form of housing pressure. Instead of having a marginalized public rental sector, there is a marginalized group who cannot afford to buy and who find few alternatives in a dwindling private rental market. While Western literature points unerringly to the general tendency of a marginalized and dilapidated public rental sector (Forrest & Murie, 1988), Hong Kong presents a different story. The public housing sector continues to receive subsidies even when government has decided to attach less importance to it.

Housing Histories and Ethnography: A Methodological Note

Part Two of this book is mostly based on ethnographical data drawn from 30 case studies of home ownership which I conducted in 1994 (see Appendix B for background of cases). Although the housing market and house prices have changed substantially since the 1997 handover, stresses and strains of home ownership still largely remain in Hong Kong. Government policy on home ownership and the domination of the property market on the economy remain intact. Hence, most of the findings and discussions are still relevant and applicable today. The following describes briefly the methodological basis of my study.

In Chapter one, I mentioned two shortcomings of the existing home ownership debates. First, existing theoretical approaches have been deeply entrenched in Marxist and Neo-Weberian rhetoric to the extent that housing studies have been detached from social reality. Second, we need to seek an intermediate framework that enables a re-coupling of the individual and society. It is also suggested that we need to pay attention to two social institutions that bear close relationship to housing and home ownership: the family and culture.

To conduct a study encompassing the above aims is challenging. It seems apparent that I cannot rely solely on the traditional social survey instrument which is popular with researchers on issues of housing subsidies and housing policy (Merrett & Gray, 1982; Van Vliet, 1990; Malpass, 1990). Both depth and richness of data are required in the study of social change. The survey method provides some good descriptive statistics but many of the questions to be addressed must go back to personal archives, through memories, conceptual re-organization and insights. A historical ethnographic method sensitive to culture and change seems in order. To choose this methodology, I am aware of the high expectation and demand on the researcher as an ethnographer, as well as the anxiety that comes with it. To this end, I share entirely with Van Maanen's earlier reminder on the relationship between culture and ethnographic fieldwork:

> Culture is neither prison nor monolith. Nor, of course, is it tangible. A culture is expressed only by the actions and words of its members and must be interpreted by, not given to, a field worker. To portray culture requires the field worker to hear, to see, and most important for our purposes, to write of what was presumably witnessed and understood during a stay in the field. Culture is not itself visible, but is made visible only through its representation (Van Maanen, 1988, p. 3).

This book is also based on two earlier social indicator research which I conducted in 1988 and 1991 on the satisfaction level of living environment and housing (Lee, 1990, 1992). The 1991 Census data and the 1996 By-Census data were also heavily used in the book. These survey data provide an extremely important housing data environment for me to work on. However, the principal method adopted in this study is one of qualitative investigation of a limited number of household experiences in home ownership. In most cases, both husband and wife were interviewed together, augmented by peripheral data supplied by elderly family members present. My concern is the housing trajectory or housing career of the individual and the family. Therefore in some cases, the interview actually comprised three separate but related housing trajectories: the husband's and the wife's own family housing trajectory before marriage, as well as their housing trajectory after marriage. Hence, it may be argued that the 30 households studied actually hinge on a much wider housing trajectories. Two criticisms against the quality of ethnographic data often raised are that: (1) they are too dependent on memories and personal recollections;

68

and that (2) there is no way to guarantee the quality of the data. While accepting these criticisms, this study took important steps to protect the quality of the data. Three levels of triangulation were built in. The first level involves the comparison of data between family members for cross-checking, for variables such as dates, names and price information (intra-family). The second level goes back to the introducer who provided background information concerning the next respondent to be introduced (inter-family). The third level involves checking on information outside the family, such as social history, government policies and house price information. My experience suggests that the first two levels of triangulation work best when the interviewer quickly responded to factual questions through on-the-spot clarifications. Interview questions were organized around four abstract levels: (1) the origin of home ownership; (2) the destinations; (3) the coping of housing situations in between tenure change, and (4) the quality of life associated with housing trajectory. The reasons for the choice of a historical and ethnographic method are twofold. First, it is only through this method that historical data on the housing trajectory could be gathered. Second, the examination of an individual household's coping strategies as reflected in the individual housing history as well the prevailing socio-political context will provide more rigorous insight into the relationship between housing and social change.

The choice of 30 cases is partly pragmatic and partly traditional. The consideration here is: what number of subjects could produce sufficient diversity in terms of data. Ideally, the intention is that the sample can reveal two levels of diversity: (1) the range of occupations should spread amongst the three common segments of the middle class, that is, the lower service class, the routine non-manual employees and the petite-bourgeoisie; and (2) the range of mortgage repayment stage, that is, early mortgage, mid-mortgage and late mortgage or out-right ownership. The resulting distribution of subjects is slightly less satisfactory with the lower service class and early mortgage owners dominating the scene. Nonetheless, as far as the range of diversity is concerned, the sample yields a broad range of subjects coming under the general definition of middle class homeowners.

Conclusion

This chapter sets out to describe the Hong Kong housing context in two respects. First, it describes the development of local housing studies in the past two decades. It identifies the transformation of housing studies from third world geography to the political economy of housing. One of the major weaknesses identified is that housing research in Hong Kong has been strongly biased towards the study of the public housing sector. The result of this uni-dimensional research tradition reflects not just a gap. At a deeper level, it reflects a structural hegemony in research culture aiming at legitimizing the role of state intervention in public housing while trivializing studies on private home ownership. Furthermore, concentration on the policy level of housing provision resulted in an inevitable neglect of individual and family experiences. Second, the chapter also describes a broad sketch of the social organization of home ownership, highlighting the housing affordability problems faced by a marginalized group within the middle class. They are mainly the first time buyers and young couples belonging to the lower service class. For those who entered the market slightly earlier, they still could shoulder up to 60%-70% of their monthly salary on mortgage repayment, but had to put up with an extremely constrained livelihood.

Evidence has revealed that, while there has been an across-the-board increase in the level of home ownership amongst all social classes, the middle class has the highest rate of growth. A number of socio-economic factors, such as speculations, affordability and mortgage, have been examined. These factors provide a first level analysis of the growth of home ownership but fail to explain the social roots underlying an individual or family decision's to become a homeowner. With a housing scene flooded by problems of affordability, speculations and housing supply shortage, a uni-dimensional research focus provides only a very limited view of social genesis of home ownership. Finally, while the chapter seeks to map out the social organization of home ownership, it has not provided a framework to interpret and consolidate these housing situations into a coherent whole. This incidentally will form the major part of the next chapter.

Notes

1. The first paper that makes an explicit attempt to focus on the development of home ownership is my own work in 1994 in *Policy and Politics;* a related work by Lui (1995); and a recent work by Chiu, R. in 1997 in *Asian Journal of Business & Information System.* (For full reference, please see Bibliography.)

2. Castells et al.'s comparative study on public housing and economic development in Hong Kong and Singapore was criticized as taking on a too simplistic view between state intervention and economic development in high-growth city-states. While accepting that massive public housing programmes of these countries do carry a labour reproduction capacity, it was suggested that the social structure of housing must be re-examined in order to clarify the relationship between economic development and state intervention.

4 Towards a Theoretical Framework

The debate on the relationship between the general tenure shift towards home ownership in Western societies (notably English speaking societies) and social change has occupied a prominent place in British housing research for the last two decades (see for example: Edel et al., 1984; Dauntion, 1987; Forrest, Murie & Williams, 1990; Murie, 1989; Saunders, 1990; Kemeny, 1992, Forrest, Leather & Kennet, 1999). Housing consumption in the form of owner-occupation has been conceived as one of the most significant social phenomena of modern societies, having potential impact on social divisions and social inequality (Merrett & Gray, 1982; Kemeny, 1981; Saunders, 1990; Forrest, Murie & Williams, 1990; Bratt, Hartmann & Meyerson, 1986). Housing consumption is seen as a major source of wealth accumulation through the dual economic processes of asset appreciation and house price inflation. The discussion of home ownership is also connected with the emergence of a salient group within modern societies that wields consumption power and a lifestyle associated with home owning. Broadly speaking, two strands of debate have evolved. First, home ownership as a dominant form of tenure has increasingly been referred to as one of the major causes of social polarization. The basic conception concerns society having an affluent majority owning good quality private housing at one end, and a marginalized minority living in poor quality residualized public rental housing at the other. They are identified as the unemployed, the single-parent families and the elderly. In extreme situation, an *underclass* develops in some societies (Gans, 1990). It constitutes one of the major social problems in recession-plagued post-industrial Western societies. Polarized housing consumption in terms of the presence of an extremity in tenure development has also been theoretically conceptualized as amounting to a new fission within society (Saunders, 1984). The root of this polarization debate lies in the proposition by Saunders that class is no longer an analytically robust concept to account for structural changes in Western societies. Social polarity is increasingly determined by one's consumption capacity rather than one's position in the production process.

Second, housing consumption in terms of private home ownership is increasingly seen as a preferred tenure, providing both as a means of safeguarding personal savings and wealth accumulation through capital gains. Longitudinal analyses of house price data and tenure preferences have shown a consistent pattern of post-war increases in the real value of property (McLaverty, 1993). Home buying for many people in Western societies is still considered a safe hedge against inflation. It also provides a source of personal security going beyond its monetary value, making it intrinsically more attractive than other tenures, notably renting (Saunders, 1990).

Over the last decade, theoretical development between these two divergent strands of development have taken on quite different trajectories, each criticizing the other as either over-generalizing the effect of home ownership on social divisions or placing too much emphases on differential housing experiences within any one society (Saunders, 1990; Forrest, Murie & Williams, 1990). A cursory view of the literature suggests that theoretical development of housing and social change is still fragmented. In recent years, housing researchers have begun to adopt a more grounded approach, aiming at exploring some of the variables which have hitherto been neglected: such as the role of the family in home ownership (Forrest & Murie 1995), the relationship between housing histories/trajectories and labour market position (Murie, 1989; Forrest, Murie & Williams, 1990), the meaning of home and home ownership in different localities and cultures (Saunders and Williams, 1988; Dickens, 1990; Forrest & Murie, 1995) and the basic epistemology of housing studies (Kemeny, 1992). The underlying idea is that housing research should emerge from a mere focus on socio-tenurial status and broaden its discussion to include other factors. While noting the importance of tenure, housing researchers have attempted to question the overall validity of a uni-focused research orientation (Kemeny, 1992; Murie, 1989). Some suggest that the concept of tenure has been fraught with misconceptions and misunderstandings and researchers have failed to appreciate the difference between taxonomic and substantive genesis of the term itself (Barlow & Duncan, 1988). Others have suggested that the future analysis of housing and social change should focus more on its relationship with bureaucracy, culture and the emergence of the middle class (Savage et al., 1992). One recent study (Forrest, Leather & Kennet, 1999) has re-emphasized the adverse consequence of a large home ownership sector during economic downturn and has begun to examine more closely the relationship between the economy and the housing system. Perhaps a common theme that has evolved from this upsurge in home ownership studies is that the relationship between housing and society is gradually being conceived as much more complex than a uni-focus on tenure polarity could possibly encompass. The urge to reconstruct a tenure-focused approach in housing studies within a broader socio-economic framework has become stronger in recent years.

This chapter will first introduce (1) the macro debate on consumption sector cleavage; and (2) the micro debate on the meaning of home and home ownership. It is argued that both theoretical strands have their shortcomings. An alternative approach focusing more on the social basis of consumption culture, of economic choice and the formation of middle class will be explored (Savage et al., 1992; Crompton, 1993; Eder, 1993). To do so, I shall rely on the strength of two theoretical strands: the theory of culture and distinction by Bourdieu (1984) and the debate on social economics of Granovetter (1985). The rationale for using Bourdieu's theory is that he attempts to treat class analysis from a cultural perspective which moves beyond occupational classification in orthodox class analyses (Goldthrope, 1987; Wright, 1985). This provides a venue for considering home ownership and social division. The rationale for choosing Granovetter's contribution in social economics is that he challenges the assumptions of traditional economic rationality. It would be more helpful in appreciating the complexity of the decision to buy home since individuals do not always make rational and free choices as is generally assumed in traditional micro-economic analysis. Hong Kong sociologists have argued for sometime about placing special emphasis on the role of the family and its network of relationship in social analyses (Lau, 1984; Wong, 1975; Lee, 1991). The implication is that economic decisions such as home buying and home financing are invariably intertwined with the family system. Three key issues relating to home ownership are explored, namely: (1) the relationship between housing histories and social change; (2) the role of the family in home ownership and home financing; and (3) the significance of wealth accumulation and consumption from home ownership.

Home Ownership Perspectives: An Overview

Before proceeding to a detailed critique of the major theoretical perspectives for home ownership, Table 4.1 should help to summarize

Table 4.1 Existing Perspectives on Home Ownership

Major Perspectives	Theoretical Debates	Social Theory Base	Major Criticisms
Home ownership as consumption leading towards major social division and polarization	Consumption sector cleavage debate:- consumption is seen as an independent force besides production, leading towards major social closure	Structural Demand side argument	a) Consumption and production are intimately linked; b) Could only enrich class analysis but not replacing it; c) Neglecting the individual/family as agents of change
Home ownership as the outcome of a control process by key institutions/ agents (state and non-state) involving in the production and allocation of housing resources	Key institutions in the housing system such as the Housing Authority, mortgage lenders, developers and estate agents are capable of shaping the home ownership process through production and distribution of housing resources by gatekeepers such as housing managers, bank managers, developers and real estate agents. These gate keepers engage themselves in both control and competition with other institutions and gate-keepers within the housing system.	Structural Supply side argument	a) The focus on the gate-keepers as the middlemen within the housing process tends to neglect the underlying processes which shape urban managers into adopting a certain allocation choice. b) The emphasis on production, bureaucratic domination and individual discretion in the social construction of the housing systems tends to undermine the importance of the social context and other institutions and processes outside the state, such as the family and the social trajectory of housing.

Major Perspectives	Theoretical Debates	Social Theory Base	Major Criticisms
Home ownership as a preferred tenure for wealth accumulation	Rational consumer behavior to maximize returns to investment	Rationality Exchange Theory	a) Only partially explains the motivation to own; b) Not all decisions on ownership are rational.
Home ownership for the enhancement of psycho-social security	Ontological security debate - socially alienated individuals seeking autonomy, freedom and self-identity through home ownership.	Sociobiology Existential-ism	a) Concept difficult to operationalize; b) Minimize the influence of culture and family and other social institutions.

Table 4.2   A Cultural Perspective on Home Ownership

Perspective	Theoretical Debates	Social Theory Base	Comments on the proposed perspective
Home ownership as outcome of interaction between Individual, family, the economy and society, against a cultural context	a) Housing consumption is seen as part of a wider social process, particularly amongst the middle class. Cultural conflicts exist amongst various social groupings. Tenure shifts seen as the outcome of competition among different groups seeking to dominate each other through the use of cultural capital.	Constructionist, emphasizing human agency and action Culture and distinction Culture and class formation	a) Debate no longer simply confined to production and consumption relationship and transcend orthodox class debate; b) Gives attention both to home ownership as a macro phenomenon and a micro phenomenon;
	b) Housing choice is seen as individual/family economic decision embedded in social networks.	Economic embeddedness	a) Treat housing decisions as affected by social relationship embedded in institutions such as the family.

major existing perspectives on home ownership. An additional perspective - a cultural perspective - based on an emphasis on the relationship between culture, class and home ownership is proposed in Table 4.2.

Table 4.1 shows a basic organization of the three major strands of debates on home ownership. On the first level, it is represented by the debate centering on the relationship between home ownership as a major form of modern consumption and its underlying social process that leads to new social divisions. The basic tenet of this debate lies in the recognition of the role of consumption in modern societies. The major social theory base of the debate is essentially structural, seeking to identify processes that lead to new social structure. One of the fundamental criticisms of this debate is that it is too constrained by traditional Marxian rhetoric of production and consumption, to the extent that the debate departs from the social reality of home ownership. The debate also confines itself to a political economy level of analysis and fails to capture the role played by the individual and the family as agents of social change.

The second level of home ownership perspective moves from a society to an institution and bureaucracy. Home ownership is conceived as the outcome of a process of bureaucratic control within key institutions of the housing system. They include the state or local government housing authorities, mortgage-lenders, banks, developers and real estate agents. Urban managers of these key institutions are seen as playing a central role in exercising control and influencing access to housing resources by households. These urban managers or *gate keepers*, exercising their power and discretion through their interpretation of state or institutional policy, are seen as playing a pivotal role in shaping the housing process. Housing managers could propose projects which aim at boosting the housing alternatives of a certain strata of the middle class while discriminating others. Banks could favour those in full-time as well as selected employment. The setting of a mortgage ceiling (e.g. 70%) could create enormous financial barrier for first time home buyers. Developers could design and promote the consumption of certain *niche* housing developments, such as Tai Koo Shing. This perspective is criticized on the ground that an emphasis on the gate keepers fails to address the more fundamental structural processes behind the execution of allocation decisions. Likewise, a focus on managers and the bureaucratic process tends to emphasize the implementation aspect of the policy process and relegate those social processes that influence the family and the individual in making housing decisions. In sum, the institutional perspective of home ownership could be regarded as a supply-side variant of a structural attempt to explain the development of the housing system. The perspective could, of course, be applicable to explain the development of public rental housing, focusing on the role of housing managers.

The third level of home ownership perspective sees it as an individual seeking to maximize utility through treating home ownership as both providing use-value and investment-value. The perspective assumes rationality of the individual and freedom to exchange in the market. One of the major criticisms of this perspective is that it amounts to only a partial explanation of the social phenomenon of home ownership. The assumption of rationality and utility maximization fails to capture the full social process that leads to a motivation for home ownership. Parallel to this perspective is another slightly different strand of theoretical development that recognizes the existence of an intrinsic relationship between the individual and home owning. The social theory base of this more individualizing perspective embraces such theory as socio-biology, existentialism and the conception of ontological security. Because of its broad theoretical base, one can argue that this particular home ownership perspective is more eclectic than those of the consumption sector and the institutional view. This perspective is also criticized as too micro-based and neglects the influence of culture, family and other social relationships that affect the development of home ownership.

Table 4.2 represents an attempt to construct a meso-framework to address the home ownership question. This perspective posits that home ownership is the outcome of a complex process of social relationships involving the individual, the family and the culture. The growth of home ownership could lead to new social class formation, but nonetheless, the discussion of class transcends traditional class analysis. Class analysis should reflect the actual conditions of every society. Culture is seen as providing the missing link between structure and action. Housing consumption in the form of home ownership is therefore seen as an important form of cultural capital. Home ownership does not merely represent an economic asset, it is also an important form of cultural assets. Differential social processes evolve as different social groups compete for cultural and economic capitals. Home ownership is part of the struggle for domination and legitimization by various social groups, particularly amongst the middle class who has a tendency to accumulate cultural capital. The social theory base of this perspective is largely derived from Bourdieu's (1984) culture theory. However, since home ownership is so often related to middle class formation, this perspective also suggests that home ownership is one of the major forms of cultural capital sought after

80

by the middle class. In this manner, the growth of home ownership is regarded as the outcome of social struggle between different consumption cultures in housing.

On the other side of the coin, home ownership is seen as the outcome of a complex decision process where the desire to become an owner-occupier reflects deeply embedded social relationships. To understand the relationship between home ownership and social change, one needs to focus on this socially embedded process. But since economic decisions take place within family space, the search for an understanding of the decision process necessarily brings us back to an interpretation of the family and cultural context. Hence, to unravel embedded social relationships would at the same time involve an identification of the cultural variables that lead to the housing decision. This perspective serves to highlight the importance of social relationships as well as family relationships in the production and reproduction of social life.

The above description provides the essential logic of the theoretical framework in home ownership studies. I shall examine these perspectives in more details in the following sections.

Macro-Perspective: Consumption Sector Cleavage and Social Division

The debate on consumption sector cleavage stems from a deep-rooted dissatisfaction with Marxist conception of social relationship based almost entirely on the sphere of production. Relations of production dichotomize social relationships and, simplify society into two extremes: those who own production resources and those who do not. Although the argument is powerful, many find it tautological, anachronistic and unable to capture the more complex social divisions of contemporary societies. Saunders (1978) suggests that contemporary social analyses have grossly overdrawn the importance of the production side of the social equation to the effect that a vital facet of modern life consumption has been generally neglected. In his analysis, an individual's life chances must not be understood solely by his position in the production process. A household's capacity to consume should form a major focus of social investigation. Saunders argues that household consumption capacity has been shaped by three key factors - the ability to earn, the right to state services and the capacity to self-provision. The following quotation summarizes the broad base of Saunder's thesis:

Just as the main social division arising out of the organization of production in capitalist societies is that between those who own and control the means of production and those who do not, so the main division arising out of the process of consumption in these societies is that between those who satisfy their main consumption requirements through personal ownership (e.g. through purchase of a house, a car, nursery schooling, dental treatment, medical insurance, pension schemes and so on) and those who are excluded from such forms of ownership and who thus remain reliant on collective provision through the state (Saunders, 1986a, p. 312).

It is apparent that the essence of his thesis does not lie simply in the identification of the consumption sector as a new focus of sociological analysis. The essence lies in the social processes that are taking place within these two main social divisions: those who can afford to satisfy their needs through private means of consumption and those who lack the means to private consumption but instead must meet their needs through collective state welfare provision. The resultant development of these two social processes is that those reliant on state or socialized consumption suffer a disadvantage parallel to that experienced by the non-owners of productive capacity, while those reliant on personalized consumption continue to thrive. The resultant social conditions witness a gradual divergence of social groupings into two socially polarized divisions. Saunders coins it *a process of social re-stratification*. Referring to the history of British social policy, Saunders argued that Britain was transformed first from a pure *market* mode of consumption when state intervention was minimal, to a *socialized* mode of consumption in the post-war era where important foundation of the welfare state was laid, and eventually to a *privatized* mode of consumption during the Thatcher period. The crux of Saunders' argument lies in his claim that the transition of Britain from a predominantly socialized mode of consumption to a predominantly privatized one was already well underway because under Thatcherism, there were clear indications that the welfare state no longer met social demands.

A New Sociology of Consumption?

Saunders' thesis has drawn many critics. Not all sociologists, particularly urban sociologists, agree with his version of the sociology of consumption. Broadly, these criticisms could be divided into *three* categories: (1) those who consider the separation of production and consumption into distinct analytical categories as not viable and unable to replace class as the major

82

analytical category of social inequality; and (2) those who accept the importance of consumption sector cleavage as a valid analytical category but think that it is too crude and needs to be further developed; and (3) those who consider his framework overly ethnocentric.

Those who challenge Saunders' thesis as not viable focus their attention on the relationship between production and consumption. They argue that the intricate relationship between the two processes does not justify treating consumption as an analytically distinct entity. This view is best expressed by Preteceille (1986). Primarily aimed at challenging Dunleavy (1979) and Castells (1983) rather than Saunders, Preteceille suggests that while accepting the separation between the work process and consumption as a material, economic and ideological reality of modern capitalist societies, it does not follow that it is an absolute separation and it varies from one city to another. His analysis of collective consumption and state intervention suggests that a person's position in the work process does to some extent influence his access to state provision and vice versa, and therefore influence the opportunity of one's consumption. Preteceille upholds the importance of production relationships as the basic determinant of structural differentiation of society, and argues that consumption cleavage is but another aspect of the complexity of class structure and could not form an independent mode of social cleavage.

Warde is yet another prominent critic of Saunders' application of the concept of consumption. He suggests that there exists a confusion in the two levels of relationship, namely: (1) the systems of production and consumption; and (2) the roles of individuals in each system. Quoting real life examples from consumption (such as shopping from green groceries), Warde demonstrates that there exists an intricate relationship the between production and consumption process. He argues that:

> No longer is it possible to think of consumption in a simple, one-dimensional way. It is not just something that happens within the household contributing to the reproduction of labour power, nor can it be reduced to the distribution of assets, nor simply treated as an area of choice and taste (Warde, 1992, p. 28).

Consumption is thus closely intertwined with work and therefore the separation of work and consumption into different analytic spheres does not seem to be justified. Proponents of the consumption thesis hold different views regarding the relationship between production and consumption. The point of departure is not whether or not production and consumption are related. It is about whether or not consumption could offer a conceptually distinct analytical tool. In a rebuttal to Warde's criticisms, Saunders challenges the whole idea of primacy of class in the determination of consumption capacity and life chances (Saunders, 1986b). His main argument is that there is something distinct about consumption in contemporary societies that gives it a unique conceptual position. An assertion of the analytic distinctiveness of consumption is not an argument for its complete autonomy from production. Indeed, production and consumption are related, but the relationship is interactive, not uni-directional. In other words, consumption is not, and cannot be considered a dependent variable of production. Although the two processes are interrelated, they are also distinct processes shaped to some extent by different factors.

Those who accept the potentials of a consumption approach argue from a more mixed theoretical stand. While accepting the importance of the overt differentiation of consumption capacity amongst various social strata, Warde considers the demarcation of two polarized modes of consumption, that is, privatized consumption and socialized consumption, over-simplified and misplaced.

Perhaps the most severe criticism from Warde concerns Saunders' failure to take into account other forms of consumption. Consumption in Saunders' thesis refers simply to either the market or the state. It fails to take account of important consumption that is delivered by way of familial obligations, for example household work and maternal care by non-paid housewives. It is essentially a patriarchal consumption and production analysis, and has neglected the gender dimension in urban sociology. Warde points out that within traditional households there are neither customers (privatized mode) nor clients (socialized mode). No accounts of consumption can afford to ignore the dynamics of familial consumption and gender divisions (Warde, 1990).

Arguing from a realist point of view and being sympathetic towards Saunders' theoretical contributions, Burrows and Butler likewise refuse to accept Saunders' polarized stand in both social science and the sociology of consumption.

> We do not accept this either/or polarity between holistic and ideal typical approaches. It seems to us that some form of rapprochement is not only possible, but actually exists within a more realistic assessment of realism. Saunders is wrong to equate realism with Marxism and holism (Burrows & Butler, 1989, p. 360).

There are also others who question the applicability of Saunders' thesis across national borders and consider his framework too ethnocentric. Citing Australia and New Zealand as examples, Thorns (1992) argues that Saunders' claim of transition from market mode to privatized mode of consumption may not be universally applicable. Both Australia and New Zealand have a long history of home ownership but never really experienced a sustained period of collective state housing provision. Hence it is two modes of consumption rather than three as suggested by Saunders. The form of consumption mode experienced by any society seems to be related more to specific social history and cultural environment rather than to a generalized conception of modes of consumption. Thorns also takes the question of *time* into perspective. He argues that the wealth accumulation effect of home ownership must take full account of longitudinal house price data. He questions the inevitability of the process of accumulation and argues that the wealth effect of home ownership could be highly fragmented over a long period of time. Quoting the work of Edel, Sclar and Luria (1984) in Boston, Thorns further suggests that working class home ownership could turn into a kind of financial entrapment rather than capital accumulation, hence further discrediting the consumption sector cleavage argument.

The Consumption Sector Debate and Home Ownership

I have thus far focused on the broad discussion of the sociology of consumption. It has not been explicitly linked with the discussion of housing and home ownership. Surprisingly, it should be recognized that all major proponents of the consumption sector thesis have their initial interest in the housing question (Castells, 1990). The built-environment and how it relates to broader social processes have caught the attention of sociologists as early as Marx and Engels. Witnessing the poor living conditions of workers in industrial cities in the late nineteenth century, Engels remarked that: '... the housing shortage is no accident; it is a necessary institution and can be abolished together with all its effects on health, etc., only if the whole social order from which it springs is fundamentally refashioned' (Marx & Engels, 1969). Being essentially a neo-Marxist, Castells' concern about the poor housing conditions of the working class of Paris helped him lay firm the foundation of the theory of collective consumption and the reproduction of labour power.

What characterizes the housing crisis is that it affects other social strata than those at the bottom of the income scale and that it even reaches large sections of the middle strata better placed in other spheres of consumption. This shortage is not an unavoidable condition of the process of urbanization, but corresponds to a relation of supply and demand, itself determined by the social conditions of production...We should not conclude from this that the housing crisis is purely conjunctural and simply a matter of the balance between supply and demand. It is a case of necessary disparity between the needs, socially defined, of the habitat and the production of housing. It is the structural determination of this disparity and its historical singularities that we wish to establish (Castells, 1977, p. 146).

It is clear from Castells' statement that the housing crisis and its underlying structure basically reflect the dominant and sub-ordinate social relationships. His exposition of the function of city in social, economic and symbolic terms illuminates the creation and structuring of space by action - administrative, productive as well as human. Moreover, the complex interaction of environment and life-style, the complex market forces and state policy against a background of traditional social practice provide a sociologically intriguing set of relationship to be scrutinized.

Saunders is another ardent student of urban sociology who has a prime interest in the relationship between housing and society. Although having reconstructed his original position in his later work, Saunders' (1978) early focus was on the relationship between home ownership and social class. Using a Weberian perspective, he examined the material and political significance of domestic property ownership on class relationships. Analysis of the social relationship of property ownership constitutes the core of his later more developed theory of consumption cleavage. Dunleavy (1979), another proponent to refocus urban sociology on collective consumption, had his genesis in the study of the allocation of housing resources at the local government level. While his concern is more with the politics of urban resource distribution rather than home ownership, his primary focus is undoubtedly about housing. Therefore it is not too over-generalizing to suggest that interest in urban sociology has primarily emanated from a concern with the impact of housing on social structure and social change. Indeed, the fields of contemporary urban sociology and housing sociology overlap with each other to a great extent.

Having realized this intimate relationship between housing and urban sociology, how did it affect the housing debate? One impact is that housing studies grew from a primary concern with housing distribution in a class society to a much broader concern with social structure and social change.

Concomitant with this is the development in urban sociology by various neo-Marxist sociologists, such as Castells (1977) and Lefebvre (1970), who were intrigued by the struggle to search for a new focus of analysis for urban sociology. Castells, Saunders and Dunleavy were amongst the most salient architects during the 1970s and 1980s to merge the housing question with the urban question.

In their celebrated study in Birmingham, Rex and Moore (1967) suggested that housing classes, alongside occupational classes, could become the marker of social status and life chances. In their view, urban development was represented by a process of struggle between competing social groups for the best quality housing. The essential social process within the city is, therefore, related to the allocation of scarce and desirable housing resources, both through market and bureaucratic means. Rex and Moore saw this as a fundamental class struggle over the distribution of life chances in the city. Their arguments were criticized on the ground that they had confused status and class (Couper & Brindley, 1975; Haddon, 1970). A further development by Saunders in the 1970s re-conceptualized the concept of housing class into the possibility of *a domestic property-owning class*. Saunders' major concern is whether or not home ownership could lead to both material and political differences for any social groupings, particularly the working class. Based on his research in Croydon (Saunders 1978) and other secondary evidence, his answer was positive - that owner-occupiers did exhibit a strong and cohesive front capable of exerting challenges to capital. However, Saunders modified his position in the mid-1980s when he substituted the domestic property class position by way of focusing on owner-occupation as a new social base.

> I would now wish to abandon the attempt to theorize home ownership as a determinant of class structuration and instead to view the division between privatized and collectivized modes of housing as one factor which is contributing to what one recent writer has termed 'a process of re-stratification' based on differing relationship to the means of consumption (Saunders, 1984, pp. 202-203).

In other words, Saunders has sought to move beyond the traditional class polemics by elevating his theoretical argument to a new platform. The ingenuity of this approach apparently lies in his success in by-passing most of the limitations one would expect to encounter within a production-oriented debate to an entirely new analytical platform, that is, consumption. This way Saunders is relatively free from the hazards of orthodox class debates thus explaining why he has to defend his position forcefully when others assert that consumption and production are in fact closely connected. Influenced by Dunleavy and others who are interested in the dynamics of new social closure and corporatism, Saunders seeks to situate his theoretical argument in the realm of sectoral cleavages (which cut across classes).

> I suggest that social and economic divisions arising out of ownership of key means of consumption such as housing are now coming to represent a new major fault line in British society, that privatization of welfare provisions is intensifying this cleavage to that point where sectoral alignments in regards to consumption may come to outweigh class alignments in respect of production, and that housing tenure remains the most important single aspect of such alignments because of the accumulative potentials of house ownership ... (Saunders, 1984, p. 203).

Owner-occupiers are seen as a new force within society which possess a common set of material interests arising out of wealth accumulation and such interests can affect political attitudes. In the words of Forrest, Murie and Williams (1990), Saunders' approach 'does not seek to rewrite class as such, but identifies an additional source of alignments and interests'. Such alignments and interests could be read off from class, directly determined by class, and so would deepen and strengthen class differences rather than cut across or confuse them.

Consumption Sector Debates: Implications for Home Ownership Perspectives

What implications could be drawn from the above critique of the consumption sector thesis? First, the debate provides new insights into the modern role of consumption and explains how certain modes of consumption affect social change. Second, it provides essentially a challenge to the traditional conception of social class as an organizing concept in exposing social inequality. However, it must be noted that the direction of development of the debate is basically tautological and circular. Much energy has been consumed or even wasted in reasserting the primacy of class. The arguments by Pretecille and Warde are good examples. The major weakness of this debate is, nonetheless, its failure to transcend the discussion of consumption from orthodox class analysis. Few have taken advantage of Saunders' bold attempt to elaborate on the relationship between consumption and modern societies. An important step along this direction is to pay more attention towards culture. This provides a new orientation to the class question - social classes emerge as social groupings involving themselves in a series of cultural battles. The consequence of these battles is represented by one group seeking eventual dominance over another. The interesting theoretical point is that home ownership could be regarded both an economic capital and cultural capital at the same time. The relative emphasis on its use should then become an interesting empirical question. But the point to be emphasized here is that property ownership becomes an exceptionally powerful form of cultural capital, alongside other forms of culture such as education and art (which are heavily emphasized by Bourdieu's analysis of social distinction). As such, the general implication of this debate is that home ownership as a modern social phenomenon must be re-examined from a consumption-culture-class axis. This then brings us to the question of how all this impinges upon home ownership studies in an Eastern society - Hong Kong.

Methodological and Theoretical Considerations for Hong Kong

When theorists conceptualize social change and structure into a framework, they aim at more than simply explaining social change within their own society. They want their framework to have wider applicability in other societies. However, theorization or conceptualization is inevitably based upon specific social institutions, systems of government, values and assumptions of both collective and individual human behaviour, and this creates problems of transferability if such framework is used to explain social change in another society in an unqualified manner. Failure to address this problem properly and adequately by researchers crossing national borders often results in truncated analyses and artificial conclusions. One example is Castells' application of his theory of collective consumption to analyze housing as a form of state intervention in a comparative housing study of Hong Kong and Singapore (Castells, Goh & Kwok, 1990).[1] One of the unnecessary evils of adopting such an approach is that it would easily stifle the search for generalization about social change. It would simply lead to the sterilization of research seeking an international sociological explanation or comparative research. It is easy to shield a particular social environment from investigation simply by resorting to protection from a mysterious cultural veil. Social research in Hong Kong has long been criticized as suffering from both an over-emphasis on the uniqueness of her socio-cultural background and a lack of concern for basic social research (e.g. class and stratification) (Lee, 1994).

Theorization of social development in the form of concepts such as social polarization of consumption reflects to a certain extent social process in a changing social context. Sociologists are not just interested in the changes per se, but also why and how certain changes are more prominent than others. In other words, the rate of change and its underlying reason constitute the core interests. For instance, one of the reasons leading to Saunders' concern with consumption is his observation of this facet of modern life which, he argues, did not exist in the nineteenth century. For the last two decades, the Hong Kong housing system has not been characterized by the kind of polarization seen in Western societies where the working class is being marginalized. A small percentage of public housing tenants also own private properties.[2] Hong Kong is not a welfare state and therefore the part of the population depending on state provision is basically small. While state-subsidized public rental housing amounts to 34% of the total housing stock, it only accounts for 24% of public expenditure. Therefore, it is difficult to talk of a two-sector dichotomy as described by Saunders. It is also not feasible to talk in general terms of a residualized public rental sector characterized by unemployment, single-parenthood and unsupported elderly. Although there are some deprived sectors in public housing, especially the old Mark I - V type of resettlement estates. But these estates account for less than 5% of the total housing stock. The quality of life in public housing estates in Hong Kong is generally satisfactory (Lee, 1990). Public housing estates are not characterized by gang-fights and crack houses. While public housing tenants generally pay less attention to home improvement when compared with private homeowners, there is no evidence to suggest that tenants consider their living conditions marginalized. Over the last two decades, urban social movements in the public housing sector have been largely organized around two main concerns: namely (1) campaigns for more public housing, and (2) campaigns against rent-increases (Ho, 1990; Law, 1988). There is little evidence to suggest that mass social movements consolidating public housing is underway (Ho, 1990).

Hong Kong does not possess the sort of polarization characteristic of Western industrial societies. It sees instead the marginalization of a *sandwich class* which finds itself excluded from the private housing market because of affordability problem, and from the state housing sector because of eligibility problem. If we take Saunders' framework again, the contradiction in consumption sectors does not fall between those who are dependent on the state sector and those who are dependent on private means. Most people in Hong Kong depend on private consumption to survive. It has been estimated that about 20% of existing public housing tenants fall within the 'rich tenants' category. Castells et al. (1990) also suggests that as a result of state intervention in housing in the early 1970s, the working class has been able to reproduce labour power even at a low-wage and minimal occupational welfare system. Public housing tenants are able to accumulate savings for consumption and investment, and therefore, become rich tenants. Likewise, those households who bought their homes during the 1980s have discovered that their properties have doubled or tripled in value. Such home ownership-related wealth has enabled many homeowners to experience a level of life-chances they have never experienced before.

Hence, when applying the consumption-sector framework, *two* theoretical issues should be noted: (1) the social polarization thesis could not be applied directly to the Hong Kong situation; and (2) the traditional debate emphasizing on class might not be entirely appropriate since there is an absence, at least on the surface, of the type of societies which have a tradition of organized labour movements and class distinctiveness. We, therefore, need the assistance of an alternative framework that sees the class from a slightly different angle.

Micro-Perspective: Home Ownership as the Preferred Tenure

Over the years, the Government has recognized the aspiring needs of the sandwich class (the middle class) in becoming homeowners. We all want to be well housed in Hong Kong. Home ownership is probably the best means to meet our society's needs (Annual Policy Speech by Chris Patten to the Legislative Council, Governor of Hong Kong, October 1993).

On a policy level, the Hong Kong government in the last decade has never been clearer on supporting and promoting a policy of home ownership. Since the introduction of the Home Ownership Scheme in 1976, Hong Kong has progressively moved towards a tenure preference for home owning. While the rest of this book attempts to provide a sociological explanation of this social process, one cannot help to be overwhelmed by the prevalence of the imagery of property ownership in Hong Kong. Take any major newspaper as an example, 25%-30% of its daily coverage is devoted to property advertisements. Turning on the radio and TV talk shows, housing policy failures, house price inflation, government land sale auctions, and the announcement by developers of new residential projects, all form a major part of the ingredients of the typical Hong Kong media extravaganza. The typical middle class 'Hong Kong Man' and his family, like it or not, are the victims of 'place promotion'- a set of sophisticated marketing strategies aiming at promotion of places (Ashworth & Voogd, 1990). The typical weekend family activities are characterized by two major modes: (1) visiting show-flats, and (2) eating out in nearby restaurants. The following excerpts from a radio advertisement on a sub-urban low-rise residential development in 1994 best illustrates the nature of 'place promotion' in fostering home ownership in Hong Kong:

A: (Calling his friend living California from a mobile phone) Hi! John. Guess what I am doing? I am sunbathing in my club's pool in Palm Spring?

B: What? Are you joking? You are really in Palm Spring in California? Why don't you come up to see me?

A: Ha Ha! I am joking. I am in Palm Spring, Hong Kong. They have this vast low-rise development. For the same price as Tai Koo Shing, you get almost double the space. So you don't need to flee your cage and go all the way to California. They have everything here, including a small garden at the back of your house in Hong Kong! Can you imagine that? Besides, it has a great appreciation potential. It has increased 15% already since we moved here 3 months ago.

B: Oh Dear! We have just arrived and you want us to be back.

A: Well! It's your choice. The price will go up soon. No place is like Hong Kong. If you don't buy it now, it would be like 'failing to catch the last ferry!'

These messages are pervasive and irresistible. 'Talking about housing', 'thinking about it', 'looking for one', and then 'worrying about price and affordability', all constitute important components of the typical Hong Kong middle class life. While most urban dwellers in large industrial cities do experience to some extent such *housing culture*, it is the intensity and pervasiveness of such culture which make the housing question in Hong Kong all the more intrigued. To grasp this housing phenomenon at an individual level, we need to move to a level of theory that is different from macro-perspectives described above. I shall examine in the next section one of the more popular micro-perspectives on home ownership - the meaning of home.

The focus on consumption sector cleavage, social class and political attitude seems to assume that there is a degree of homogeneity amongst homeowners of the way they view *home*. This, in fact, is not necessarily the case. An owner-occupier could make his house a *home* while a tenant could equally make his dwelling his *home*. Home ownership does not necessarily monopolize *home making*. How far an individual treats his dwelling as home depends to a large extent on how an individual or family relates to a particular socio-spatial environment called *home*.

Sociologists have long been interested in the meaning of home to individuals and households (Williams, 1984, 1986, 1987; Saunders & Williams, 1988; Dickens, 1989). While they may be focusing on specific aspects of the meaning of home, nowadays it is widely accepted that an individual's home means much more than bricks and mortars. It represents the centre of reproduction of a set of family and social relations, without which the household as a social unit would not be able to survive. Home in this sense becomes one of the most significant social settings outside the workplace that contributes to social dynamics. Williams (1987) suggested that it is essential to think beyond the workplace to other settings (or locales) where social interaction takes place and where social relations are composed and contextualized. To this end, perhaps Giddens' conceptualization of a *locale* best summarizes this. He defines a locale as a physical region involved as part of the setting of interaction, having definite boundaries which help concentrate interaction in one way or another (Giddens, 1984). The home is one such locale. In other words, the house is not simply the container within which households live their lives, but is the medium through which these lives are realized (Saunders & Williams, 1988).

Having accepted this broad conception, contemporary interest in the meaning of home could be grouped into four areas: (1) home as the centre of family life; (2) home as a place for privacy, retreat, relaxation and recreation; (3) home as an indicator of social status and success; and (4) home as a place of freedom, autonomy and personal identity. What is interesting here is whether these meanings of home have bearings on the preference for home ownership? In general, there are fewer controversies amongst sociologists regarding the first two areas, for the apparent reason that both tenants and owner-occupiers could reproduce social relationships under the same roof in terms of family life and relaxation, regardless of the nature of their tenure. As to the third area, it is intricately related to the issue of wealth accumulation and there are many debates concerning the fragmentation of asset appreciation within the owner-occupier sector (Forrest, Murie and Williams, 1990). In this section, the focus is thus on the fourth area: whether or not home is regarded as a place of freedom and autonomy, a place where one could exert control on one's immediate environment, a place where one could feel particularly secure and hence come to identify with it. And if all these are positive, would it then lead to a preference for home ownership?

Saunders' three-town home ownership study in England has revealed interesting variations between owners' and tenants' images of home (Saunders, 1990). His study has indicated that tenants are more likely to associate home with neighbourhood ties while owners are more inclined to associate their house as home. Accordingly, an important question could be generated from this finding. Does that mean that ownership can provide a sense of personal security, identity and autonomy that may be denied to tenants? Does home ownership generate greater expression of self and identity?

This leads us to the question of *ontological security* - a term which has been taken up by Giddens (1984), who defines it as confidence or trust that the natural or social worlds are as they appear to be, including the basic existential parameters of self and social identity. His view is that life in modern society has been marked by gradual erosion of the ties between human beings and nature. Modernity is characterized by a process of time-space distanciation that systematically drags the individual away from harmony with the physical and social environment. This results, as far as the individual is concerned, in a sense of rootlessness and meaninglessness. In order to regain equilibrium in life, the individual will resort to a renewed search for a sense of ontological security, particularly in the private realm (Saunders, 1990). Since one's own home constitutes the most important private domain of an individual, home ownership may be one aspect of this search for ontological security. However, one of the problems confronting researchers is that they find it extremely difficult to operationalize the concept of ontological security in empirical research. It is likewise difficult to identify the roots of anxieties, fears and paranoia as relating to the lack of security. Researchers could only deduce it from other indirect indicators. Two frequently used indicators are the degree of attachment to one's home and the presence of self-provisioning. Saunders' studies suggest that owner-occupiers exhibit a higher degree of attachment to their home while council tenants invest a lot less in home improvement.

Saunders' ontological security thesis is, nonetheless, not without its critics. Harloe (1984) argues that the concept of ontological security is too vague and it is difficult to empirically test the existence of a real link between the thesis and tenure preference. Franklin (1986) goes further to suggest the whole idea as a mere *academic fantasy*. Forrest and Murrie (1988) indicate that there exists a wide disparity of ownership pattern and it is difficult to generalize the link between ownership and ontological security. While recognizing the yet unsettled nature of the debate, one of the key weaknesses of this concept is that it fails to relate the 'individual-at-home' with the wider society. It emanates from a concern with the alienation of the individual in modern life and seeks explanation in the individual's response. However, it could suffer from the same misfit when compared to another strand of debates on human nature advanced by Dickens (1989) which focuses entirely on the bio-social nature of human beings and argues that home ownership is the result of an innate desire to possess within a certain territory. The problem of these approaches is that the deeper you get into the private realm, the farther away you are from the social context. It is my argument that we need a framework which, on the one hand, reflects the dynamics of the individual within the home and, on the other hand, seeks to bring the *individual-at-home* back to a societal context. A home should represent an intersection between the society and the individual. It is definitely one of the important interfaces between the individual and the society. The *individual-at-home* is the carrier of social structure and social change. It is this relationship which I seek to explore. Before moving on to another framework which seeks to link the individual-at-home with wider social process, it is appropriate to note some of the similarities and differences in terms of the meaning of home and home ownership between Western and Chinese societies.

The Meaning of Home and Home Ownership in a Chinese Society

There are two common expressions about home in Chinese: (1) *Uk Kei* which literally means 'the house in which we live'; and (2) *Lou Jar* which literally means the 'old family home'. The first expression - *Uk Kei* is a colloquial expression of home commonly used in the South China region. *Lou Jar* is a more formal term. The essence of these two expressions lies in the primacy of family within the home. In Western societies, *returning home* means returning to the place where you live. In a Chinese society, those living independently do not regard themselves as having a home. Instead, they say they have a shelter. *Family* and *home* become a practical synonym in the Chinese language. Comparing this with the Western conception of home: such as, *home is where the heart is*; *home is one man's castle*; and *home sweet home*, the Chinese meaning of *home* signifies much less attention to its physical entity - the house. Whereas the Western meaning of home emphasizes on individual *freedom*, *autonomy* and *identity*, the Chinese meaning of home emphasizes much less in this respect. If the Chinese regard *home* and *house* more or less synonymous, it follows that we should look at the Chinese meaning of the house. *Uk*, as suggested earlier, refers to the physical entity of a house. A few Chinese idiomatic expressions give rise to interesting cultural meanings attached to the house. First, it is often suggested (across all social classes) that 'if one studies hard, one should be rewarded a golden house; if one studies hard, one should be rewarded a beautiful woman'. Although the idiom primarily signifies the attachment of a high social value in achievement through education, it likewise reflects the importance attached to the house as a property. Second, 'When one gets married, one must be *propertied*'. On the surface, this expression bears no difference from Western values. The difference could only be revealed when it is practised. It is still common in Hong Kong that when parents of two to-be-wed people come to meet for the first time, the parents of the girl would ask whether the young man has already bought a flat. In contemporary gender-sensitive Western societies, this sounds awkward. Nonetheless, property ownership as a status symbol is generally tied to the family life cycle and is widely recognized. It is still practised in many Southeast Asian countries (e.g. Singapore, Malaysia, and Indonesia) where the Chinese become one of the major ethnic groups. Third, in considering marriage, there is a traditional saying that 'a bamboo door must match a bamboo door; a wooden door must match a wooden door', which essentially means that the social status of two marriage partners must match. The point to note here is that the 'door' represents status, carrying strong class connotation.

In sum, two elements could be deduced from a general consideration of the Chinese conception of home and property ownership: namely (1) home is intimately blended with the concept of family; and (2) house and property ownership are closely associated with family, wealth and status. The Chinese meaning of home has much more to do with family and property than with individual security. The distinctive elements of individual freedom, autonomy, and the expression of self-identity, which are placed prominently in the discussion of the meaning of home in Western societies, are relatively weak in Chinese society. Home ownership as a manifestation of the search for ontological security amongst Chinese is thus not strong. This does not mean that Chinese people do not ask existential questions as expressed by Giddens (1991) in his *structuration theory*, nor that they do not feel anxious and alienated from the society. This only reflects the fact that home ownership is not a major medium of expression in this context. Such claim must be carefully qualified here. What is referred above deals with the Chinese people in a historical and general context. It does not apply to specific regions or specific times. *Chinese people* is basically a very broad concept, because it represents far too many intra-ethnic variations. Take Hong Kong as an example, the late 1980s and 1990s were marked by a prolonged period of uncertainty in the socio-political arena. This could actually generate a period of acute ontological insecurity. As suggested by Giddens:

> The ontologically insecure individual tends to display one or more of the following characteristics: such as when an external environment is full of changes, the person could be obsessively preoccupied with apprehension of possible risks to his or her existence, and paralyzed in terms of practical action (Giddens, 1991, p. 53).

If this applies to Hong Kong, the frantic search for emigration opportunities after the 'June 4th Event' in Beijing in 1989, as well as the craving for property ownership in the ensuing years, could well mean the existence of such kind of insecurity.

Class, Culture and Home Ownership: An Alternative Perspective

In the beginning of this chapter, two strands of debates in home ownership were mentioned: one links the growth of home ownership with macro changes in social inequality as manifested by polarized living environment and social divisions in consumption, and the other suggests that home ownership has fast become a cherished way of life-style, particularly amongst the middle class. While these two strands of debates could be easily read off as focusing on different facets of home ownership and social change, this section will demonstrate that their relationship is much more complex. Superficially, the way people consume reflects an individual's taste and personal preference. But on a deeper level, sociologists have long been interested in the relationship between patterns of consumption and social stratification. Veblen is amongst the earliest to study the socio-economic effect of consumption and introduces the concept of *conspicuous consumption* (Veblen, 1970). Each person's repertoire of cultural practices might be distinct, yet a given practice sometimes is widely shared, and individual differences in repertoires are neither random nor the product of personal taste alone. Hall and Neitz (1993) suggested that although each individual's cultural practices are unique, the dazzling variety of culture become surprisingly coherent when we view it through the lens of social stratification. While the consumption sector cleavage debate has dominated the theoretical scene in housing studies throughout the 1970s and the 1980s, the 1990s have seen an emerging interest in focusing on home ownership as a consumption practice or culture and seeking to relate it to changing life chances and class formation (Crompton, 1993; Savage et al., 1992). If we criticize the Saunderian thesis as too conclusive to suggest that home ownership constitutes a distinct base for social alignment, the cultural perspective seeks to address more fundamental questions in a less deterministic manner. What else determines social inequality in modern societies other than one's labour market position? Could housing consumption become an independent variable, capable of effecting aggregate social change as salient as those emanated through production and work? The cultural perspective seeks to reformulate Saunders' question on home ownership and social alignment from an angle that prevents itself from falling into the Marxian trap of production versus consumption.

Consumption, Culture and the Work of Bourdieu

As a distinct theoretical perspective, the relationship between home ownership, consumption culture and social class is still very much in its infancy. Compared to the overtly more developed debate of consumption sector cleavage, the cultural perspective looks at an individual's living style in society from a broader perspective. This section will first examine the ideas of one of the most important proponents of the cultural perspective - Pierre Bourdieu. This is then followed by a discussion of how contemporary sociologists' attempt to apply Bourdieu's theoretical contributions to the debate on class formation, consumption culture and home ownership. Particular attention will be drawn towards the formation of modern middle class, as this would hinge on the discussion of middle class formation through home ownership in Hong Kong. This chapter does not attempt to apply Bourdieu's concept in a wholesale manner as his research was done largely within a certain historical period of the French culture. However, the insight brought about by Bourdieu's thinking on consumption and social change is simply too costly to be overlooked.

Bourdieu's perspective raises important questions on traditional work-based class analyses. It is argued that current debates in home ownership suffer severely from a predisposition towards inherent Marxist and Weberian constraints, and Bourdieu's conceptualization offers an opportunity to view social class from a slightly different angle. I shall first delineate the basis of Bourdieu's idea as extracted from one of his major works: *Distinction: A Social Critique of the Judgement of Taste.*

The Interplay of Different Capitals

The basic tenet of Bourdieu's conception lies in his construction of the idea of *capital*. He conceptualizes society as comprising four major types of capital, namely: (1) economic capital (based around the classic Marxist principle of relationship to the means of production); (2) cultural capital, e.g. education attainment, family background and life style; (3) social capital (based on social network - who you know? etc.); and (4) symbolic capital (based on reputation, respectability, honour and generally related to fame) (Bourdieu, 1984; Crompton, 1993). Substitutions could occur within and between capitals, e.g. education to some extent substitutes poor family background; economic capital to some extent substitutes the lack of education attainment. In Bourdieu's world, an individual is conceived as wielding a combination of these capitals and struggles hard to accumulate more of one capital in order to substitute the lack of another. The underlying assumption is the existence of a dynamic process of struggles between various capitals, particularly between economic and cultural capitals. Struggles between social groups wielding different capitals constitute a process whereby the boundaries of existing social classes are blurred, reformulated and eventually disintegrated, hence, forming the basis of new social classes. Class, in Bourdieu's sense, is not simply a conglomerate of occupational groups. It is not conceptualized as having clear boundaries. It is something that is constantly reshaped to reflect new equilibrium between various aggregate capitals. If Marxist and Weberian analyses aim at conceptualizing and constructing clear class boundaries, Bourdieu's construction seeks to depict a scenario of classes in flux. Bourdieu apparently has given more attention to economic and cultural capitals. In the words of Crompton (1993), these capitals together empower individuals or agents in their struggle for position within the *social space*. And as a result of this empowerment, individual class come to develop and occupy a similar *habitus* - a concept developed by Bourdieu meaning 'a system of dispositions shared by all individuals who are products of the same conditioning' (Bourdieu, 1984). Summarizing in a simple mathematical formula: [(habitus)(capital)] + field^3 = cultural practice], Bourdieu sees class formation as reflecting constant struggles between people with the same social conditions as well as between groups of different social conditions. Conceived in this manner, the habitus is the dynamic intersection of structure and action, society and individual. The concept enables Bourdieu to analyze the behaviour of agents as objectively coordinated and regulated without being the product of rules, on the one hand, or conscious rationality, on the other. Unlike Lockwood, Goldthrope and Wright, who seek to identify a clear class structure through occupational categories, Bourdieu sees social class more as a generic name for social groups distinguished by their conditions of existence and their corresponding dispositions. Bourdieu's work, therefore, is primarily concerned with the active processes of class formation rather than paying attention to whether or not emerging occupations could fit into existing occupation classifications.

Taste as Marker of Class

'Taste classifies, and it classifies the classifiers' (Bourdieu, 1984). In more simple terms, Bourdieu's contribution lies in his deep analysis of a society's taste pattern. He proposes that we adopt a dual perspective to view *taste*: one level of analysis attempts merely to reflect simple personal preference; the other attempts to unravel an individual's predisposition and social conditioning which underlies one's taste structure. The fact that one goes for Mozart's piano concertos while the other goes for Mahler's Symphony No.8 or Wagner's Das Rheingold reflects not simply a difference of taste in music. More fundamentally, it reflects a difference in social conditions and hence a difference in class.

In Hong Kong, a preference for Pekingese Opera rather than Cantonese Opera usually reflects the choice of a middle upper class of Northern China origin, either from Shanghai or Beijing, while the preference for the latter usually reflects the taste of a working class family originating in Guangdong.[4] Likewise, in the case of homeowners, the traditional middle and upper middle classes, largely comprising owners of medium-sized commercial or industrial corporations, are concentrated in the Kowloon Tong District. They seldom attempt to move to areas such as Tai Koo Shing where the *new middle class* - young professionals and semi-professionals such as teachers, nurses, social workers, advertising agents and real estate agents - live. It is not because of affordability, as house prices of these two areas are more or less the same, but rather for the difference in predisposition and social conditioning. We can find more old-fashioned markets, restaurants and food shops in the nearby district of Kowloon City. They are much more traditional in their decor and shop keepers adopt a more personalized approach in doing business. Shops and restaurants in Tai Koo Shing are more of an avant garde style, and they are in general more briskly decorated and obviously more refined in packaging. In terms of education, the upper middle class in Kowloon Tong would send their children to old fashioned primary schools such as the La Salle Primary School, Heep Yan Primary School and the Munsang Primary School that all stress discipline and austerity as educational principles. On the contrary, the *yuppie* middle class of Tai Koo Shing and Whampoa Garden like to send their children to new primary schools that stress openness and creativity rather than discipline.

While there seems to be a common culture shared by the Chinese middle class in the way they eat, the way they live and the way they educate their children, there are in fact subtle differences amongst them. These fine distinctions in consumption could not simply be regarded as a coincidence of taste randomization. In the words of Bourdieu, they are not *culture* in the restricted sense. They are culture in the broad sociological sense and their choices are very much governed by one's class predisposition.

> However, the predispositions which govern choices between the goods of legitimate culture cannot be fully understood unless they are reintegrated into the system of dispositions, unless 'culture' in the restricted, normative sense of ordinary usage, is reinserted into 'culture' in the broad, anthropological sense and the elaborated taste for the most refined objects is brought back into relation with the elementary taste for the flavour of food (Bourdieu, 1986, pp. 99).

The identification of one's taste is essentially the unravelling of one's social origin. Residents of the new middle class in Tai Koo Shing or Kornhill Estates find it difficult to penetrate into the traditional middle class area of Kowloon Tong. As a result, a new middle class culture and living styles are thus established in Tai Koo Shing and other areas, which stress avant garde coffee shops and trendy boutiques. Evolving in the early 1980s with the development of these modern estates, this new middle class consumption culture has now effectively overshadowed those in Kowloon Tong, to the extent that house prices of Tai Koo Shing are now higher than

Kowloon Tong (traditionally the most representative middle class residential area).

Class, Culture and Social Action

Three elements can be discerned from Bourdieu's conceptualization. First, consumption as an independent variable is capable of reflecting one's social predisposition. In other words, one's life history, consciously or unconsciously, forms the basis of one's social conditioning, and is capable of bringing direct effect on the shaping of one's social predisposition. Following this logic, the aggregate of individuals' predisposition would form the basis of social dynamics - minute changes in people's trajectories leading to social change. Second, an individual's consumption is not fixated by a single series of social predisposition. The changes in resources brought about by the struggle between and within various capitals introduce a dynamic element into an individual's social predisposition. Third, while all consumption choices reflect individual predisposition, some forms of consumption are more significant. Consumption choice in housing is no doubt more significant than the consumption of coffee, even though the choice of coffee brand name might reflect a certain degree of conditioning. While Bourdieu only highlights the consumption of art, education and the consumption of luxurious goods, it is evident that housing consumption occupies a central position in an individual's ladder of consumption. The theoretical implication of Bourdieu's work is that if we can establish the link between consumption culture and class, the link between middle class formation and the consumption of housing in the form of home ownership could then be theoretically established. Eder's (1993) theoretical work on new urban social movement provides a good example of such link. He argues that the primary reason for the decoupling of class and social action essentially stems from the lack of a meaningful link between class and collective action. He maintains the importance of class as an organizing concept in social theory but accepts the limitation that contemporary class analysis does not take account of the cultural texture that gives specific meaning to social action.

This theoretical insight carries special meaning for Hong Kong. Many local sociologists (King, 1972; Miner, 1975; Lau, 1977, 1984; Lee, 1993) have long concluded that Hong Kong takes on such a unique path of social development that it renders class analysis irrelevant to understanding social inequality. Local social movements tend to be short-term, issue-oriented rather than reflecting collective class interest (Ho, 1990; Lui &

Kung, 1985). This reinforces the accepted position of decoupling class from social analysis. As a result, many sociologists have demonstrated the tendency to avoid the class question in local social research (Wong & Lui, 1992b). However, Eder's proposal serves well the purpose of highlighting once again the importance of the debate on the relationship between structure and action, even for a society that is known overtly to be much less diverse politically than many Western societies.

Three Major Themes: Housing Histories, Family and Capital Gains

The exploration and critique of home ownership perspectives bring forth a number of themes that need to be tackled in greater detail conceptually and empirically. The first concerns the role of housing histories and housing trajectories. As discussed above, one of the major criticisms of the consumption sector cleavage is that it confines its discussion to home ownership and the tenure question. The focus of analysis always remains at a rather macro level, thus failing to appreciate the effect of individual and family history on housing development. To remedy this shortfall, Bourdieu's proposition suggests that we need to identify an individual's predisposition in social conditions and also the social processes reflecting such predisposition. This theory implies that if we are to understand a fuller and richer account of the social phenomenon of home ownership, there is an apparent methodological necessity to look into individual and family housing history. It is only through such historical examination that we are able to reveal more fully the social conditions that lead to contemporary cultural conflicts amongst various social groupings.

The second theme concerns the role of family and family network in influencing the growth of home ownership. Two sub-themes are evolved: (1) the Chinese meaning of home and home ownership; and (2) the way the Chinese families cope with the housing needs and how it influences home ownership. From a micro perspective, it has been mentioned that the Chinese do have a different meaning and interpretation of their relationship with home and housing. Both Bourdieu (1984) and Eder (1993) have pinpointed the importance of identifying the cultural context if we are to understand the social dynamics of class formation. A broader framework to capture social change is thus essential. A thorough examination of the Chinese family in Hong Kong will provide the cultural context on which home ownership and socio-structural changes could be meaningfully situated.

The third theme concerns the whole issue of capital gains from home ownership to which existing theoretical perspectives give a great deal of importance. Two fundamental issues are being addressed here. First, to what extent home ownership gives an individual wealth advantages over other tenures? A more specific question is to what extent the money tied up in home ownership benefits the individual household? Second, assuming some gains can be made, are all homeowners able to benefit or are the rewards unequally distributed? These two questions have been fundamental to most Western home ownership research. By examining these three variables, that is, housing history, family and capital gains, I think we should be in a better position to grapple with the fundamental research agenda.

Conclusion

This chapter attempts to tackle three fundamental theoretical questions of home ownership and social change. First, what are the weaknesses and limitations of the current theoretical perspectives on home ownership? Second, how useful are these perspectives in explaining the growth of home ownership in Hong Kong? Third, what other alternative perspective could we use? While the macro perspective of consumption sector cleavage provides fruitful debates on the relationship between consumption and social division, it has been criticized for being too confined to the relations of production and consumption and failed to take account of other facets of modern life. The micro-perspective offers a hopeful turn. The ontological security argument seeks to describe how an individual develops an innate relationship with home and housing. The rational consumer perspective provides an economic model of decision-making in home-buying, bases largely on neo-classical economic theory. These two micro-perspectives prove extremely useful in understanding individual behaviour with respect to home ownership. However they are criticized on the grounds of failing to account for other important social institutions such as family and culture. Thus, they could only be regarded as partial perspectives, providing partial explanations. Likewise, one of the criticisms against them is that they fail to link up clearly with the macro debate.

To resolve this problem amounts to tackling the third question - finding an alternative. To do so, we need to identify a framework that deals with the interface between the individual and the family on the one hand,

and with the wider social structure on the other. In some way social theories are products of the time when they are developed. The ecological school, for example, reflects the conditions of market capitalism in America before the New Deal. The urban managerial school as proposed by Pahl (1975) and others was in many ways reflective of post-war welfare capitalism in Britain at a time when welfare expenditure was expanding. The growth of Marxist urban theory came out at a time when the world began to experience recession and it seemed to provide prospect of new urban sociology. Hence, the consumption sector cleavage debates grew out of dissatisfaction with the failure of Marxist urban theory to account for urban change. The presence of social fragmentation within modern society seems less able to warrant a sweeping explanatory framework.

This chapter explores a meso perspective - the cultural perspective, which seeks to redress this theoretical gap. A cultural perspective does not treat class as a mere occupational conglomeration. It sees class formation as a struggle between various cultural and economic capitals. The strength of this perspective is that it retains the usefulness of consumption as a modern social phenomenon, while escaping the seemingly futile controversies on denouncing class as an analytical category. The cultural perspective of home ownership affirms the usefulness of structural analysis and therefore, the importance of class analytic is retained. It also affirms the primacy of agency - the individual in the house and the home, and the value of constructionist method. However, a constructionist method is empty if it lacks a cultural context. What then constitutes the cultural context in home ownership debates? If we see organized or disorganized social action in relation to housing, what then is the link between social structure and social action? Besides, how could the home ownership framework be applied to different societies and yet still find meaningful interpretation given the difference in cultural contexts? Using Bourdieu's ideas, this chapter suggests that the answer lies in the adoption of a cultural framework which seeks to merge the individual and the society. Home ownership decisions at an individual level are linked to cultural predisposition on the one end, and class formation on the other. The family is seen as a carrier of culture that actively reproduces an individual's cultural predisposition. The importance of home ownership lies in the fact that it is a double-edged capital - meaning that it is both an economic capital and a cultural capital. In the case of Hong Kong, it is suggested that middle class formation is very much affected by the variable uses of this particular type of capital. Segmentation within the middle class in fact reflects the different uses of home ownership as a capital to struggle for class formation.

Notes

1. Castells' conclusion that post-war economic success of both Hong Kong and Singapore being a consequence of active state intervention in housing was criticized as over-generalized and essentially unsubstantiated. Details of the critiques could be found in Lee (1993), Book Review, *Housing Studies*, Vol. 8(2).

2. In October 1994, the Housing Authority estimated that 17% of public housing tenants owned private properties. A special task force was set up in the government to consider ways to encourage these 'rich tenants' to vacate their flats and to make way for more needy people (150,000) on the public housing waiting list.

3. Field refers to the sites of collective symbolic struggles and individual strategies, the aims of which are to produce valuable cultural goods. The value of a symbolic goods depends upon the value assigned to it by the relevant consumer community.

4. In Chinese history, the Southern provinces: Guangdong, Fukein and Guangxi were denoted as places where peasants grow their crops. The gentry class or officials would regard coming to work or settle in the south as a form of exile. The Southern provinces were once dubbed as the 'land of the smoke and mud'. People from the south were regarded as uneducated and rude. Cantonese and Hokkein, two major dialects of the south were never regarded as having the same national regard as Pekingese, now forming the basis of Putonghua - the national Chinese language.

Part Two

HOUSING HISTORY, FAMILY AND THE MIDDLE CLASS

5 Housing Histories as Narratives of Social Change

Hong Kong is a cruel society in which very little assistance is given to the poor. The government has consciously pursued policies designed to foster economic growth, in the conviction that the economic prosperity of the whole Colony would inevitably, in due course, filter down even to the poorest. An early appropriation of funds to social welfare could only be achieved by high taxation, which would, it was claimed, frighten away capital investment. Since the government is composed almost exclusively of permanent officials, it has been able to follow these policies unhampered by the conflicts of representative government. ... It is amazing that this overt paternalism has survived the wave of nationalism and self rule which has swept China and the rest of the world. ... A large proportion of the population has accepted exceedingly cramped living conditions without creating serious disorder or political agitation. What is more surprising is that these same people have so meekly tolerated mass evictions both from squatter huts and private tenements. The ease with which eviction was secured through the courts contrasts with the difficulty of the same process in other countries (Hopkins, 1971, p. 271).

Written in the 1960s, Hopkins' statement clearly encapsulated the early social sentiment of Hong Kong. It was characterised by a paternalistic and minimalist government that held a very pragmatic conception of social responsibility. Hong Kong people are largely passive, tolerant and inward looking. Between speaking up and feeling desperately helpless, they have chosen to bury themselves into hard work. The 'forty-something' middle class should be able to remember well their childhood as a period marked by a number of social imageries: take-home work, poor pay, the 1967 riot, water supply restrictions, hawkers, family renting a 50-feet cubicle, squatters and Mark I resettlement estates. Life was extremely difficult in the 1950s and 1960s. However, there were certain unique cultural characteristics prevalent during this period which dominated daily discourse and shaped people's livelihood. Lau (1977) described this situation as *utilitarian familism* and went on to explain why the former British colonial government managed to rule with ease. But this chapter

109

will begin from another direction. Instead of asking how the colonial *government* ruled and why Hong Kong sustained political stability, this chapter will question the way Hong Kong *people* develop into what they are today.

The Social Meaning of Housing in Hong Kong

The above questions will be explored from a housing history and trajectory method. In particular, I shall look into individual and family histories to appreciate the uniqueness and particularity of the post-war housing situation in Hong Kong and how it affects the current housing crisis. The rationale behind the approach is that housing problems in Hong Kong could not be isolated from its particular socio-spatial context. One can describe Hong Kong as overcrowded. But that does not mean much other than the usual conception of urban congestion. Tokyo, London and New York are all overcrowded. The meaning of over-crowdedness in Hong Kong is relative even when compared with Singapore, despite the fact that the two small city-states are strikingly similar in many respects. Such difference is important and significant not merely in relative terms. It is important because deeply embedded in this difference are social values unique to Hong Kong. Unraveling these values entail a close examination of the interplay between physical, cultural and socio-economic conditions which give rise to a particular outlook in housing by its people.

The last chapter suggested that housing studies in Hong Kong have been heavily influenced by a uni-dimensional perspective which assumes that all societies move along a similar housing path. And it will eventually converge in a housing system having a dominating owner-occupier sector and a declining public rental sector (Lee, 1991). Such a perspective is weak and simplistic. There are unique cultural and historical elements that shape a society's housing path. Housing oneself and one's family means more than a choice between tenures, mortgages and locations. Housing, above all, is a social experience. It is continuous, contextual and contingent upon many facets of life and society. The underlying assumption is that each society has its particular *social meaning of housing*, the construction of which represents a long process of complex interactions between variables such as space, culture, social history and government policy. This is not to herald the simplistic view that history determines the development of housing. The housing question is too complex to take on such a deterministic stand. Rather, the historical context of a society must be taken as part and parcel of the whole housing analysis. In this respect, my interest is to identify the cultural predisposition of Hong Kong people and the process through which they cope with their housing environment.

In order to fully appreciate the housing process in Hong Kong, a chronological mapping of individual and family housing histories will be constructed, spanning from the early 1950s to the 1970s. This period roughly extends from the era when the housing system was dominated by squatter huts, old inner-city tenements to the early phase of public rental housing. My purpose is to set the stage for subsequent discussions of those cultural predispositions as reflected by the housing histories of individuals and families, as well as the evolvement of certain indigenous cultural concepts. My argument is that the early phase of post-war housing experiences impacted tremendously on housing choices in later life. It will also be shown that contrary to many Western studies of home ownership which place great emphasis on the intrinsic value of owning, the high motivation for home ownership is a more complex issue in a Chinese society. It calls into question the role of the family and kinship support, the social meaning of home ownership, capital gains as well as the role of the state.

The housing history of Hong Kong dwellers could be roughly divided into four phases. These include: (1) the old inner-city tenements period prior to 1950, (2) the squatters period from late 1950s to early 1960s, (3) the resettlement period 1954-72, and (4) the new public housing era from 1973 to present.

Living on the Threshold: the Old Inner-city Tenements

It is difficult to describe Hong Kong's early housing situation with any degree of accuracy because during its first hundred years or so it was marked by a constant inflow, and at times outflow, of population to and from China. The population increased from approximately 627,000 in 1921 to nearly a million in 1936. This was then followed by an even larger influx of refugees from China after the war, so that by 1947 there were some 1.8 million people. With the exception of the period of the Japanese occupation during the war, the population has increased at a rate that far exceeds its housing capacity. Soon after the Communist takeover of China, Hong Kong's population made a quantum leap to 2.5 million in 1956. As far as housing is concerned, two main problems were encountered. First, there was the acute problem of urban congestion. Second, there were the health hazards arising from poor house sanitation.

The early population was largely concentrated on the northern waterfront of the Hong Kong Island as well as the southern tip of the Kowloon Peninsula, mainly in the form of old tenement blocks of 3-4 storeys high with no toilets and very few windows. As recorded vividly by Pryor in his historical review of Hong Kong's housing:

> In terraced houses, only the front rooms had windows so that the inner compartments were dark and airless. At the rear of each floor was a cookhouse, normally about 2 metres deep, which also frequently served as a latrine, storage room and even sleeping quarters. Chimneys were the exception and smoke escaped by means of holes, usually about 1.2 square metres, cut in the upper floors and roof. Such smoke holes were not very effective with the consequence that fumes permeated the living space...Tenement houses were constructed so that each floor was one undivided room. On the ground floor a space was boarded off in front of the kitchen for a bedroom or store and above this a platform was often erected as a workplace or for sleeping. While the regulations required the provisions of latrines, these were rarely to be found. Women and children normally used a pot kept either under a bed or in one corner of the cookhouse. The menfolk had to resort to the use of public latrines which, although supervised by the government, were run as a business enterprise with the products being shipped to China and sold at considerable profit to farmers (Pryor, 1973, pp. 10-11).

During the war, some 20,000 houses were either damaged or destroyed. The post-war housing shortage was exacerbated by the Communist takeover of China in 1949 when a large number of refugees flooded into Hong Kong from various parts of China. The population suddenly soared to a record level of 2.1 million in 1951 - 100% increase compared to 1936. Any government could not have foreseen such rapid expansion in population. Nonetheless, the population somehow managed to squeeze into the existing old tenement blocks. This resulted in doubling the number of households in the already crowded old tenement flats. Others simply lived in squatter settlements by the hillside. A flat of a tenement block of the size of 800-1,000 square feet used to house two families. With the refugee influx, it was expanded to house about six to eight families under one roof.

The appalling living conditions in those days were most vividly portrayed by one of the residents now well into his forties:

I can remember as a young boy those horrible summer months in Sai Wan (Western District). We rented a room on the 2nd floor of an old tenement. It was about 50-60 square feet. The ceiling was high and the whole place was dark even during daytime. Our cubicle had no windows. Only the two rooms in the verandah facing the street had windows. The landlady and her family lived in the rear room. There were altogether four big rooms. But after sometime, the landlady put up three double bunkers along the corridor leading to the kitchen at the rear part, hence narrowing the already narrow corridor. Each bunker housed 1-2 persons. Mum said these poor people walked all the way from Guangzhou and came to know the landlady through some remote relatives. My brother was very naughty! He would peep into those bunkers covered by worn out sheets and always got scolded by the old lady who smoked heavily in her bed. She must be quite sick because she coughed heavily during the night (Mr. Fung (a)).[1]

The living conditions in these old inner-city tenement blocks were so deprived and congested that personal space was an impossible luxury. Another homeowner remembered how, as children, he and his siblings were even denied space for playing and taking bath.

As a child I can remember my mum didn't allow us out for fear of bad elements on the streets. During weekends and holidays, we usually played together inside the room where we lived. There were other families in other rooms. When my mum cooked in the kitchen, my brother would drag out a wooden panel from the bunker and use it as a slide at a corner of the room. That's all we had in the childhood as 'playground'. We had no toys because they were expensive. We played with stones and tiny bags filled with sand. In the evening when bathing time came, all three of us, including my sister, bathed in the same tub of water. Not exactly a tub in the modern sense, mind you, it's just a big wooden basin. Because there wasn't a bathroom and we were too small to go to the public bath, we bathed either in the kitchen or in the corridor where everyone passed by. We did that all the way until I was about ten and my sister about eight, when we began to feel a bit shameful of exposing our bodies like that. At night my brother slept on the top of the double bunker with me. It was a small bed: 3' x 5'. I always woke up in the middle of the night and discovered my brother charging his toes right into my mouth (Mr. Chan (b)).

The Concept of 'Ngei' - Extreme Endurance as Virtue

Two observations emerge from such appalling living conditions: (1) the ability of people to adapt at all costs through the concept of *Ngei* - meaning extreme endurance;[2] and (2) a feeling of insecurity arising from being a tenant and the craze for personal space.

In order to survive, people must heighten their adaptability and flexibility to an extreme. They must shun whatever form of life habits they had in Mainland China. In fact, many refugees (particularly small landlords and the petite-bourgeoisie) from both the rural areas and Guangzhou city had a comparatively better living environment before fleeing to Hong Kong. The convergence of refugees from all parts of China in the early 1950s made a war-devastated Hong Kong a safe haven for all. There was a prevalent culture of *inwardness*, mainly as a result of the unwitting ethos of a sojourner. Nobody should be responsible for anybody's well being or misfortune, except oneself or one's family. The colonial government was definitely not a target of blame, nor was misfortune or bad luck. It was fate! This transient character of the place was best captured by the famous words of Hughes in his celebrated book, *Hong Kong: Borrowed Place, Borrowed Time*.

> The Hong Kong mood is one of masterly expedience and crisis-to-crisis adjustment and recovery. It is partly a gambler's mentality, partly fatalism...no one came to Hong Kong to make a home there; he came to make a living and get out. ...After all, Hong Kong is the city of the present (Hughes, 1968, p. 112).

This inward-looking attitude forms the most important base of the concept of *ngei*- the idea that since the world is no object of blame, one should become the centre of gravity and the pivot. This complex concept essentially means more than just endurance or tolerance. It refers to the unquestioned willingness of the individual to sacrifice personal comfort and old values in order to survive in the new environment. One accepts enduring of the most unfavorable conditions of life without repentance. It also means the readiness to live anywhere as long as there is shelter and to take up any work that comes along, even if followed by personal degradation. This also partly explains why post-war Hong Kong was able to absorb its massive refugee influx into its housing system without having to rely on state intervention. The concept of *ngei* has gradually evolved to become a social value and a quality for employment. One is praised both for intelligence and the potential of *ngei*. Interesting enough, this concept is still widely practiced today in many sectors of the society. It is a well-accepted part of the social repertoire, regardless of social class or employment.

Concomitant with this concept of extreme tolerance is a craze for personal space. While people in Hong Kong quietly swallowed their predicaments, few took it to be perpetual.

Looking back to those days in Sai Wan (Hong Kong Western District) old tenement when our family moved from one block to another because of nasty landlords, I said to myself: when I grow up I shall never become a tenant. My mum used to say that when we grow up we need to have a decent life - a life that would not be looked down upon by our relatives and friends, a life which would be free from landladies, a life that we could have our own say (Mr. Fung (a)).

The more one is deprived in early life, the more one will seek to compensate in later life or realize it through their offspring. This may not be universally true. However, evidence from homeowners shows that parents coming from a squatter and old tenement background are more inclined to influence as well as to provide financial assistance for their children in home purchase. Housing experiences in extreme congestion during childhood seem to have affected the housing attitude and preference in later life. Mr. Cheng's vivid memories certainly explain such strong desire:

The two things I dreaded most were the kitchen and the heat. The kitchen was always flooded with people, mostly women, smoke and non-stop chattering. Often bitter quarrels surfaced when people competed for the use of the only basin for washing. When cooking time came, it was the best time for my brother and I to sneak out to the nearby waterfront to watch pier-side fishing. Later we could have a cold shower in the nearby public lavatory if we were lucky enough to get a space. The heat was still on when we went home for dinner. My brother and I usually left home again after dinner, heading again for the waterfront. A group of our friends were already waiting for the night to begin. Looking back, I always wonder why I wasn't made a triad member (Mr. Cheng).

Young people in those days were greatly deprived of private space. In the late 1950s and early 1960s, there was a general absence of recreational venues for young people. For a population of nearly 3 million, Hong Kong had only two public swimming pools, two large parks and a few youth centres run by religious groups like the YMCA. Besides schooling under a rather sterile colonial grammar school curriculum, young people had absolutely nowhere to use their excess energy. More important, the home was not somewhere they looked forward to returning to. The long summer was the worst time of the year with a usual upsurge in youth vandalism. The seeds of social discontent had already been laid. Social disruption was well in sight. It was not a question of how, simply when.

> The air was always filled with a strong odour in summer: it was a mixture of sweat, cheap perfume and herbal medicine. I slept with my brother on the upper deck of a bunker while my sister slept on the other upper decker. My parents were sleeping on the lower deck of my sister's bunker. There were all sorts of quirky sounds in the next room where a butcher's family lived. The room partitioning was so low and I could easily peep into the other side of the room when I lay awakening on the upper deck of my bunker. I used to dream: when can I afford my own place? (Mr. Cheng)

Squatting as a Way of Life

If the 1960s were the period of resettlement estates, the 1950s was, the period of squatters. When a massive influx of refugees arrived in Hong Kong in the years after 1949, they first went to live with their friends and relatives in the old urban tenements. But when hospitality ran out after a few months, they had no choice but to resort to squatting in the urban fringe areas, meaning illegally erecting your own home on the hill side anywhere in town. As suggested by Bishop:

> The housing stock had been badly depleted by damage and neglect during the war and this, coupled with the dramatic increase in numbers, meant that those unable to afford what accommodation was available had little choice but to become squatters (Bishop, 1971, p. 111).

In the early 1950s, the size of the squatter population fluctuated in relation to the growth of the total population. During the period 1956-58, the estimated number was about a quarter of a million, in addition to over 60,000 rooftop squatters, and about 4,000 in resettlement areas established by the then Resettlement Department before a 'tolerated' system came into being:

> Since 1954 squatting has been controlled by demolishing new squatter huts when discovered. Inevitably, control has not been completely effective and it was agreed in 1959 and 1964 that illegal structures presumed to have been erected before 1954 or expressly tolerated as a result of special survey made in those years should be tolerated and allowed to remain, although new ones would be demolished (Dwyer, 1971, p. 112).

116

Squatter areas were mainly found on the northern side of the Kowloon Peninsula below the Lion Rock (which more or less separates Kowloon and New Territories). They were found in some 130 squatter villages ranging in population size from 29 persons in Tai Tam Village in a rural setting to something around 40,000 persons in the Hok Lo and Sai Tau Village in Kowloon North. A majority of these villages were located close to each other, forming clusters of squatter areas to the north fringe of Kowloon. In Hong Kong Island, the squatter villages mainly took up the eastern fringe of the waterfront and were largely concentrated in Tai Hang, Shau Kei Wan and Chai Wan (Wong, 1976).

Early studies of squatter living conditions in Hong Kong have invariably emphasized the poor living conditions, such as unsafe structures, poor sanitation, lack of space, poor access, absence of sewage disposal and drainage system as well as extreme fire hazards. This is true in many respects. However, most studies tend to over-concentrate on the problems of living standards (Drakakis-Smith, 1973; Hopkins, 1971; Pryor, 1973) and spatial distribution (Drakakis-Smith, 1979) but fail to pay attention to lives and social organization within the squatting community. Such neglect amounts to a skewed understanding of the situation of squatter living in the early years, and fails to locate adequately its significance in relation to social change.

One researcher made an early attempt to depart from this perspective. Wong (1971) did a detailed study of a small squatter area - Aplichau Squatter Area. It was a small island south of the Hong Kong Island with fishing and farming as its main economic activities before the war. With the influx of refugees in the early 1950s, Wong discovered that the island was gradually transformed into an area of light industries, including boat building and machine-making and repairing. These early small industries had successfully formed the industrial base of the nearby Wong Chuk Hang Industrial Estate which was developed in the late 1960s when the government made a major attempt at industrial development of the Island South, including Aplichau. Because of the increase in the immigrant population, a host of service industries thrived, for example: hawkers selling cooked food and clothing, retail and wholesale trades and small restaurants. There was also an increase in amahs (domestic helpers) and waiters for the original non-squatter sector of the population who relied on the availability of the relatively cheap labour of the new immigrants.

Wong's study, although pioneering in terms of focusing only on a particular community of squatters, is essentially descriptive in nature, seeking a spatial overview rather than unravelling the social process underpinning squatting. Subsequent studies of squatter living have made an overt attempt to link squatter living to broader structural processes (Kehl, 1981; Chan, 1985). In his study of the process of squatter clearance in Diamond Hill (a squatter area in Northeast Kowloon), Smart (1986) demonstrated two important elements heavily affecting social change. First, he discovered that while squatter huts were either illegal or 'tolerated' properties not capable of legal ownership or exchange, there existed in fact a rather open illegal market for home ownership. Second, squatter clearance by the government and hence the building of resettlement estates have been more directed towards making land available for industrial use rather than the commonly conceived objectives of social housing for the poor. Smart's (1989) subsequent studies further explored the role of the Hong Kong government and suggested that it actually fostered the growth of an illegal squatter market. He further indicated that in appraising the role of the state in housing, its relative autonomy should not be underestimated.

While Smart's analysis contributes significantly towards linking up the process of squatter clearance and the operation of the squatter black market, his exclusive concentration on the structural aspect of squatter clearance has failed to take into account the ways in which individual and family housing experiences were linked to other aspects of the broader social process.

Among the 30 cases in Smart's study, five lived in ground squatters; four lived as rooftop squatters while the rest were all in old tenement blocks in the city in their early years. Only one lived in the New Territories in his childhood. This is not surprising as we probe into other family housing histories later and find that many housing movements are bound by family networks within a certain locality.

People who arrived from Mainland China shortly before or after the Second World War were mainly trying to seek refuge from the Communist regime. While there is difficulty in getting precise figures, the general picture is that 80% of these refugees came from Guangdong and its vicinity. Most of them were ordinary working class, small businessmen and landlords. The rest were professionals and rich businessmen from Shanghai and Northern China. For the small businessmen and landlords, the capital they brought along could provide them with access to renting or buying private tenements. However for the majority of the refugees, squatters had become the most common housing alternative since most of the old inner-city tenement blocks were already fully occupied.

Mr. Chung, a restaurant captain, and Mr. Mok, a social worker, both lived in squatter settlements when they were young: one in Ho Man Tin (Kowloon Central) and the other in Tai Hang Sai (Kowloon East). They share one common characteristic, that is, they moved to their respective squatter hut without going through the tenement experience. Chung's father was a farmer in Shun Tak, a village in Guangdong Province, who came to Hong Kong in 1949 with his family (wife and mother). With no friends or relatives and about $300, which was barely sufficient for the purchase of materials, they built a small hut near Ho Man Tin, now the site of a large public housing estate in Kowloon. Later he became a fresh fruit hawker near his house, where the number of illegal squatters tripled in the span of one year.

> Life was difficult in our early years. My father used to say something like this: 'The Communist came to strip us of everything in our village: house, land and live stocks, but here we are again! We have nothing from the outset and yet we are thriving again. I knew nothing about hawking and fruit selling, and now I manage to bring you up like that. Building your own house (squatter) is something you should be proud of. Your grandfather also built his own village house in Shun Tak.' We always thought dad was a very self-reliant man. He didn't depend on anybody, not anyone, not the government of course. He said we must use our own hands. Nothing could be worse off than living under Communist rule. One must bear in mind that they are (the Communist) never to be trusted (Mr. Chung).

Squatting for the Chung family was seen more as a way of living, a way of surviving Communist menace. It was something to be proud of. For Mr. Mok, the story was slightly different. His family used to live in Guangzhou and his father had a small furniture business. They used to own a rather large flat in the town centre. Unfortunately, his family assets were all frozen during the Communist uprising and the family wealth was lost during the flight to Hong Kong. The family rented a squatter hut in Tai Hang Sai (the largest squatter area in the 1950s) after three months of chilly reception by Mok's uncle. As he painfully recalled life in the early 1950s:

> Our family had really fallen into pieces. My father was sick after the trauma of the closing down of his business and my mother was really neurotic about people knocking on our door in the middle of the night. She felt so ashamed of living in that 'hole' and all the time hid herself in the corner of the house. Things didn't get any better until my brother got a job as a machine apprentice and my sister worked as a cleaner in a nearby restaurant. We were quite lucky to have some very good neighbours and

because the rent was cheap, as long as we had work our life was okay. My brother and I began to build an extension of the kitchen so that the original kitchen could become another room. We knew that was not allowed because our hut was one of those 'tolerated' but who cared. My brother always had his ways with those 'resettlement' folks. Years later when we moved to a nearby resettlement estate, we kept coming back to meet our friends and neighbours. Some of them are still friends today (Mr. Mok).

While the Chung and Mok families were of different origins and heralded different processes of adjustment, squatting as a way of living all began to take shape quite naturally. It seems rather obvious that both families suffered greatly under political turmoil and Hong Kong was regarded as the much-wanted *refuge*. Ironically, the anti-Communist stance by these families has provided them with a rather positive impetus for work and survival in their new environment. It has also provided these families with an opportunity to construct a new identity, based on self-reliance and acceptance. This partly explains the prevalence of an inward-looking attitude and a general political acquiescence amongst the people, for whatever welfare systems bestowed upon them by the colonial government during the early period. The family and the social network were the two things they trusted most. Parallel with these was the unconscious development of an inbred inclination to alienate from the government. There is this common Chinese saying from the 1950s: 'When you are alive, never get involved with the government, and when you are dead, never go to hell!' Such public sentiments provided the British colonial government with much ease in public administration. In King's (1975) conception, political absorption by way of co-opting a few Chinese dignitaries into the legislature, mostly big family names, was sufficient to amass legitimacy in governance, because legitimacy was basically there. However, such ease in administration bred complacency and shortsightedness among colonial officials. The seeds of social discontent were unconsciously laid. The refuge in Hong Kong, no matter how temporary and unbearable, was regarded precious and irreplaceable. It has provided people with the impetus and drive for survival. Indeed, what had come to be known as mutual help and neighbourliness amongst Chinese people could sometimes be transformed to extreme greediness, egocentricity and selfishness. While some would regard it a kind of cultural schizophrenia (Bond, 1991), others would think that this actually provided Hong Kong with the necessary impetus for its subsequent growth and development (Lau, 1984; Lau & Kuan, 1988). These attitudes are captured by the following typical remarks about child rearing amongst the working class:

Never stay near to any crowds in the street and if it ever happens, come home quickly. Remember the saying that 'each household should only be concerned with sweeping snow from their front yard and should be least bothered with the snow on the roof of his neighbour'. People in Hong Kong are all in the same boat. If anyone is in trouble, we will eventually be in trouble as well. So we should really help out when we can.

It was within these seemingly contradicting values, armed with a desperate desire to survive, seasoned by a general disregard of the government, and backed by an intense fear of Communism, all lumped together to form a jam-packed living environment for the young people. Poor housing conditions in squatters and old tenement blocks represent just one facet of this context in which people of the 1950s and 1960s lived out their lives. So it was not housing alone that mattered in those days. All other physical and social conditions posed hardship of a greater or lesser extent on the livelihood of people. By examining the housing histories of the individuals, social changes are videolized and played back. Housing provides a window to understand the past.

Life in Early Public Housing Estates: Mark I - VI Blocks 1954-1972

...if Hong Kong rehoused the mass of its population at Parker Morris standards as laid down for state housing schemes in Britain, the actual volume of building would increase by at least four or five times, possibly more. This does not take into account the complementary open space standards, but merely those of actual habitable building. It may be many years before we are in a position to aim at such standards, but should this not at least be considered possible? (Prescott, 1971, pp. 14-15)

Of course a Parker Morris standard of housing was not possible. It was quite apparent that early colonial administrators of the Housing Department had other things on their minds. In the Christmas of 1953, when they were faced with the daunting task of resettling 50,000 families displaced by a fire in Shek Kip Mei (a Kowloon East squatter area), what was the ideal of a young English planner turned out to be the mass construction of seven-storey H-shaped housing blocks named Mark I - II, swiftly relocating 120,000 people within four years (Pryor, 1973). These early resettlement blocks, with only communal toilets, communal water supply, and the absence of cooking and laundry facilities became the dominant mode of dwellings in Hong Kong for the 1960s and 1970s. They took on the enormous task of mass resettlement of squatter population with little or no planning at all. With the provision of only 24 square feet per adult and about 100 square feet per unit, there was hardly any space left for cooking and washing. It was merely a room, or a 'pigeon hole', in Cantonese. As suggested by Prescott, life in a resettlement estate could be comparatively worse than that in a squatter area because tenants had to pay rent, electricity as well as to comply with a set of stringent rules for the use of communal facilities. However, according to a Resettlement Department survey in 1964, only 2%-3% of squatter households refused resettlement. It was also discovered that an unknown number of *impostors* were present at most clearances. They were usually members of a squatter family who did not actually live in the squatter hut and were therefore not eligible for resettlement, but nevertheless claimed resettlement when the area was screened for clearance (Dwyer, 1971). Resettlement, however traumatic and painful, was much desired. Life in squatter areas was too hazardous and unhealthy. During winter, there were incidents of fire caused either by kerosene cooking stoves or improper electrical wiring from illegitimate sources. In summer, there were horrendous typhoon attacks, resulted in landslides and collapsed houses. People looked forward to a more permanent kind of housing. Smart's (1989) study of squatter exchange clearly indicated that one of the prime reasons for illegal exchange of squatter ownership was the fact that squatter occupation amounted to future entitlement for resettlement. Mr. Cheung (a), now a university administrator, clearly recollected the experience of resettlement and how the family moved into a Mark II estate in Tai Hang Tung (Kowloon East), one of the first resettlement estates.

> I can remember the 1960 Typhoon Wendy, you know, which killed many people and made 10,000 homeless. At that time our family lived in a squatter hut in Tai Hang Tung. It was one August evening, I don't remember exactly when. Signal No.10 was hoisted. During dinner time my father and I were trying to stabilize the hut by some more external wiring...and you know what, by ten, the whole roof was blown off, just like that! We all clutched together under a plastic sheet for 2 hours before the rain turned light and then we ran for cover in a nearby school. One day in 1963, my dad came home with a letter from the Resettlement Department saying that we could move to the new Tai Hang Tung Estate within three months. We were allotted a cubicle of a monthly rent of $20. Mum was so delighted and she bought roast duckling and beer for celebration and instantly burnt incenses for our family ancestors. Soon we moved in our new place. Apart from the fact that we didn't have a kitchen as we used to have, it was much more convenient for mum to buy stuff because downstairs there were shops and clinics. Between Blocks 8 and 9 there was

also a market as well. You know in Tai Hang Tung Squatter Area mum used to climb up and down those slopes and had to walk for 30 minutes to the market. That was always a bit too much for her. Later on my sister and I enrolled in the school on the rooftop, quite convenient, you know, one of those 'rooftop' primary schools. It was located in the same block so that we didn't even need an umbrella during rainy days (Mr. Cheung (a)).

Other housing experiences during transition from squatter to resettlement block carried a similar tone. Life stresses and attention were seemingly diverted from a concern for environmental safety (whether one's house would be blown away or burnt down) to interpersonal conflicts. The lack of individual household facilities in their new homes, such as washing, cooking and toilet, invariably gave rise to a great deal of neighbourhood tension, for example, deciding on the right time to take a shower or who should have the priority to use the toilet and the shower room. These personal tensions sometimes erupted and caused serious consequences, with people attacking and injuring one another, particularly during extreme situations, such as those frequent droughts in the 1960s when water supply was restricted to only four hours per day. Behind all these ordeals, perhaps, what often passed unnoticed by researchers on Hong Kong housing issues was that kind of extreme competitiveness to survive in the living environment. As recollected by Mr. Wan, an airport technician, the constant alertness or vigilance started young:

> When I was about 10, I was assigned by my mother as a 'sentry' for the washing tap and the toilet. I developed a system of warning and communication with my family so that they knew exactly when to come forward to the communal place (we called it the 'pit') for washing. I mustn't let the fat lady next door get it first because if she did, we wouldn't be able to have the shower room before 10. I was extremely good at that, and nobody in my family could beat me... (Mr. Wan).

This kind of competitiveness was not present in Guangdong, where most people in Hong Kong originated and still have relatives. Indeed, even with the opening up of the Chinese economy and after Hong Kong's handover, people living on the other side of the border are still rather 'laid-back'. Such competitiveness emanates only from Hong Kong.

The Concept of 'Shingmuk' as a Survival Value

The transition from squatter to resettlement estates and subsequently to home ownership marks a progressive shift in challenges and can be regarded more aptly as a training ground for subsequent life challenges. Indeed, this contributes to the formation of a much-debated Hong Kong ethos.

> Looking back, life in those periods, I mean the 1960s and 1970s, was extremely difficult. I wouldn't expect it to be possible to live in those Mark II estates any more. But after all, we didn't feel all that bad at that time. Life was more often preoccupied by survival rather than sadness or anguish; we just had no time for that anyway. You had to be alert and *shingmuk* all the time, don't you? Even now, even when I am doing much better than 20 years ago, you still have to be *shingmuk*. Otherwise I could easily fall prey to 'crocodiles'. That's Hong Kong! Some of my toughness in business comes from that training. I don't know how on earth my family survived in those days. But that was really no big deal for us (Mr. Lai).

Shingmuk, like *ngei*, is a Cantonese slang, meaning a combination of smartness, vigilance, swiftness, worldliness, assertiveness, agility and independence. When somebody is described as being *shingmuk* and also capable of *ngei*, that somebody is almost certainly destined for success. This mundane set of cultural concepts carries a wide impact across all social sectors. The interesting point to note is that they do not apply to other areas of China, not even Guangzhou, the capital city of Guangdong Province. They are unique to Hong Kong. In recent years, they have been elevated to such a level of eminence that employers continue to regard them as key qualities they should look for in staff recruitment, particularly in the business sector. The comment that would be raised by a prospective employer is something like this: 'Well! He looks good on papers, but is he *shingmuk* or can he be *ngei*?' These concepts have emerged since the 1960s and have since remained an integral part of Hong Kong culture.

Social Tensions and the Riots of 1966 and 1967

It was during this part of the housing history that the infamous riots of the 1966 and 1967 broke out. Social tensions had been mounting in the preceding years of the riots. Anti-government feelings progressively built up from the late 1950s to the 1960s as a result of poor social conditions, for example, unemployment and poor housing. There was widespread hatred for the way the colonial establishment handled its business, particularly concerning the way police and housing officials handled people.

For some homeowners, the shifting dynamics of the society as well as the seeds of discontent among the young people are reflected in these thoughts:

I hate the policemen, especially those *gweilo* (expatriate) inspectors, they just came to kick at my father's fruit stall, with oranges and apples running all over the place and many of them squashed by cars passing by. Not just the police, those guys from the triad society as well, they're all over the place and police took no note of them. My father had to pay 'protection fees' to them daily, otherwise we wouldn't be able to have our stall there. What he earned was already meagre and still had to serve all these interests, I didn't know where we were heading for. To help out with the family income, my mum took on some take-home work, usually assembling plastic flowers. After school, the whole family worked for a few hours before dinner. We applied for resettlement housing a long time, but nothing happened. We were desperate. But we cannot blame anyone. We can only blame that we were poor (Mrs Liu).

I was 14 years old and was in Form 2. I worked daytime as an office boy and studied in an evening school. My family lived in a resettlement estate in Tze Wan Shan. We were all working hard. My father worked as a casual worker in transport and my mother did take-home garment work. Life was stringent. We never ate out. During Chinese New Year, we must borrow money from my auntie to pay for some repair work in the flat. I remember on Sundays we usually gathered at this hideout place in Yau Ma Tei with a group of fellow-students. We shared news about what was happening in China and there were distributions of notes of revolutionary songs about the Communist Party. We sang Mao songs and then a 'big brother' came forth and talked to us about how corrupt the government was. At first I had no interest in Communism or China, but the *we* feeling did matter to me somehow. I always had the feeling that the government didn't care a shit about whether my family was dead or alive. For a while I thought I took pride in knowing that China was stronger, so that British won't look us down anymore. Of course, I kept these meetings to myself. My father would be mad to know that I talked to the Communists (Mr. Chung).

I can remember the riot started in May 1967 and ended in January 1968. There were numerous casualties mainly as a result of homemade bombs by the leftists. I knew it was coming because my friend who worked in the union told me. The government had always underestimated the Cultural Revolution. At first it was only a small group of people. But it got worse as the summer of 1967 wore on, with all the kids in the street, things went out of control. I didn't think the public really support the red guards, but they were amused to see the chaotic situation the police found themselves. I remember running after a crowd one evening and almost got caught by the police. I didn't throw any stone at the police but as a young lad, I found that exciting (Mr. Chan (a)).

In these recollections of three separate homeowners, it is clear that tension was beginning to emerge between the people and the government. There was an inclination that young people identified more, albeit haphazardly, with the Chinese Government. The Cultural Revolution gave impetus to the already restless and disgruntled youngsters. Nonetheless, it was never clear whether their temporary identification with the leftists was more the result of political conviction or merely seeking an alternative identity, to displace the then corrupt and uncaring colonial administration.

Social eruption finally came as two consecutive riots in the late 1960s. In the Report of the 1966 Kowloon Riots, the following conclusions were drawn:

> ...there is evidence of a growing interest in Hong Kong on the part of youth and a tendency to protest at a situation which their parents might tacitly accept....the degree of misunderstanding of government's aims and problems exposed by the inquiry emphasizes the importance of ensuring that its policies and problems are clearly explained and the public's cooperation in their implementation actively pursued (Report on 1966 Kowloon Riots, p. 129).

The riots were a painful lesson for Hong Kong. Many businessmen fled Hong Kong in 1968. The government began to take a more serious approach towards her knowledge of the local community. Unfortunately, like many other official inquiries during that time, the purpose was to scale down the issue to a mere problem of communication. To tackle the problem, government departments should improve their communication channels with the local community. What the government failed to realize and appreciate were the immense stresses and anxieties the people had to put up with in their struggle for a living. It was not until a long lapse after the 1967 riot that the government finally acknowledged the existence of much more deep-rooted problems. In another report to the Legislative Council in 1968, the following comments were made:

> ...the Far Eastern Economic Review maintained that Government had not given the people a sense of belonging...there was no feeling of participation between the people and Government...the governor had failed to reach the targets which he had set himself at the beginning of his tenure of office -

reforms in education, medical and health services, housing and administration in general... (Report on 1967 Riots, pp. 269-297).

Like it or not, the genesis of a more comprehensive public housing programme in the early 1970s was conceived soon after the riots. The belief was that, if the people were sufficiently sheltered, they would not take it to the street, or at least the young people would not. The famous 'Blake Pier Modern Dance Party' was organized every Friday evening in the early 1970s by the Urban Council to help young people air their excessive energy, if they found their home environment unbearable.

The New Public Housing Era: Low Cost Housing Estates

By 1971, the public housing programme had firmly taken shape. If the 1950s and 1960s could be termed an era of reluctant state intervention in housing, the 1970s marked the first decade when the government began to take a more serious role towards meeting people's housing needs. Why? Lessons learnt from the riots were certainly one impetus of a more proactive housing policy. The findings of various studies also indicated three reasons for this shift in the role of the state. First, there was the failure of the Ten Year House Building Programme (1964-74) which prompted much public criticisms (Pryor, 1973). In 1964, the government appointed two committees to review the housing problems of the colony: the first to deal with slum clearance and the second to assess the policies aiming at squatter resettlement and the provision of low-income housing. A White Paper was later produced which aimed at a quantitative planning target of housing 2.2 million people up to 1974. However, as a result of poor implementation and lack of coordination between the old Resettlement Department and the new Housing Authority, coupled with the world economic downturn, only one million people had been rehoused, meeting only half of its original target (Chan, 1982).

Second, a new governor, Sir Murray MacLehose arrived in 1971. Being more inclined to the social interventionist approach and also grasping a sense of urgency in the housing situation, the new governor launched a far more comprehensive and ambitious public housing programme. Two elements stood out most prominently during this period: (1) the government was to be responsible for the building of better quality, self-contained housing for both rental and ownership (Home Ownership

Scheme); and (2) six new towns were to be developed in the suburban New Territories in order to ease urban congestion (Bristow, 1989).

Third, Hong Kong, which had an export-led economy, began to grow in the early 1970s and naturally people desired for better living standard as their income rose. The government also recognized the growing need to revamp the housing programme (Fong, 1986). While evidence of rising expectations was more speculative, evidence of the growth of the economy was abundant. As indicated by Chen (1979) in his study of comparative growth rates of Asian economies, the rate of Hong Kong's income growth was highest during 1960-66. In order to meet the new housing targets, the Housing Authority was reorganized into a semi-autonomous statutory body with a high degree of financial independence. Government funding would go to the new Housing Authority in the form of a loan from the Development Loan Fund and it had to be repaid with interest over a period of 40 years.

Two significant changes were noted in public housing. Extensive renovation and reconstruction of the old resettlement estates were launched. Small cubicles were combined to form larger units, and toilets and kitchens were added to these enlarged units. From Mark IV estates onward, self-contained units with standard facilities have been introduced. The following responses are indicative of the changes that were taking place.

Many families in our resettlement block had been relocated to a newly built public housing estate in the New Territories. My father was selling dried foodstuff in the neighborhood market and he had built up a network of customers. So he didn't want to move away although we understood that the new estates would have improved facilities. The other reason we stayed was that the Housing Authority would be renovating our block very soon. We were later allocated an improved unit in the same estate. It was a 'combined' unit of two old units. We had a toilet and a cooking place inside the unit. That was a very small toilet without shower or bathing facilities. We had to install a detachable shower to the tap. But you see that was a very big improvement already. We didn't have to go out for bathing and toilet any more. Also we didn't have to cook outside along the corridor any more. But it's funny that for a long time many people didn't quite get used to the idea of abandoning the public corridor as their own living place. We still put some of our unused belongings such as buckets, old stoves and pots outside (Mrs. Poon).

We moved to the Wong Chuk Hang Estate from Tin Wan Resettlement Estate (both in Hong Kong Island South) in 1973. The blocks were much taller and with lifts. The living condition was improved in terms of space and the neighbourhood. We also had a private toilet and a kitchen. Since the estate was newly built, it was cleaner and better planned than Tin Wan. But I think the built quality of the blocks was quite primitive. The cement ceiling, walls and floor were very rough and poorly painted. We didn't really have a kitchen. I would call it just a cooking place. The stove was built in the balcony where it was very windy. It was impossible to cook there because the flames of the stoves would be put out pretty soon by the wind. I remembered my parents had to spend a few thousand dollars to renovate the unit and to install plastic wind shields in the balcony so that we could cook there. (Mr. Yuen)

The improvement of housing conditions in the renovated or newly constructed public housing estates was obvious but yet far from satisfactory. Another problem facing the government in the early 1970s was that all urban land had been largely developed. Castells et al. (1990) and Smart (1989) suggested that the real reason behind the restructuring of the housing system was due to structural demands for land from a booming industrial economy in the late 1970s. This means a great demand for industrial and commercial land, and hence resulting in an intense competition for urban land between industrial, commercial and residential use. The demand for industrial land is well confirmed by studies into the source of economic growth. Shea (1989) suggested that the main reason for growth in the manufacturing sector in the 1960s and 1970s was the result of a successful concentration of industrial production within a few products having comparative advantage in the world market (such as garment, textiles, footwear, plastics, toys and consumer electronics). The impact of this was a greatly heightened demand for suitable industrial land as evident in the increasing revenues from land sales for the period 1970-98. From Table 5.1, we can see that revenue from land sales, though fluctuated during the last three decades, by and large produced on average 10%-13% of the total revenue, providing a steady income to the government. It is important to note that upturn in the economy was accompanied by an increase in land sales. The late 1970s and early 1980s marked the boom years in property and therefore land revenues. Mid-1980s and early 1990s marked the low period in land sales revenue as a result of a declining property market. This was followed by another boom period starting from the mid-1990s, reaching its apex in 1997. It should be noted that the demand for residential land was low for most part of the 1970s. It was only in the late 1970s and the early 1980s that the demand for residential land became keener. Table 5.1 also dispelled a common belief that land sales form a major part of public revenue and that the government has put great emphasis on land sale receipts. In fact, the major source of revenue has always been direct taxation from corporations and wage earners.

Table 5.1   Revenue from Land Sales (1970-1998)

Fiscal Year	Revenue from Sales (HK$ million)	% of Total Revenue
1970-71	814.9	7.0
1971-72	269.3	7.6
1972-73	669.5	13.6
1973-74	287.7	6.1
1974-75	345.9	4.9
1975-76	345.9	4.7
1976-77	557.3	6.8
1977-78	1831.3	18.9
1978-79	2007.8	14.4
1979-80	2845.2	15.4
1980-81	10769.8	35.2
1981-82	9676.5	27.3
1982-83	5048.1	12.9
1983-84	2267.1	6.0
1984-85	4267.2	10.3
1985-86	4481.0	10.0
1986-87	3086.0	6.0
1987-88	3974.0	7.0
1988-89	6758.0	9.0
1989-90	7211.0	9.0
1990-91	4243.0	5.0
1991-92	9486.0	8.0
1992-93	9224.0	7.0
1993-94	19376.0	12.0
1994-95	20586.0	12.0
1995-96	22896.0	13.0
1996-97	29508.0	14.0
1997-98	66368.0	24.0

Source: Hong Kong Annual Reports (various years).

Conclusion

This chapter depicts a painful and tortuous social trajectory of housing. The gradual development from old inner-city tenement blocks to squatters, resettlement estates and then public rental housing has been portrayed. The individual and family housing histories of the respondents are reflections of the housing history of Hong Kong, which is interwoven at the same time with social history itself and the changing society. Through these individual homeowners' histories, we witness how the social, political and economic situations in Hong Kong and its housing development have come to influence each other. The policy of the colonial government gradually evolved from an apathetic to a more proactive role, although pragmatism and the overriding concern for economic development still largely dominated.

Most of the homeowners in the study recalled different degree of socio-spatial deprivation in the early history of Hong Kong's habitat. Poor housing was not the only thing Hong Kong people suffered from in the 1950s and 1960s. The society was plagued by unemployment, low wages, poor personal and environmental health, insufficient school places and an uncaring government. This chapter highlights only one of the most serious predicaments, that is, housing. The question I am raising here is: how significant are these social conditions in housing have come to shape people's life? Evidence from my case studies indicated at least two types of responses. The first type of response was characterized by a form of stoicism. Respondents seemed to have accepted life as it was. The appalling housing conditions did not seem to have created any great disturbance to their life and livelihood. In fact, some of them had shown gratitude to the colonial government. This was best echoed by Mrs. Chow's mother, aged 65, joining our interview from the kitchen:

> To be able to come to Hong Kong is already our family's greatest fortune. Nothing is worse than being persecuted by the Communists. Our squatter in Ho Man Tin was not much different from our village hut in Shun Tak (a small village in rural Guangdong). You know: 'All crows under the sky are black.' One shouldn't ask too much for life. That's how I teach everybody in my family.

The above comments reflect a deep-rooted refugee mentality that is still widely shared amongst people over the age of 55 in Hong Kong, irrespective of class and origin. The desire to live and survive has come to outlive any other personal sentiments, resulting in a pervasive culture of *ngei* depicted earlier. They are contented with status quo, accepting *ngei* as a way of life and seldom demand for more from others. The second type of response, which is more representative of the group of homeowners in my study, is a sentiment suggesting toughness, endurance and a kind of forward-looking attitude. For them, the refugee mentality is somewhat subdued by a more proactive survival spirit. For them, the refugee mentality belongs more to their parent generation. It is more a cultural predisposition than something emanating from their hearts. Hence the poor housing condition in childhood is seen more as a form of transient mishap rather than permanent misfortune. Mrs. Kwok recalled her childhood experiences in rural Yuen Long.

> Our family lived in a small farm hut in Ma Tin village near Yuen Long. There were grandma, my parents, three sisters and one brother. The house was always dimly lit because my grandma wanted to save electricity. There was frequent power failure, so kerosene lamp was always used. The kitchen and toilet were very crude cardboard extension built by my father who knows very little about woodwork. The toilet was simply a hole in the ground and it was chilly cold in winter. Once a typhoon came and some time in the middle of the night the whole roof was blown off. We went to stay in our neighbour's house for the rest of the night. The next day we went to school as usual and after school I helped my father to fix the roof. All our furniture and electric appliances were badly dampened. My mother borrowed a thousand dollar from my aunt to pay for the repair. Within a week, our life went normal again. It's funny. We never felt really bad about what happened. I thought I have a wonderful childhood. We had lots of friends and good neighbours (Mrs. Kwok).

My middle-aged subjects may use different forms of expressions, some vivid, others factual and a few vague. But none of them related their childhood life experiences as sad and painful. A childhood deprived of good living space and environment does not seem to be negatively related to later life development, or at least at the surface analysis. What is perhaps most striking is the determination and acceptance of the value for individual and family betterment. Unlike their parents who are contented with what they have, this younger generation is highly motivated to work hard to achieve a better life for themselves and their family. In Cantonese, this represents another popular cultural concept - *pok*. It stands for the combined meaning of pro-activity, fierce competition and risk-taking. The well known Cantonese saying goes like this: 'In Hong Kong, to succeed means to *pok*.' When homeowners were asked what they wanted most after they had succeeded, most of them invariably suggested that they wanted to improve their living conditions. The dictum perpetually mentioned was that: 'You can only work well when you live well.'

My exploration into homeowners' early housing histories has led to two tentative conclusions on the relationship between housing and society. First, the middle class homeowners unmistakably reveal a childhood of extreme deprivation in housing and space. Such deprivation predisposes our subjects to a corresponding crave for a better living environment in later life. Second, deprivation in living environment also predisposes Hong Kong children to a culture of endurance, diligence and pro-activity, as represented by the three core values of survival, which could be rightly coined - 'the survival trio': *ngei* - endurance, *shingmuk* - agility and shrewdness and *pok* - pro-activity and risk-taking. While it is premature and judgemental to suggest a direct relationship between these core values and housing consumption, many homeowners have indicated a high motivation for improvement of living environment. If we are not satisfied with this indirect bearing of housing history on home ownership, the next chapter will turn to a much more direct aspect of middle class homeowners: that is, how middle class people are influenced by their families through home financing and home buying.

Notes

1. Unless otherwise stated, all quotes are from author's own fieldwork.

2. The concept of *ngei* basically comes from Guangzhou, the capital city of Guangdong Province, which is very near to Hong Kong. It is interesting to note that for many people who have an ethnic origin from the north, such as Shanghai or Beijing, once they are in Hong Kong, this concept is quickly picked up and practised.

6 Family Support, Culture and Home Ownership

Chinese people are known to have strong family ties. They tend to support each other and stick together in times of difficulty. They depend not just on members of the nuclear family, but also on the stem family as well as the *modified extended family*, where a cluster of related nuclear families live in close vicinity to facilitate interaction and support. More important, mutual dependence manifests itself more in the form of material and financial transfers, in addition to moral or psychological support (Lee, 1991; Wong, 1975). Such a notion of family and kinship stands in stark contrast to accepted views in Western society where, ostensibly as a consequence of industrialization and modernization, families are heading towards a reduced family network and hence, less dependent on the kinship system for help. As a result of weakened kinship support, the nuclear family relies more on state welfare support (Gans, 1962). That is the traditional view of modern family and the state. Nonetheless, a more modern development of the sociology of family since the early 1980s has seen a rediscovery of the importance of family networks in contemporary urban society (Segallen, 1984; Wilson, 1987; Qureshi & Simons, 1987; Ungerson, 1987; Lewis & Meredith, 1988). Extensive practices of kinship mutual support are found in family networks, stemming from duty, responsibility and loving care (Finch, 1989). Concomitant with this development is that housing researchers in the West also witness a developing interest in the role of the family in home ownership and home financing (Madge & Brown, 1981; Henrietta, 1984; Finch & Mason, 1993; Forrest, Murie & Williams, 1990). One of the key findings of these studies is that kinship support as a variable contributing to the growth of home ownership has been grossly underestimated and under-researched. The role of the family, with regard to housing decisions and its influence on the development of an individual's *housing careers*, has been neglected or taken for granted. To properly understand the role of the modern family in housing consumption and its influence on society, researchers have begun to question the validity of the traditional unitary vision of housing studies, which assumes a high degree of independence of the rational housing consumers. Instead, they endeavour to incorporate a more broad-based perspective that sees the individual as an interdependent subject within a complex matrix of familial, economic, cultural and state relationships. This way, housing research could then be reinstated in the broader discussions of the dynamics of modern and post-modern societies. An emerging literature is being developed to further the debate on the relationship between modern family networks and housing choices (Forrest & Murie, 1995). Tosi (1995), for example, has noted that 23% of owner-occupiers in Italy achieve home ownership through inheritance, suggesting that the family is an important, yet often under-rated social institution which directly affects the growth of home ownership.

In recent years, research in Hong Kong also has also seen the resurgence of interest in the roles and functions of the modern families, partly as a consequence of the rapid increase in social problems associated with the family, and partly as a result of the government's plan to roll back welfare expenditures and the controversial *new* policy to reinstate the importance of a self-reliant and self-supporting Chinese family. While there is still an absence of local literature focusing on the relationship between family ties and home ownership, a renewed emphasis on the extent of intra-familial support is becoming popular (Lui, 1995).

Against this background, this chapter attempts to examine more closely the relationships between housing, home ownership and kinship support within the Chinese family system in Hong Kong. The broad theoretical question being addressed here is: how far family network support and cultural practices in housing contribute to the development of home ownership, and what is the impact of this development on the society at large. In particular, the following three theoretical questions are explored: (1) Assuming family mutual assistance in home financing does exist, how far and in what form does it take and under what conditions are such family aids transferred? (2) How does this family assistance in housing consumption influence and shape the housing system? And (3) how far do aids in home ownership shape contemporary social processes? This chapter is divided into two parts. The first part briefly reviews the recent literature on the roles and functions of the contemporary Hong Kong family. The second part sets out key empirical evidence from my case studies of homeowners. The conclusion highlights the significance of such findings for current debates on home ownership and the family. The major argument being advanced is that kinship assistance in home ownership not only provides families with enormous help in meeting housing needs, but also effectively shapes middle class culture and identity, reinforces class differences and furthers social inequality.

The Hong Kong Chinese Family

From social indicator research carried out in 1988 (Lau et al., 1991), it is evident that the nuclear family is the most prevalent type of family in Hong Kong. There are as many as 78.4% of the population in nuclear family form, of which 84.5% are nuclear families with couples and their unmarried children. The next most prevalent type is stem family (13.5%). Amongst them, parents living with a married son are three times as common as parents living with a married daughter. In a study by Lee (1991), it is indicated that the traditional norm of performing obligations to immediate kin and relatives is still widely shared by Hong Kong people. The majority of respondents (70.9%) reported that they had rendered financial and other assistance to their parents in the previous six months. On the contrary, only a quarter of them said that they had received financial assistance from their parents. The study has indicated that mutual financial help between parents and children seems to be rather active, much more so from children to parents. However, such a conclusion must be read with caution because the study does not specify the size of the financial aid. It should be noted that there is a tradition for working children of Chinese families in Hong Kong to contribute regularly small sums of money towards their parents as an indication of the commitment of care. Hence, it is not surprising that the findings indicate assistance more often flowing from children to parents. However, as revealed in later findings, transfers from parents tend to be more sporadic and in much larger amount in order to meet specific needs, for instance home buying. In a follow-up study in 1992, Lee focused his question more on the origin, destination and size of intra-family help. It is revealed that while financial help only forms part of the research question, parents stand out as the key donors and recipients of help. Likewise, when making important financial decisions, a relatively high percentage of respondents would turn to parents for help and advice (Lee, 1992). No doubt the nature and form of this aid vary considerably, and the size and complexity of kinship help differ widely. Some have a much more consistent pattern of help whilst for others it is more sporadic. Hence, the question is not whether or not there exists mutual help, but in what form it takes and whether it is growing or diminishing.

Kinship Help in Home Ownership: A General Profile

Of the 30 cases studied, 18 indicated that some form of mutual kinship help existed in their process of home buying. This ranged from the transfer of $10,000 to more than $200,000 towards down payment of home purchase, or a few thousand dollars to meet partial monthly mortgage installment. Likewise, the case histories suggested an extensive inter-generation flow of non-material aids in home buying such as information on the reliability of real estate agents, conveyancing solicitors, interior decorators and bank mortgages. More important, inter-generation flow of non-material help not only provides help per se in the home buying process, it also provides important, sometimes decisive, influence in the decision-making process of home ownership. The extent to which an individual's kinship network influences the home buying process has often been taken for granted or relegated to the backstage in contemporary Western housing literature. The tendency is to assume housing consumption as more a rational-individual decision-making process rather than treating it as the product of a complex process of family-network decision-making. For better exposition of the various facets of kinship help in housing, empirical evidence from this study is grouped under the following headings: namely (1) home ownership as a family project; (2) mutual family support as domestic banking; (3) proximity of nuclear families as a way of living; and (4) kinship aids as a means to reinforce cultural distinction.

Home Ownership as a Family Project: Individual versus Group Ownership

Home buying is costly, especially when a family is moving from rental to ownership. For many families, a decision to buy a flat instead of renting involves a complex process of financial planning. Assuming a *right place* has been identified, buying a *home* involves a down payment, stamp duty, fees for conveyancing, fees for real estate agents and the costs of moving and settling in. With a mortgage ceiling of 70% of the house price, a prospective homebuyer must be able to mobilize a considerable sum of money. In 1999, this roughly means that a middle class family needs to have something in the region of $750,000. This is a very large sum of money for many young middle class families. Yet, from the case studies, more than 75% of the households had a housing trajectory originating in public rental housing and 60% of them were first-time owners. Of course, it is true that most of them bought their first flat well before the 70% mortgage ceiling was in force, and hence the amount they had to summon for first-time purchase was comparatively small. Nonetheless, the shifting of tenure from public rental housing did imply that most families were first-time buyers and hence not in the position of having the asset benefit of a second-time buyer. This somehow suggests the existence and practice of intra-family resource support at various stages of one's housing career. The following are some of the findings that confirm this trend.

Mrs. Lee (a), married with two daughters and a senior secretary of a large welfare organization, now lives in a flat she bought with financial help from her retired parents. She has an elder brother who was married and lives in a flat that was previously their family flat. Her family's housing history marks two distinct periods where kinship financial aids for home purchase are both significant and active.

> For a long time my family lived in a small public rental unit in Chai Wan (eastend of Hong Kong Island). My father was a sailor so he came home about twice a year. My mother worked as a part-time housemaid to supplement the household income. Things began to change when my elder brother got his first job as a junior electrician at the China Light and Power Company and I also began to work as a clerk. My father retired from the shipping company with a lump sum gratuity. That was 1978. He suggested that we should buy a flat with the money and all the children should live there. I thought what he had in mind was to have a place for my elder brother who was about to get married. We bought a second-hand 2-room flat in North Point in 1980 for $220,000. My father paid a 10% down payment. Including other expenses, he spent about $25,000 on the flat, which was almost his entire fortune. Since the interest rate was quite high at that time (15%), my brother and I basically shared the monthly mortgage. I paid about $600 while my brother paid $700, my mum and dad paid the rest. All the children moved there while my mum and dad continued to stay in the public housing unit. Of course we didn't inform the Housing Authority because my dad still wanted to use the unit in exchange for a future Home Ownership Scheme flat (Mrs. Lee (a)).

Two observations could be made here. First, when the father bought the flat it was never meant for personal consumption. It was for his children's use. The flat was registered in the son's name. Second, the question of 'who owns the flat?' did not seem to matter. Although the son was the legal owner, he was not expected to sell it without prior agreement of his entire family.

> No one thinks seriously about my brother owning the flat. He won't dare to sell it any way. It's my parent's flat, or I think more correctly, it's our family flat! (Mrs. Lee (a))

Everyone automatically shares a responsibility in contributing to the family flat when they could afford to. And whoever has the more pressing need for it is entitled to live there. The idea of individual property ownership seems to be subsumed by a broader concept of *family ownership* with a *variable user right* by individual family members according to different needs occurring during different stages of their life cycles. The purchase of a Home Ownership Scheme flat later by Mrs. Lee (a) further illustrates the primacy of kinship help in home ownership.

> I planned to get married in late 1983. John was fresh from abroad after his mid-career return to study for a degree in a Canadian university and his parents weren't in a position to help because there were already too many problems in the family. At that time this Home Ownership Scheme (HOS) project near our Chai Wan public rental unit was open for application. My father suggested that we should apply for a large unit, something like 800 square feet. But the problem was that my parents must then give up their public rental unit if they decided to benefit from the priority in allocation. At the same time my mother was getting seriously ill. We thought that it was a good idea for our parents to live with us. So we were finally allocated this HOS flat in Wan Chui Estate. It's a 3-room flat. My father lent me half the money for the down payment, which was about $20,000. He said we didn't have to return it because he would be living here as well. Now my parents sometimes live with us and sometimes with my elder brother, when they want to spend sometime with their grand children (Mrs. Lee (a)).

One may argue that in the case of Mrs. Lee(a)'s parents, they were only helping their children in order to help themselves. Through helping Mrs. Lee(a) to buy a Home Ownership Scheme flat, they would be able to live with her and be taken care of in their later years. In a competitive society without a universal social security system, helping one's children to attain home ownership does seem to be a rational and viable way of guaranteeing one's future abode. While such a view may run the risk of being over-generalized, it is extremely difficult to empirically test it since parents would not reveal their intention in those terms. However, there are other families that do exhibit a keener interest in family ownership. They do so more out of economic interest of the family as a whole rather than the simple mutual-help function. Mrs. Cheng, the mother of one of the flat

140

stir-fryers, had developed an early interest in properties. She acted like a development manager who would look out for buying opportunities and set up projects within the family. She may or may not be involved in the project herself. She would go around and put heads together to make the buying possible.

> My mum's grandfather was a landlord in Guangdong who owned lots of land and property. I guess my mum was greatly influenced by that tradition. She has many mahjong friends and they exchanged information about real estates. Mary and I had no intention of buying our first flat if not because of her persuasion and help. She practically arranged everything for us. She took us to see the flat, introduced us to a bank manager, suggested lending us $100,000 to meet part of the down payment and even showed us a hypothetical lay-out plan for the first five years and how it would be cheaper to buy than to rent. In fact, for the first flat we bought since my father's retirement, all my brothers and sisters were required to contribute to the mortgage. I still go back sometimes to make repairs and repainting in the flat. I consider it very much my own property as well because I did contribute towards buying it. My mum always takes pride in telling our relatives the number of flats the family now owns and who else would be buying in the near future (Mr. Cheng).

One important theoretical point to note here is that how much family support in home buying is a result of personal character and how much is that a result of family traditions and values? Questions of this nature are difficult to disentangle. The answer could be both. The findings of my case studies suggest that family traditions and values in mutual help carry an overriding influence on the way families help each other. Individual characters and personalities facilitate, but cannot provide the primary force, if the tradition does not exist in the first place.

Family Mutual Aid as Domestic Banking: 'Better to Benefit Folks than Outsiders'

In contemporary Hong Kong, most people take out a mortgage from a bank for home purchase. All the 30 cases in my study indicated that they had gone, at some stages, particularly during their initial purchase, to a bank for mortgage. Nonetheless, two situations deviated from this norm. First, a household could mobilize idle kinship financial resources in order to pay-off an outstanding mortgage loan early. Second, an individual could seek loans from the family to cover a large down payment when they faced problems of securing a high percentage of mortgage loan, either as a result of the lack of appropriate employment reference or the nature of property itself qualifies only for a smaller loan. From the case studies, families having a close relationship have a higher tendency to maximize idle financial resources within the family network for home financing.

Mr. Ho, a restaurant worker, comes from a family with such a tradition. His father runs a small business selling dry seafood in Western District with his eldest son acting as his deputy overseeing the business. Because of cash flow problems, his father usually depends on loans from his sons and daughters and in turn lends them money when they need it. There is a long history of intra-family loans and sometimes they are not fully recovered. The family motto is 'when there is fortune, every one shares. When there is adversity, every one bears'. Mr. Ho bought his first flat in Western District with a loan from his father because he had problems in securing a large enough mortgage loan from the bank.

> I bought my first flat in Western District in 1986 because I was planning to get married later in the year. I knew my father or my eldest brother would be able to help some way but I went to the nearest Hang Seng Bank to ask for a mortgage. It was a rather old flat, 500 square feet, quite near to my father's shop. After valuation, the Bank only agreed to provide me with a 60% mortgage, on the condition that I produced an Employer's Guarantee of Character and Repayment ability. I was really disappointed. I knew the Bank didn't respect people working in restaurants because our job was not stable. But I was just asking for about $200,000, no big deal! My father was mad at me when he learnt that I didn't go to him first. Later he loaned me all that money and I was required to pay him only 5% interest, which was much lower than the market rate of 12%. In 1990 when my father's shop faced acute financial problems, I sold my flat at $1 million, making a profit of almost 100%, and returned all the money to him with the full interest. Together with help from other brothers and sisters, my father managed to overcome the crisis (Mr. Ho).

It may be argued that Chinese families with a business tradition tend to draw on whatever available resources existed in the family. It is therefore not surprising to see the presence of a maze of kinship financial relationships, particularly among families of small business establishments such as shops and restaurants. However, it is interesting to note that families without a tradition in business are even more inclined to help each other through substantial sums of financial aids in home purchase.

Miss Leung's father was a primary school teacher for 25 years before he retired in 1990. Upon retirement, he was given a lump sum amount from his Provident Fund Account (about $500,000)[1] He owns a flat in Tsuen Wan which he bought in 1988. Miss Leung, herself a teacher, used to live with her parents, later also bought a flat in the same housing estate in 1989 when she eventually got married. Initially she was paying a rather heavy monthly mortgage of $9,000 for one and half years, consuming nearly 50% of the household income. Later her father lent her $300,000 to repay half of her mortgage loan. As a result, her monthly mortgage was reduced to about $3,000 per month, enabling a welcome relief from the mortgage burden.

> I didn't want to accept the money from my dad because that meant a lot to him. But he told me that he didn't know what to do with his money. He didn't think it's safe to put it into the stock market because of political instability. He said it didn't pay at all now to put money in the bank because of the low interest rate. Dad had no intention of buying another flat because of the high price and high mortgage repayment. Knowing that I had a heavy mortgage burden, he thought the best idea was to help me out. He said why we should let the bank benefit from this while the family could afford not to. I remembered he quoted the old Chinese saying: 'one shouldn't allow good water to flow into the neighbour's field.' (Miss Leung)

Miss Leung's father never set down any clear terms for her daughter to return the money. All he said to her was that he did not need the money then and told her to take her time in returning it. It becomes quite clear that while the transfer of kinship help in housing is contingent upon rational economic reasoning, the manner in which the transfer is made is often rather irrational. Family business is usually conducted in a family manner: trust, rather than any other consideration comes first. In Miss Leung's situation, it is difficult to know if her father would expect her to reciprocate help to him in any form in the future. In traditional Chinese culture, there is a general expectation that grown-up children should take care of their elderly parents, even though their parents may not have helped them at all in home buying in the first place. In fact, some parents may never be able to do so. So is it meaningful to argue that middle class parents in Hong Kong exercise more individualistic values and hence are less inclined to impose their value on their children in family exchanges? Lee (1992) has already demonstrated that there is no evidence to suggest that modern Hong Kong families begin to depart from traditional family values. It is therefore difficult to suggest at this stage that financial aids within middle class families in Hong Kong are based more on reciprocity, rather than on familial bondage, duty and responsibility.

Kinship help in home purchase does not flow simply between parents and their children, but also between brothers and sisters. About a third of those households in the study had at some stage sought financial help from their brothers and sisters. This assistance is transferred in conjunction with assistance from parents or simply on their own. There is again no evidence to suggest that age or status in the family hierarchy is related to the flow of family assistance. It is often much more contingent upon the availability of extra financial resources from a certain family member.

> It is difficult to expect everyone within the family to be able to offer help when you need it. You know even within the family, one is more inclined to ask help from a specific member. In my case I am closer to my elder sister. But it all depends on the kind of help you are talking about. For instance buying this flat, I borrowed $100,000 from my younger brother to meet part of the down payment. I am not very close to him but I asked him anyway. My brother was single and he didn't need the money at that time. I never expect him to refuse me. You know within a family, there shouldn't be any question about help! We're one family! (Miss Fok)

The family network as a banking system sometimes needs a coordinator because, unlike banks where information can be highly centralized, the amount of resources available at any one time is not always fully known. In some situations, the parents or anyone keen to organize within the family would be able to coordinate such activities. This function is vital because it keeps the family system working, without which the family network would be much more distant and segregated. Of course it is difficult to be conclusive here, but there is evidence that families with a higher rate of intra-family transfers of monetary help as well as having a good family 'manager' do exhibit a more lively and congenial family relationship. Reciprocity of help within the family system provides the best cement for tying the Chinese family together. At a time when a family cannot obtain social or political assurance from the state, increasing family bondage through mutual financial help very often provides the best form of security a family needs.

> When I need help about anything, I would naturally go to my eldest sister. She keeps very good contacts with everybody and knows what's happening between them. Besides, she is taking care of our parents and so we often go

to her place for dinner during weekends. I mean when I need money or anything, I would speak to her first and she would say whether it's a good idea to go to the bank or whether my mum has some money idling in her savings account. If I need the money from my brother she would have a word with him first before I do so. You know you do need somebody to organize these things and initiate within the family (Mrs. Chow).

My mum usually organizes things in the family. She talks to everybody over the phone during the week and then at the weekend dinners where everybody meets, things get sorted out. I wouldn't talk to my brothers or sisters directly about anything I need, except my little sister, with whom I have a closer tie (Mrs. Liu).

Two broader questions arise here. First, why is it necessary for the family to get organized in order to maximize resources for housing for its members? The answer is simple. There are *mutual advantages* for family members to participate. Finch (1989), in her celebrated study of family obligations, suggests that mutual advantage forms one of the most important elements in shaping English family support: 'the common ground between historians is that reciprocal exchange on the basis of mutual advantage is the essence of support between kin, making the family a group whose relationships are rooted in material imperatives and ties of affection.'

The above statement appears to be well-supported by empirical evidence as suggested in previous discussions on *home purchase as a family project* where family members would be able to share both the use-value as well as the exchange-value of the house they jointly bought. Nonetheless, this is not entirely applicable in the case of family as domestic banking, because there is no evidence that all family members would benefit and that even when they do, the benefits are quite unequally distributed. This casts doubt on the general applicability of established views of Western family historians on the prevalence of kinship help on grounds of mutual advantage (Anderson, 1971; Humphries, 1977; Roberts, 1984) and also the second question: is it possible for kinship help, particularly substantial help such as loan for home buying, to be based purely on kinship ties rather than reciprocity?

The answer to this question lies in the existence of a priority of family values. Evidence suggests that family obligations do have certain priority. The basic denominator of family help is always *familial bondage, duty and responsibility*, followed by the prospect of *reciprocity*, while the consideration of *mutual advantage* is the last on the list. There is also a hierarchy of needs, with those of the parents always coming first. The value of *filial piety* is still widely accepted as the pivot of the relationship between parents and their children.

Proximity as a Way of Life: Family Support, Culture and Home Ownership

In Chinese, the term *kar ting* (family) usually means one's own home and one's family kin group while *kar yan* means members of the nuclear as well as the extended family. When someone is referring to his family, he does not simply mean his *own* nuclear family. He may also talk about his parents, brothers and sisters and the in-laws. In this way there is a slight distinction from the Western usage of the term *family*, which also means one's *home*. In addition, the Chinese notion of a family also denotes a sense of *proximity* and *togetherness*. This raises an interesting question about the spatial distribution of blood-related nuclear families. The case studies suggest that families exhibit a strong tendency to live in close proximity.

Hong Kong is, by international standards, well served by an efficient and reasonably priced public transport system. Besides, it is a very small place. However, it is not uncommon to find all or part of the family system residing within one private housing estate. Even when it is not possible to live within the same estate, we can see that nuclear families belonging to the same family system would choose to live in nearby estates; or if that is untenable, within the same district.

> I moved away from my parental home years ago when I began my studies at the University of Hong Kong, which is located on Hong Kong Island. Most of my family: my parents, two brothers and two sisters have been living for years in City One Estate in Sha Tin. I wanted to move there as well when I was planning to get married three years ago. My wife and I began to look around for suitable accommodation in City One, but the price was too expensive for us. So we looked at Riverside Plaza, which is just a stone throw away, developed by one of the less well known developers, China Chem. But we really didn't like its built-quality. Since there was really nothing available at the northside of the Shing Mun River, we decided to move to the south of river, which is cheaper, but a bit farther away from my mum and others; but anyway, we are still in Sha Tin. If there is likelihood of a market downturn, we might be able to buy a flat in City One (Mr. Kam).

It can be conceived that one of the decision-making processes for housing among Hong Kong Chinese families would be to establish a concentric sociogram where families of the same kin group have the tendency of moving as close as possible to the centre. Spatial-temporal decision-making regarding where to buy one's home emerged as an interesting issue in the case studies. For a married couple with two relatively *normal-size* kin groups, the decision of where to buy their home would involve a location which would command the maximization of social exchanges within the family network. Even if it is not possible to achieve maximization in one move, the interim decision is to lay the foundation of progressive maximization in the future.

> For a period of time shortly after we got married, we rented an apartment in central Kowloon. That was chosen because it was convenient to where I worked - Tsim Sha Tsui. But it's so far away from our two parental homes, mine in Tsuen Wan and my wife's in Yuen Long. It became such a nightmare to travel back and forth for family dinners during weekends. Every one in our families wanted us to move nearer to them. The best place for us to minimize travelling and to maximize the opportunities of seeing both of our families is Tuen Mun, because it is situated between our parental families. But because there was nothing to our liking available in that area, we finally opted for Castle Peak Road, which is slightly farther away; it was cheaper and more practical for the interim period, but our final aim is still Tuen Mun (Mr. Fung (a)).

For Mr. and Mrs. Fung (a), the major problem facing them is to choose a location that could maximize interaction and exchanges between the two sets of kin groups between husband and wife. Contrary to conventional belief that a Chinese wife would merge more with the husband's kin group rather than her maiden family, the case studies have shown that a strategy of maximization of exchanges for both families is normally adopted. But how far do members of the same kin group aim to optimize their location in relation to centre of family gravity despite all the spatial and economic constraints in home owning? The case studies, whilst not claiming to be representative, do convey a general feeling of how serious they are about living close to the family. Of the 30 cases studied, a third of them have at least one close relative living in the vicinity and five have their parents living within close distance, although only three actually have parents and relatives residing in the same estate. This phenomenon has both practical and theoretical ramifications regarding family functioning and home ownership. In practical terms, the modified extended family provides the convenience of support for domestic chores and childcare. While many middle class nuclear families in Hong Kong depend on the help of Filipino domestic helpers to take care of household work when the couples are both working, they do have doubts leaving child-rearing to the domestic helpers. Many Chinese, especially elderly people, believe that children must be brought up by the family.[2]

> ... having a Filipino maid to take care of my baby boy Che Ming, is not something we would like to have. What we do like to have, of course, is for Mary to take care of him. But you know that is practically out of the question. We need two incomes to survive. At present we are paying about $12,000 per month for mortgage, and to be frank with you, my salary, everything included, is only around $20,000. How could Mary stop working? Her teaching job fetches about $15,000. That settles the mortgage as well as the maid. Of course the best thing to do is to let our parents take care of the child, but they are quite old and frail. I dare not think about what would happen if one of them gets very sick. Mary's parents died a long time ago, so it's also out of the question. It's just not the kind of situation I would like as I told you (Mr. Chan (b)).

Also, proximity of living between parents and children could mean enormous savings in resources on weekly travelling and also encourages more interaction within the family because, irrespective of class origin, it is customary for a Chinese family in Hong Kong to visit parents weekly or fortnightly.

In theoretical terms, proximity of living within the family implies at least two things, namely: (1) the benefits of an extended family in terms of mutual care and support could still be efficiently practised, while the integrity of the nuclear family, that of independence and privacy, is still being maintained; and (2) as a result of this urge to live near to one another, an enormous demand for housing can be created for a certain locality.

> Having been in Mei Foo Estate all these years,[3] I realize why so many people keep coming and why prices keep rising. It's not just because it is convenient. It's because families kept growing. Once the parents move here, then followed by the son, the daughter, and eventually the whole clan. Funny enough, people didn't actually have the experiences of living in large family because our parents mostly fled China when they were young and arrived Hong Kong in small family or just by themselves. Therefore, their children shouldn't be looking forward to big family togetherness. You know what: they said it's easier to get mahjong players this way (Mr. Cheung (a)).[4]

Another reason for middle class family to live in close proximity to each other, which is often overlooked or underestimated by researchers of family and housing, is the existence of intra-family competitions, that is, between siblings and in-laws. Middle class children in Hong Kong often face very high expectations from parents since childhood. Such expectations can be manifested in their concern for their offspring's education: which school do they attend? How do they perform at school? In employment, concerns would focus on the level of pay, perks, status of the company, etc. In social life, the focus would be on who they befriend with and where they have recreation. Finally, the main concern would be on how and where they live. In Hong Kong, competition begins early at home. Such motives are often successfully masked by other more practical reasons.

> For me and my wife, choosing Kornhill three years ago was largely because I thought it was always safe to put your money into popular estate. Besides it is so convenient for shopping and the transport. My parents and two sisters are just around the corner. The choice is so obvious! But to be frank with you, I also like to live near to the university. I have friends living there as well. I do sometimes think about moving away. I guess my mum exerted enormous pressure on us when my sisters moved there some years ago. My wife used to get quite edgy when my elder sister began to nag about our having no property over family dinners and about how her flat in Tai Koo Shing got appreciated in value. You know. We just hate to take any more of that! (Mr. Tse)

Intra-family competition in housing matters very often is a source of family tension and conflicts. Evidence from this study suggests that housing decision seems to be less gender-specific within a nuclear family because both husband and wife would call into the same set of questions which should hinge upon economic, social and family considerations.

> I don't really mind where we live as long as it is convenient. But I just don't understand why Joan is so concerned about how her family thinks of that. I mean I am quite happy with our flat in Wan Chai. It's central and the restaurants around are wonderful. The only thing you can criticize, I think, is that the place is getting a bit old and not very well managed. This is understandable because it is just a single private housing block managed by a very small company. But Joan is so persistent about wanting a change. She wants to move to Tai Koo Shing for no apparent reasons. The only reason I can think of is she doesn't want to be looked upon down by her sister-in-law because she has a sea view flat there (Mr. Ho).

149

Looking back, I think the most difficult time between me and my husband was during that time when we were trying to decide whether we should opt for the Home Purchase Scheme offered by the government. I don't belong to the kind of people who attach great importance to owning a house in Hong Kong. I am quite happy with the place where we were renting then. It got good schools around and some very good neighbours as well. I think the flat had got very good *Fung Shui* and it's not easy for us to find another one. [5] My children never suffered from any major illness or anything bad since we moved there five years ago. But John was so adamant about buying a flat in Whampoa Garden. While I agree that real estate investment is a good way with money, what I think at the bottom of his heart is that he doesn't like to be seen as the only one in the family without owning a flat (Mrs. Sze).

Family Support as Reinforcement of Cultural Distinction

Besides the promulgation of mutual support, shared advantages, maximization of family resources and the general preservation of the family system, one of the most pertinent theoretical questions being addressed is: what is the social significance of this family support and how does it relate to the question of *middle class* and *class formation*? With the help of Bourdieu (1984), we have arrived at a better grasp of the relationship between economic capital and cultural capital. How do people actively invest in cultural capital in order to realize economic capital, and vice versa? Savage et al. (1992) argue that one of the most important contributions of Bourdieu is to show that the dominant and subordinate groups within the middle class are engaging in endless processes to assert their group identities. Through the use of the concept of *habitus* (sets of internalized predispositions which govern people's behaviour), one of the most important strategies being used by the middle class to assert their identity is through home ownership. Cultural assets in the form of a life style associated with home ownership would then be stored and transmitted through the family system to the next generation. Hence, the empirical question being asked here is whether the middle class in Hong Kong exhibits such a tendency, and to what extent their children are exposed to a culture of home ownership? Using Wong and Lui's (1992b) broad representation of the Hong Kong class structure on the basis of Goldthrope's schema, it is interesting to note that families in the lower service class, routine non-manual workers and the petite-bourgeoisie manifest a keener culture of home ownership, much more so than the upper service class. Managers and professionals manifest a more practical or pragmatic attitude towards home ownership. Thus, it is argued here that this tendency would further fragment the already loosely defined service and intermediate classes. The following is some of the evidence from various class backgrounds.

The New Petite-bourgeoisie

Unlike UK, the Hong Kong class structure is less dominated by landlords and traditional small shopkeepers, who are often grouped under the so-called old middle class. Historically, their position in the middle class is blurred. Modern petite-bourgeoisie are characterized by a mixture of small self-employed businessmen such as contractors and sub-contractors in the construction business, artisans who utilize their exclusive skills as capital (e.g. typesetters, book-binders, antique-watch repairers) and small traders in import/export as well as retail/wholesale trade. Many of them are of working class origin and a high percentage of them own properties. Two elements characterize the significance of their existence. First, while their position in the occupational structure is invariably marginal, they have always been a dominant force in the urban environment. Second, in the brief history of the Hong Kong class structure, the self-employed have always been fragmented. They have never emerged as a cohesive social class as in Western societies (Savage et al., 1992)

Mr. Fung (b)'s life history represents a typical case of petite-bourgeoisie. He started as a self-employed untrained electrician at the age of 20. His family fled China in 1949 and his father was a small landlord in a Guangdong village. To expand his business, he later rented a small shop-space in a public housing estate in Yuen Long, New Territories. For many years, he did small contract work for estate residents, mainly in electrical wiring and fitting out works. When the contract became too large, he subcontracted to other self-employed electricians. He has three sons and two daughters. The eldest son was a school dropout and later became his only part-time employee. His family was allocated a small rental unit in a public housing estate nearby. In 1975, he bought his first private flat for his wife and children while he continued to live in the public housing unit by himself. He did not give up his rental unit because he needed a warehouse for his retail electrical goods, something he expanded as his business progressed. He managed to hide the real purpose of the flat from the Housing Authority for 18 years. Since then, he had frequently bought and sold flats for profits and it had become a very important source of capital for his small electrical business. He now owns a government Home

151

Ownership Scheme flat in Tuen Mun (in his son's name but mainly financed by him) and two private flats in Yuen Long which he rented out for profits. He now lives with his wife in a private flat near his shop. It is a flat at the low end of the market and the family apparently does not spend much on decoration and furnishing. Over the last decade, he has encouraged his children to buy flats. He now owns two flats jointly with his two elder sons.

> Mr. Lee, although I haven't had a fair chance of education like you had. I do know a few basic principles in life in order to survive in Hong Kong. Rule No. 1 - no matter what one does, one has to be a propertied man. I don't mind whether you are filthy rich or just make do with life. If you don't have paper qualifications in this society, the only judge on you would be whether you are propertied. Rule No. 2 - you should never be contented with just one property. You should always use your property to exchange for a better property. 'Better property always finds better people, better neighbourhood, better life.' Rule No.3 - don't ever rely on the government to help you. I have seen enough of this government. How can you trust a colonial government that is leaving us behind? I don't trust the Chinese government either. Just look at all those corrupted governments in Chinese history. Rule No. 4 - the only thing to keep the family together is through helping each other to buy their own property. If they have a good place to live; they will have good kids and good schools to go to and they wouldn't think about emigration all the time. Look! How can you expect kids to grow up somebody in places like Sham Shui Po (a run-down inner city area)? Having spent a good part of my life here (Fung fled China with parents in 1949), I can tell you that the family is the only thing one can lean back in Hong Kong (Mr. Fung (b)).

Two important points could be deduced in Mr. Fung (b)'s housing career. First, a life wrung around properties is essential because it provides the necessary life opportunities for self-advancement for the family, such as education, capital and good environment. Second, a life depending on property assets also signifies a way of survival with the minimal state intervention. One of the interesting attitudes generally held by the working class and also to a great extent by the middle class is the pervasive acceptance of the notion that the government should not be responsible for an individual's welfare. There is a strong belief that the fate of an individual lies very much in his own hands. For the working class, it also amounts to a disgrace among family members if one has to beg for help from the government. That explains why so many working class people still resist applying for social security in times of temporary hardship.

Yes I did have hard times. I think everyone here had been through times without a meal for the day, living in cramped squatter areas. Even then I had never resort to dough. I don't think I shall have the 'face' (a complex Chinese concept of social relations: in this context it means *courage* plus *personal integrity*) to face my family and my relatives. There are times when all you can do is to swallow everything and get back on your feet again. I always remember the motto my dad once said to me: 'Heaven[6] always shows you a way to live.' (Mr. Chung)

However, one may argue that the petite-bourgeoisie's attachment to a life of property arises more out of economic rationality and they are not genuinely after a culture of home ownership. At least the Fung (b) family does not exhibit strong investment in cultural capital, such as furnishing and interior decoration. There is an arguable point here. It is both a theoretical and an empirical question. Theoretically, Bourdieu (1984) demonstrates that, through a series of cultural battles, dominant and subordinate groups within social classes would be able to assert and legitimize their status quo. And it is this constant interplay of economic and cultural capitals that leads to and reinforces class identity, social position and self-worth. What is unclear is the exact process of the interplay of these two types of capitals - economic and culture. Therefore, empirically it is difficult to distinguish the relative influence of each type of capital. What remains meaningful is the outcome of the process itself. In the case of Mr. Fung (b), it appears that a relatively higher level of economic capital has been invested relative to cultural capital. However, when we turn to the routine non-manual white-collar class in the next section, a much more distinctive pattern of cultural practice emerges.

The Tai Koo Shing Syndrome: Social Construction of Cultural Distinctiveness

The lower middle class in Hong Kong is largely composed of non-manual office clerical workers, personal service workers (e.g. air hostesses, travel guides, hairdressers, policemen, firemen, ambulance men, etc.), sales persons (e.g. wholesale and retail salesmen) and lower grade professionals (e.g. nurses, teachers, social workers, para-medical etc.). The heterogeneity of the lower middle class is probably as diverse as its occupational types. While class theoreticians are still busy wrangling with the contradictory position of the middle class (Wright, 1985), the concern in this section is more modest. I want to see whether or not there is a distinct cultural practice within this diverse group regarding home ownership, home buying and the life-style associated with owner-occupation. The purpose is to ascertain whether or not there exists a high level of investment in cultural capital and how it relates to family values and practices. The empirical evidence from the cases studies, while varied, does indicate that cultural practices and family values are being blended in such a way as to reinforce the individual household to pursue a life style closely associated with home ownership.

Mrs. Chan is a senior clerk of a government office. Having been brought up in a Chai Wan (Hong Kong Island East) public housing estate, the whole family moved to Tai Koo Shing in the early 1980s. Since then, her two brothers and a sister bought separate flats in Tai Koo Shing when they got married. Mrs. Chan got married in 1985 and moved also to a flat in the same estate where her husband and his parents lived before their marriage. Mrs. Chan's maiden family, particularly her father, a retired government driver, has a special kind of fondness for the Tai Koo Shing life style.

> My father likes the Tai Koo Shing environment hugely. He wouldn't agree to go anywhere else. He likes the green landscaped podium where he goes every morning to attend his *Tai Chi* class and read his newspapers. He also likes the huge shopping mall with those bullet-shaped glass lobby lifts. It's just like a five star hotel lobby. In the hot summer months, the whole place is air-conditioned and it's really pleasant to shop after a hard day's work and getting out of the jammed-pack subway. My father also likes the Jade Garden Chinese restaurant there where he usually has tea and dim sum after his morning round of exercise in the nearby Golden Hill Country Park (Mrs. Chan).

A Clerk's Dream

Mr. Hui is also a clerk in a government department. The family has a household income of approximately $25,000. They are paying a monthly mortgage of $12,500 for their 600 square feet 2-room flat. While the mortgage burden is heavy, they have a different way of interpreting their situation.

> I think it is worthwhile to put up with this burden. Aside from the fact that we want to stay quite close to our parents, I think this place has a great deal of uniqueness; it has a class of its own. That means a lot to us. Tai Koo Shing is just different. It's different from Mei Foo; different from Wah Foo and it's just different from anywhere! That's why the price keeps going up. I don't bother so much about the price really, because that's the only flat

154

we've got, but it's this whole feeling of being here, you know, you can say a hundred good things about this place but that's not exactly what I mean. It's funny. I won't dream of buying a place in Shau Kei Wan, which is just 5-minute drive down the road. It's so different there, the atmosphere and everything, and most important of all, the people are different. It's expensive here, but it's great! (Mr. Hui)

Cultural distinctiveness within a certain locale is always the product of a two-way process. Tai Koo Shing was built in the late 1970s. When it was first developed, there were only 15 high-rise blocks without any central shopping facilities but only a few small shops downstairs providing the daily necessities. Now the estate boasts 40 high-rise blocks with 30,000 residents, and it is a self-contained community. The middle class characteristics of the estate have gone through a slow process of progression over one and a half decades. The first group of inhabitants was mainly low grade, white-collars who invested their first savings in the housing market. It was followed by the civil servants in the mid-1980s who had reached their housing allowance eligibility point (who usually rented and hence pushed up the rentals), then the yuppies (insurance salesmen, travel agents, real estate agents and stock brokers) of the late 1980s who wanted health food and sauna clubs. Augmenting those groups in the late 1980s were the Japanese and Korean expatriates. The latest addition are business cadres from the *new rich* of Communist China, who find buying up flats more profitable and efficient then renting cheap hotels. Through this process, Tai Koo Shing is, to a certain extent, *gentrified* by the arrival of the *new middle class*. It is the conglomeration of these various groups, which triggers the proliferation of health clubs, exotic restaurants, designer boutiques and exclusive kindergartens.

In fact, many developers, such as Sun Hung Kei, Cheung Kong and Hong Kong Land, follow the Tai Koo Shing model and developed similar large private housing estates all over Hong Kong (Whampoa Garden in Kowloon, Laguna City in East Kowloon, and South Horizon in Island South). In order to sell successfully to various middle class niche groups, developers concoct images such as 'the love nest', 'the holistic community', 'the garden city', and 'the country club'. Modern facilities such as indoor and outdoor swimming pool, gymnasium, resident clubhouse with exclusive membership, squash and tennis courts and round-the-clock security system, are now standard items in any new estate sales promotion.

Properly evaluated, Tai Koo Shing today means much more than a modern condominium complex with avant-garde living facilities. Tai Koo Shing means *status*, *identity* and *class*. Those who live in Tai Koo Shing are the well educated, the professionals and the health-conscious group. They are the people who give up Honda Civic for Accura Legend; Corolla for Camry; and Ford Laser for BMW 3-series. They are the people who shun oily Chinese food and go for vegetarian. In sum, Tai Koo Shing represents something symbolic and yet tangible. Put in another way, it is a tacit demonstration of cultural power. It has become the bulwark of Hong Kong middle class value and life style. The possibility of transforming a living environment into such a powerful social imagery is what makes the pursuit of home ownership there so tempting.

Neighbourliness

However, behind the socio-spatial glamour of Tai Koo Shing lies one of the saddening characteristics of modern Hong Kong life. Neighbourhood relationship is, similar to all middle class people in suburbs in Western societies, minimal and distant. Spatial distance or proximity has come to bear little on the level of neighbourhood interaction. Few of those interviewed knew the names of their immediate neighbours (the adjacent ones and the opposite) and only one in ten of them had been invited by neighbours into their homes.

> I don't talk to our neighbour much. That's something I don't like this place. What I like it here is that people take care of their place nicely. You know. There are really decent people around. You won't see scruffy people much. There are a huge variety of gates and doors with different colour and design, always giving the place an expensive look. In Mei Foo they are uniform and monotonous, although it's one of the more established estates (Mr. Lai).
>
> Tai Koo Shing is a place for many people. You have common names such as Wellcome and Park-In supermarkets, but you also have up-market places like Delicatessen, Uny, and also some very good health food shops. I like to go to one of these health centres where you can work out or do aerobics, and also do 'facials' (special skin care). It's costly but make you feel really good afterwards. Also there are children centres where they can have piano class, Chinese calligraphy club, and ballet as well; by the way, they are not those run by the charity or the government! The teachers are well qualified. My husband is one of those hi-fi enthusiasts. He likes to go to these exclusive shops which sell very rare stuff, you know, those black-boxed amplifiers and speakers...I don't have a clue. But he likes them. He says Tai Koo Shing is the only place he can find those shops. That's where all his money gone (Mrs. Cheng – wife of Mr. Cheng).

The social construction of Tai Koo Shing as a safe middle class fortress in Hong Kong has made it one of the most sought after properties by the middle class. Over the last decade, it has developed into something beyond a middle class housing estate. The existence of Tai Koo Shing has marginalized other residential accommodation within the same area (that is, Hong Kong Island East), such as those in Shau Kei Wan, Chai Wan and North Point. Hence, the process of cultural distinction could be seen as a process of one class marginalizing the other through the use of dwelling type, resulting in the reinforcement of existing social distinction.

Conclusion

The matrix of family and kinship relationships is both complex and intricate. It is often complicated by different elements, such as personal character, ethnic diversity[7] and cultural values. For instance, the Chinese have rather unique interpretation of concepts such as *face, shame, guilt, yan* (kindness), *yi* (reciprocity) and *chung* (loyalty) (Li & Yang, 1976). They represent the backbone of Chinese family values and greatly influence and shape individual and family actions. To explore adequately the impact of these values on family practices would mean moving beyond the boundary of this study, though intellectually tempting, but practically not feasible. What I am concerned with here is the relationship between intra-family actions (in the form of mutual support) and the development of home ownership, within the current cultural context. In this context, certain themes concerning the process of kinship help and housing do emerge, namely: (1) the concept of private property in the Chinese family; (2) the idea of family obligation and reciprocity; and (3) mutual advantages and kinship ties. Evidence from my case studies suggests that the Chinese treat property as *family property* more than *personal property*. Within the family system, ownership of a certain property is much less discrete than Western families. This is especially true for families that demonstrate a complex history of housing finance. Family traditions and values in mutual help do carry an overriding influence on the way families help each other. Individual personalities facilitate, but cannot provide the primary force. As regards the practice of the principle of mutual advantage as a prime motivation in family mutual support, the findings challenge the established view. From my case studies, although I discover the existence of some degree of mutual advantage, nonetheless, evidence is not strong enough to support such a view, because there exists also unequal distribution of benefits and advantages. There is also insufficient evidence to say that this is an accepted value. When asked why this is so, one common response of the homeowners was that: 'Well. This is a family business. How can you calculate within the family? How can your hands calculate with your legs?' Evidence also suggests that there is a hierarchy of family values and they are commonly practised in the subjects under study. The basic denominator of help is familial bondage, duty and responsibility, followed by the prospect of reciprocity, and then the consideration of mutual advantage. There is also a hierarchy of needs priority, with parents on top of the list. It also suggests that proximity of family dwellings as a functional necessity when community facilities are limited and when family mutual help must be efficient. Within the extended family, there may also be expectations for home ownership and living within close proximity, and sometimes this may have created pressure on individual family members. Such demand for conforming to family culture may however be seen as growing out of genuine concern for the welfare of the family members. The economic consequence of this urge for home ownership and proximity is an unwarranted demand for space within a small locality, hence, providing enormous opportunities for developers and speculators to influence the magnitude of house price increases.

Given this intimate family support system, a great desire for family property and a strong urge to live near to each other, how do we connect the family and larger societal change? Family mutual support in home financing serves as an effective means to foster a culture of home ownership. However, since individual family aspirations and values differ substantially, it results in different engagements in terms of cultural battles. These various cultural battlefields represent both the process and the end results of groups trying to distinguish themselves from one another. Hence from an aerial view, we can imagine atomistic families migrating over time and space, displacing other less competitive families and converging on a locality which best suits their cultural needs. The transition of Tai Koo Shing originally from a lower service class community to an upper service class social imagery clearly depicts the prevalence of this process. Likewise, the case of Tai Koo Shing also signifies the usefulness of home ownership as both a cultural and economic capital. For lower service workers without higher education, they can now use their house in Tai Koo Shing as cultural capital, to be qualified for entry to the 'middle class club' they so aspired. From a Bourdieu sense, home ownership is both a symbol and a process of class formation. In the case of Hong Kong, some middle class people also benefit from home ownership economically. How this affects life chances and social division will form the focus of the next chapter.

Notes

1. In Hong Kong, teaching is probably the only profession that provides a compulsory savings scheme similar to a Central Provident Fund. Contribution from employees is usually limited to 5% of their income while contribution from employers would range from 5% to 15%, depending on the employees' years of service.

2. There is a general feeling among middle class people that young children under the care of Filipino domestic helpers will have their Chinese language development delayed as they are exposed to two different languages, Chinese and English, at the same time. No research has yet been done to prove this.

3. Mei Foo is one of the oldest private housing estates in Kowloon. It used to be much sought after by the middle class. However, in recent years its price has gone down apparently because of ageing facilities. Now it becomes one of the second rate old estates sought after by young couples who find it relatively cheaper and with more space.

4. Mahjong is a very popular game amongst all social classes in Hong Kong. It is not uncommon to find families devoting their entire weekend to playing it. It is both a social game and a family game.

5. *Fung Shui* is a branch of Chinese superstitious beliefs on the location and direction of one's house. It is a common practice for Hong Kong people to hire a professional man to read *Fung Shui* of a certain site or house before they decide to buy or to build. It concerns about things like the number of doors and windows and the direction they are facing, etc.

6. The word 'heaven' is not the best translation. The original text should be 'sky'- *tin*. It denotes a summation of everything omnipotent, everything beyond human anticipation. It stems from a Chinese trilogy of *'sky - land – man'*, where land stands for the physical environment and man - the human society. The idea is that these three entities must be related in a harmonious way and their balance must not be upset.

7. For instance, the *Chiu Chow* as an ethnic group in Guangdong Province is famous for their exceptionally high level of family mutual support and intra-clan support. Many Chiu Chow people become very successful businessmen and politicians in Hong Kong.

7 The Middle Class and Home Ownership: Capital Gains and Class Formation

On an individual level, capital gains from property ownership not only enable homeowners to reap windfall earnings, hence fitting neatly into Pahl's prophesy (1975) that 'one may gain more from the housing market in a few years than would be possible in savings from a life time of earnings', but also encourage them to reinvest their money into the housing market and other things. Hence, a strong pursuit in capital accumulation, coupled with a highly entrepreneurial real estate exchange system, has made Hong Kong one of the world's most speculative housing markets.

On the society level, home ownership seems to be closely related to the rise of the middle class. Mammoth private housing estates with modern shopping centres and landscape planning have sprung up since the late 1970s. The life style and consumption culture of homeowners in Tai Koo Shing, Kornhill, Whampoa, Hang Fa Chuen and Mei Foo cannot simply be passed as trendy. Places and people are often blended seamlessly. They represent one of the most conspicuous social imageries of Hong Kong since the early 1980s. Homeowners' consumption behaviour, their values and aspiration, together with their wealth, inescapably bring important bearings on the formation of the middle class. The purpose of this chapter is to examine more closely the relationship between middle class formation and home ownership within a rapidly changing society. I shall first focus on some local debates on class. This is then followed by analyses on the findings of homeowners on capital gains. Finally, the chapter will examine how such gains have impacted middle class formation.

A Truncated Social Research Tradition

It has been widely accepted that there is a dearth of local studies on class and stratification in Hong Kong. A popular explanation is that basic social research is not generally supported by the academia. Unfortunately this only partially explains the situation. What is more important is that there is another distinctive contributing factor, notably a long-standing bias in local social research that emphasizes on the *uniqueness thesis*. Lau's study in political stability (1977) and his later studies on Hong Kong society (1984) are good examples of this genre. The assumption is that Hong Kong is such a unique society that prevalent Western theoretical analyses are not relevant or applicable. Two reasons might account for this phenomenon. The first reason, as suggested by Agassi and Jarvie (1969), is that in the early days of social research, Hong Kong is often regarded by Western sociologists as a 'colonial fossil' and that one is always better off studying Chinese society in Taiwan or Singapore. The second reason is almost common sense and applicable to other branches of local research - the lack of research personnel and institutional support. Nonetheless, a more recent explanation advanced by Wong and Lui (1992a) has pointed to an interesting clue. They suggest that researchers in the 1970s were too pre-occupied with the desire to explain the uniqueness of Hong Kong as a success story. This standpoint has been so vehemently pursued that later on a plethora of theoretical constructions such as Lau's (1984) suggestions of a *minimally-integrated socio-political entity, the social accommodation of politics* and *utilitarian familialism* have become part of the popular discursive structure of Hong Kong society. These concepts have been applied to explain why Hong Kong is so successful in maintaining her political stability without having a strong state. The main contention is that the Chinese society largely looks after itself. It is a society relying on centripetal relationship, and thus is extremely inward looking and self-reliant. Hong Kong society is conceptualized as consisting of a myriad of family networks, each concerns mainly with its own self-perpetuation. There is an absence of horizontal integration among these familial groups and therefore political leaders would find the task of forging links between groups and organizing them difficult. Lau and Kuan (1988) have asserted that 'social class as structural forces in shaping interpersonal and political actions are relatively insignificant in Hong Kong'. It could be seen that subsequent social studies have been heavily influenced by Lau's general framework, for example, the study of community service delivery (Lau, Kuan & Ho; 1986) and the study of bureaucratic and community leadership (Lau & Kuan, 1988). Wong and Lui (1992a) have argued that it is not the nature of these studies that is problematic. Rather, it is the intensity of this approach that has eclipsed more orthodox ways of studying society, and hence resulting in a neglect of fundamental social studies such as class formation and social mobility. On the whole, in the words of Wong and

162

Lui, 'we feel there is an inadequate self-awareness and reflexiveness on the part of local sociological studies, with regard to their forefather tradition'.

The Hong Kong Class Structure

Stemming from this dissatisfaction with local research, a group of young sociologists have sought to reinstate the debate on class and stratification (Cheung et al., 1988; Tsang, 1992; Chan, 1991; Wong & Lui, 1992a; Wong & Lui, 1992b; Leung, 1994). These researchers have tried to ascertain two things: first, to draw a class map of the Hong Kong society; and second, to identify the dynamics of this class structure over time. Drawing on a random sample of 1,000 male household heads between the age of 20 and 64 in 1989 and using Goldthrope's class schema, Wong and Lui (1992b) have come up with a class map as shown in Table 7.1.

From the class map, we can see the limitation of Goldthrope's Class Schema since it has completely left out the upper class which, although quite small in Hong Kong, is widely known to be powerful and influential. Setting this aside, however, a rough class picture emerges. Hong Kong, similar to many Western societies, is characterized by a sizable middle class.[1] It has been explained in Chapter two that the emergence of the middle class is mainly the result of the restructuring of the Hong Kong economy in the last two decades. With the opening up of the Chinese economy and the incessant supply of relatively cheap labour, many manufacturing establishments in Hong Kong have gradually moved to the mainland in order to reap cost advantages. Hong Kong's economy is now dominated by a large service sector with the professional and managerial personnel forming a significant part of the middle class. In addition, the thriving service sector also creates a large pool of intermediate support service workers as well as a sizeable number of small proprietors providing technical support for the service sector. This also accounts for the relatively large Intermediate sector. It is true that, depending on the definition and theoretical genesis of the concept of middle class, the actual size of it might vary. Nonetheless, the middle mass of the Hong Kong society is still highly visible.

Drawing on the findings of their study, Wong and Lui have suggested other areas that signify class difference. First, more than 80% of the service class were of Hong Kong origin since childhood, while only around 50% of the working class were of Hong Kong origin (many

Table 7.1   The Hong Kong Class Structure

7-Fold Class	Brief Description	N	%	3-Fold Class
I	Upper Service Class: higher-grade professionals, administrators and officials, managers in large establishments, larger proprietors	81	8.6	Service
II	Lower Service Class: lower-grade professionals, administrators, higher-grade technicians, managers in small business and industrial establishments, supervisors of non-manual employees	107	11.3	
III	Routine non-manual employees in commerce and administration, personal service workers and sales personnel	90	9.6	Inter-mediate
IV	Petite-bourgeoisie: small proprietors, artisans, contractors, with or without employees	132	14.0	
V	Lower-grade technicians, supervisors of manual workers	150	15.9	
VI	Skilled manual workers	149	15.8	Working
VII	Semi-skilled and unskilled workers, agricultural workers	234	24.8	

Source: Wong & Lui (1992b), *Reinstating Class: A Structural and Developmental Study of Hong Kong Society*, Occasional Paper 10, Social Science Research Centre, University of Hong Kong.

working classes are emigrants from Mainland China in the 1970s). They have argued that, other than suggesting a *late-starter* character for the Hong Kong working class families, more attention should be paid to the successive waves of immigrants from Mainland China and the ways these families made their way in the new environment. Second, amongst the younger age group (25-34), nearly one in three had had his primary education interrupted once due to various reasons. Third, with regard to education attainment, class differences were evident with 80% of the class I people having attained at least upper secondary qualification, and nearly half of them having undergone university education. Most important, class differences were also significant in the type of housing and housing tenure. Not surprisingly, more than 60% of the service class were in private housing and almost three quarters of them were owner-occupiers. In stark contrast, 57% of the working class lived in public housing blocks and few were owner-occupiers. In terms of the ability of different classes to accumulate wealth, only 27% admitted they had one or more investments (be it shares, foreign currency, or property). As far as investment is concerned, it was revealed that 50% of them belonged to the service class while only 17% belonged to the working class.

A Selected Profile of Capital Gains of Homeowners

Given this broad class picture, it is evident that there exists an intricate relationship between the middle mass and home ownership. In the 30 cases in my study, it is possible to say that except for those who entered the housing market after 1991, most of their properties had attained a certain percentage of capital appreciation. In Table 7.2, a group of 16 homeowners have been selected from the 30 cases on the basis that they represent a broad range of capital gain experiences. This selected group shares a few common characteristics. First, they are all over 30 years of age and belong to the service and intermediate class. Second, a majority of them entered the housing market in the 1980s where the biggest property boom prevailed. Third, the size of their flats ranges from 400 to 1,000 square feet, representing the kind of dwelling a middle class family in Hong Kong normally has. Fourth, most homeowners in this profile are in various stages of mortgage debts and only two of them are outright owners. These two exceptions are the 'early starters' in the sector. This implies that, by and large, the home ownership sector in Hong Kong lies very much in the first generation of home ownership and none of them inherit their

165

Table 7.2 Selected Profile of Households having Capital Gains from Home Ownership in 1994 (In Hong Kong $)

Name and Family Status	First Home Price Size (sq. ft.)	Current Home Price Size (sq. ft.)	Home Purchase Since 1st Home	Estimated Price of Current Home (94) Net Capital Gain Appreciation Rate
Mr. Chan (a), married for 10 years	1988 0.22m 430	1990 0.85m 670	3	2.5m 1.65m (2.9)
Mr. Chan(b), married for 6 years, 1 kid	1987 0.35m 700	1990 0.4 m 700	2	1.4m 1m (3.5)
Mr. Cheng, married for 12 years, 1 kid	1980 0.40m 350	1990 4.8m 1,000	3	6.5m 1.7m (1.35)
Mr. Cheung (b), married for 15 years, 1 kid	1983 0.19m 330	1989 2.4m 900	4	4.0m 1.6m (1.7)
Mrs. Chow, married for 20 years, 3 kids	1976 0.15m 500	Same as left	1	0.4m 0.25m (2.6)
Mr. Chu , married for 7 years	1991 1.5m 900	Same as left	1	3m 1.5m (2)
Mr. Fung (b), married for 25 years, 6 kids	1972 0.15m 450	1988 0.60m 650	4	1.35m 0.75m (2.25)
Mr. Ho, married for 10 years, 2 kids	1978 0.30m 600	1986 0.65m 600	3	1.85m 1.2m (2.8)
Mr Hui, married for 5 years	1989 0.85m 550	1992 1.3m 800	2	2.4m 0.5m (1.8)
Mr. Kwok, married for 7 years, 1 kid	1989 1.2m 850	1991 1.8m 700	2	2.8m 1m (1.6)

Name and Family Status	First Home Price Size (sq. ft.)	Current Home Price Size (sq. ft.)	Home Purchase Since 1st Home	Estimated Price of Current Home (94) Net Capital Gain Appreciation Rate
Mr. Lai, single	1988 1.2m 650	Same as left	1	3.0m 1.8m (2.5)
Mrs. Lee (b), married for 8 years	1987 0.6 m 500	Same as left	1	2.5m 1.9m (4.2)
Mr. Mok, married for 5 years	1990 0.6 m 500	Same as left	1	0.7m 0.1m (1.2)
Mr. Tse, married for 15 years, 2 kids	1991 2.8m 750	Same as left	1	3.8m 1m (1.4)
Mr. Wan, married for 6 years	1987 0.4m 650	Same as left	1	0.6m 0.2m (1.5)
Mr. Wong, divorced	1971 0.8m 1,000	1978 0.35m 500	2	1.3m 0.95m (3.7)

properties from their parents. The major difference in the group lies in their residential change over the years. They spread out to all parts of Hong Kong Island and Kowloon as well as to suburban new towns. This distribution pattern of the homeownership cases enables a more rigorous comparison for differential gains over a wide area.

Likewise, the homeowners come from a rather broad spectrum of life stages, ranging from single persons and divorcees to homeowners married for over 25 years. Many of them also have more than one dealing with properties. At least two of them have bought and sold properties for four times since the 1970s. This reflects a rather high frequency in home buying. A review of the background of these more frequent home buyers suggest that they belong to the private home ownership sector, and on average they move to a new residence once every five years. Although this observation could not be used strictly to suggest that homeowners in the private sector have a higher motivation to invest through property, it does point to a higher tendency for people in the private housing market to change their residency more often to suit either their job or preference for community facilities. In contrast to private home ownership, homeowners in the public sector (subsidized sale flats) are more stable. At least three of them remain in the same tenure since they bought their home from the Housing Authority in the late 1970s and early 1980s.

Capital Gains and Home Buying

In Table 7.2, we can see that for houses bought in the 1980s, there was an appreciation rate between 1.2 and 4.2 (average = 2.3) times and an estimated net capital gain of $100,000 to $1.9 million (average = $1.1million). Although this is a crude estimate (it has not deducted transaction costs such as commission for real estate agents, stamp duties, legal fees etc., which normally account for about 5% of the total transaction costs), it still provides a picture of capital gains rather than losses. The most important difference between these home owners lies in three important aspects of housing transaction: (1) the timing of purchase; (2) the frequency of transactions; and (3) trading-up.

In the Profile, it is clear that those who entered the market after 1991 made lesser gains because of market fluctuation in the early 1990s. In general, homeowners who traded up for more than once had better capital gains. Homeowners buying their homes in newer housing estates in the 1980s also had better appreciation potentials. In Hong Kong it is common for developers to sell all new flats off the plan before construction actually begins. Such practice allows developers to raise funds for the building construction, hence, reducing burdensome interest payment. To the buyer, a flat sold off the plan could enable them to delay payment of the outstanding balance. In effect, many speculators made use of this time gap to resell their yet-to-be-built flat and made quick profits in an extremely buoyant market. In practice, a home-buyer could opt for one of the following three methods of payment in the case of a flat sold off the plan: (1) pay the full cost of it at a discount of 15% - 20% of the house price, OR (2) pay a 10% down payment and then pay the rest in mortgage schemes through the banks, OR (3) pay a 10% down payment and then pay the rest through the bank when the property is ready for occupation, which would be a year or more later. No discount would be given in the case of the third option. The implication for speculative activities of such a system is paramount. Speculators, usually opting for the third payment method, would be able to amass great profits by simply putting down a small sum of money to cover the deposit. The time gap is usually long enough for house prices to appreciate to a level which lures them to buy a few off the plan properties in one purchase, if they can raise sufficient capital for the deposits. In general, there are actually three different modes of speculation for flats sold off the plan, depending on the motivation and capital outlay of the speculators: (1) the sparrows, (2) the night owls and (3) the falcons.

The Sparrows

The sparrows are small speculators who have only a small amount of capital outlay. They usually concentrate on new developments. In the course of property transaction, one is usually given a period of one month to complete the contract. Buyers are also required to pay a 10% down payment as deposit. The sparrows would try to sell the flat to another buyer for a quick profit within the one-month transaction period. The risk is that if they cannot sell it within the short time, they would get 'hooked' and hence, need a much bigger capital outlay for subsequent mortgage repayment. Hence, the sparrows would only flock to very popular new developments that have great appreciation potentials. At the height of the market, many real estate agents became sparrows themselves. They might work either individually or as small groups.

The Night Owls

The night owls are the genuine *stir-fryers*. They have more money and with a slightly longer-term interest in property investment. They take great care to spot the right property and watch the housing market intensely. Since they have up to date market knowledge, they are able to detect properties that are under-priced or having very good investment potential. They put their money into one, two or three flats, pay the down payments, and get mortgages from different banks (legally there is no limit on the maximum number of mortgages one could obtain; an individual is not legally liable to inform banks of their involvement with other banks). They may even live in one of the flats, and then wait for the right moment to sell. The best time for the night owls is the period just prior to completion of the development as this is usually the time for substantial price appreciation. The night owls actually receive the best benefits from capital gains, although they often stretch their capital to extremity and are often required to pay the highest amount of property tax.

The falcons are mostly not individuals. They are those medium-sized real estate agencies. Small real estate agents are more or less like individual stir-fryers, lacking the necessary capital for large investments. The falcons do something like snatching up to 50 new units under construction or a whole building block. When flats of a certain size or a certain locality are in great demand, they would try to take stock of their flats in store, snatch up as many vacant flats in the area, keep them until they appreciate up to a predetermined level and then have them sold. In Hong Kong, this is commonly known as 'making a market'.

Home Ownership, Differential Gains and Class Formation

From the profile of selected homeowners, it is clear that most of the households had an average of two to three home purchases over the last two decades. They were not asked directly as to how much they had gained altogether from home purchase for the reason that it was part of Chinese culture, especially for the middle class, to be modest about their wealth. It is even considered rude and impolite to ask about one's precise amount of wealth. In any case, it would be difficult for homeowners to come up with a correct figure of their profit and loss account. Hence, net capital gains were only estimates based on the market value of their present home in relation to their prices at the time of purchase, as well as information disclosed with respect to previous transactions. Hence, it is important to note that there is high possibility of under estimation of the net capital gains in the study because it did not reflect net capital gains from all property transactions. Although none of the homeowners indicated speculations as their prime motive, their progressive interactions with the housing market over the years had somehow shaped their original motive of home purchase. A much higher expectation on capital gains was apparent for homeowners in the later part of their experience with home ownership.

Homeowners in Hong Kong are far from being a homogeneous group. Difference in the time of entry to the market shapes different home ownership trajectories. Different homeowners struggle differently to survive, often with diverse motivations and consequently different life opportunities. While most homeowners have gained wealth, their gains are different and carry different implications for life chances. I shall group them into five categories for ease of understanding: (1) the *flat stir-fryers*;

(2) the pragmatic homeowners; (3) the catching-up homeowners; (4) the old tenement homeowners; and (5) the Home Ownership Scheme (HOS) homeowners.

The Flat Stir-fryers

If one of the reasons for Hong Kong's economic success is the result of an ample supply of self-made entrepreneurs, the thriving housing market certainly produces a few good examples. The focus here is on a distinct group of people within the society, who are not necessarily the best-educated, although they like to be regarded as such; who are not exactly the most-talented, but certainly the most aggressive and assertive social group one can find. In terms of class structure, they are either the lower service class or the petite-bourgeoisie. They are mostly found in the insurance, real estate, advertising or marketing business. They can also be small factory owners or simply doing small trading business with Mainland China. They are always visible in public places such as restaurants, cafes and clubs. For more than a decade, they have been involved in the housing market both in a personal and professional capacity. In the case studies, Mr. Cheung (b) represents one of the best examples of this distinct group of middle class. He owns a small factory in suburban Tuen Mun producing and exporting gloves. He lives in Tai Koo Shing, one of the most popular middle class private housing estates in Hong Kong Island East. His flat in Tai Koo Shing is estimated to fetch about $4 million in 1994. He also owns another flat in Kornhill (a nearby private housing estate) and rents it out. Over the last two decades, he has been actively involved in the buying and selling of flats. He disclosed that he had bought and sold for at least three times, with some being sold long before they could be occupied.

> Please don't ever call me a flat stir-fryer (a term generally applied to small investors who speculate on the housing market by quick buying and selling), because I never think of it that way. This is called sound investment. I think everyone in Hong Kong must do that and ought to do that. Who is really going to care for you. The British government? No way! They are leaving. The Chinese government? Oh I think they are even worse. You know Mr. Lee, we are not working for the government. We have no job security. So we've got to make money. Nothing is more important than to make money in Hong Kong. You know this old Chinese saying: 'if you don't work for yourself, even God won't forgive you.' And for me, the work comes from the housing market (Mr. Cheung (b)).

171

Interestingly, there is a certain stigma against *stir-fryers* in Hong Kong. People like to be regarded as good investors and always appear to avoid being labelled as speculators. This is in fact contradictory to what happens in the stock market where all stock brokers are proud of their role as a *stir-fryer*. In the case of Mr. Cheung (b), the genesis of his motivation and interest in the property market stem more from his parents' early ownership experience.

> I first got involved with the housing market in 1980 when I saw my parents selling their flat and making around $300,000 within five years. My mum used to say this: 'nothing is more real than real estate - not even gold'. Since childhood, my mum always said that she couldn't take on anything from those stingy and mean landlords. We must own our flat, no matter how small it is. And so my family had a long history of buying and selling and moving house after a few years. Each time we moved into something slightly larger than before. The motto of my mum: we mustn't go back (Mr. Chueng (b)).

To many Hong Kong people, one of the most critical social events of the 1980s was the political uncertainty on the future of Hong Kong. The effect of this fundamental change on the society is certainly unparalleled and its influence could be reflected in Mr. Cheung (b)'s process of home buying:

> I got married in 1981. For a couple of years, Mary's family was talking about moving to Canada all the time so we weren't really sure we were going to buy ourselves a flat. And you know, that was the time when MacLehose was visiting Beijing and how he got snubbed by Deng. We figured that Hong Kong was not going to be very stable after all, so we rented a small flat in North Point. Besides it was also very practical, because it's near to Mary's work. Things changed when Mary decided not to follow her family to Canada. At that time, I remembered we had to pay about $3,000 for rent. But the average price for a flat during that time, 1983, was about $500 per square foot. With a 90% mortgage and a 20-year loan, the amount of mortgage monthly was slightly higher than the rent. We figured that it might be a sound idea to buy a flat instead of renting one. So we bought this small flat in Kowloon which was basically a studio flat on the top floor. The former owner converted the rooftop so we had an extra room to use as well. It cost us $190,000. It was a rather old flat and we couldn't get 90% mortgage from the bank. So instead we paid about $70,000 and the rest over 15 years. In fact we already managed to pay almost half of the loan in the first 5 years, because Mary got her first promotion (Mr. Cheung (b)).

172

That was just a rather uneventful beginning of home buying for the Cheung (b) family. Their attitude towards home ownership has changed enormously since their first taste of capital gains. While some would stick to their own positions, others began throwing themselves into the housing market.

> I think my views on property changed quite a bit when I decided to look for a larger flat because of the arrival of our first daughter Melissa. That was 1987. The property market was just beginning to pick up. We put up our flat for sale. We asked for $400,000 initially and later raised the price to $420,000 on the advice of Mary's friend who was a real estate agent. We sold our flat to the first buyer. He looked like a small businessman and said that he bought it because he had some extra cash. He didn't even bother to bargain at all! We thought he was a stir-fryer! So paying back $120,000 to the bank, we made a clean profit of $300,000. Adding up my own money and Mary's savings, it would take us 10 years to come up with that amount of money (Mr. Cheung (b)).

It is clear that the first experience of capital gains from selling marked the turning point for the Cheung (b) family. Investment in housing became the major aspiration for them to transform their life chances.

> We began to realize the importance of the real estate market and how ineffective our paid jobs became. With the money, we bought a slightly larger flat in a new development near the old Hung Hom dockyard - the Whampoa Garden. At that time only the Phase One project was on sale. We bought it when it off the plan and moved in about six months later. It was 900 square feet with 3 bedrooms. It was well layout and we could afford to hire a Filipino maid to take care of Melissa. They occupied a smaller room. It was the first time I could afford a study for myself. The price was $850,000. Including the 10% down payment and all those legal and tax fees, we paid about $130,000. We spent another $50,000 on the furnishing and decoration. Our family was thrilled when we moved into our new flat during the Christmas of 1987. Deducting everything, we still had about $150,000 for any future contingency (Mr. Cheung (b)).

After 1987, the Cheung (b) family became semi-experts on the housing market. They read through most of the newspapers and made cuttings on all new developments, paying particular attention to the movement of a few major developers: Cheung Kong, Sung Hung Kei and Swire. Their policy was never to buy a junk flat: 'Property is a bit like bonds, never buy poorly located properties. The best property would always fetch the best price.'

> We spent most of our weekends driving around Hong Kong to inspect new developments. We built up a small library on all sorts of property promotion brochures with the price lists etc. In the second-hand market, it's always important to know the original selling price. Otherwise the estate agents would just brag any price they want. We went as far out to Sha Tin and Tsuen Wan. Some people look down on these new towns but I always think they have an opportunity because the urban centre is so small. The New Territories is the only hope for the middle class in future (Mr. Cheung (b)).

It is interesting to note the transformation of Mr. Cheung (b) from the level of meeting one's housing need to the level of investment portfolio management. He is apparently moving beyond his immediate needs. Like gambling, many people find home buying and speculation compulsive, especially when one encounters some windfall gains in the initial purchase. Cantonese are notorious for being fond of gambling. Speculation in the housing market is always indirectly linked to this habit. Together with mahjong playing, horse racing and the Macao casinos, property speculation has become the fourth most popular gambling pursuit in Hong Kong. And so the Cheung (b) family marches onwards.

> An opportunity finally came when Kornhill - a new development - came on the market. Mary and I lined up in front of the sales office in Causeway Bay one Saturday morning. We thought we were early. But by the time we arrived, there were already 50 or so people before us. 300 new units were snapped up in the morning. We paid a nominal deposit of $20,000 and secured a 750 square feet unit for $1.2 million. The Hong Kong Bank and Hang Seng Bank had already set up desks in the sales office, ready to accept preliminary applications for mortgage. As I already had a mortgage with Hong Kong Bank, I naturally opted for Hang Seng. The mortgage application was completed in less than 15 minutes. From the time I got into the office, bought my flat and got my mortgage of $1 million something, it took less than one hour. I was absolutely amazed at the pace and ease the transaction was completed. But a business decision is always a business decision. It doesn't pay if you linger on too long. It has to be sharp shooting! There was a model flat next to the sales office but I didn't even bother to take a look. As I walked away from the office, I could see estate agents setting up temporary desks outsider the premises, offering to resell some of those new units with an added-on value of $50,000-$100,000. I couldn't believe what I went through and what I had seen (Mr. Cheung (b)).

Mr. Cheung (b) did not just move from a position of no gain at all to a position of gains. Through actively involving himself in the housing market, he created more opportunities for himself. Not merely that, he was also developing chances for his ensuing career.

> The flat subsequently rose to about $1.5 million at the beginning of 1989. I was fed up with advertising. A few friends suggested that we pulled together some money and set up a firm on exporting gloves to US and Europe. I wanted a change. And because Mary got another promotion, I decided to quit my job. I sold the Kornhill flat quickly and got about $450,000 minus all other expenses. I pulled together some of our family savings and that's how I got my business started. Well. There were ups and downs at first, particularly for a year after 1989, but we are on a very firm footing now. If I had never got into the housing market, I would still be a second grade advertising agent. I bought another smaller flat after 1989 when the price went down a bit. And with the flat I am living now in Tai Koo Shing, the flat in Kornhill and my business, I think I have a gross asset of about $8 million. It all began with the first flat we bought (Mr. Cheung (b)).

In Mr. Cheung (b)'s case, one can easily discern an element of calculation and rationality in each of his moves towards capital gains. He was not stretching himself to an extreme and in each instance, he reserved some money for contingency. This certainly wasn't the case for Mr. Chan (a) who fought his way through the hierarchy in a small foreign exchange company.

> There's a Chinese saying that: 'men cannot be rich unless there is some windfall money and horses don't get strong unless they are fed with "night" meadows (a special kind of grass).' In 1988, I was so fed up with my work in the foreign exchange firm. I was obviously not going anywhere because I used to get crossed a lot with my boss. A very close friend suggested to me that we should pull some money together to do some *stir-frying*. He began to tell stories of his friends making millions from the property market within a year or two. I was never really serious about property because I thought it took too long and it was too serious a commitment. I used to think the stock market was where money should go. But my friend had a completely different view on the property market. He said if we could pull together about half a million and go for a few *Lau Fa* (new flats under construction), we would be able to double our investment within half a year (Mr. Chan (a)).

Two elements stand out quite clearly in the process of home buying and selling, namely: (1) internal allocation of new flats - *Lau Fa* by major developers through their own staff in a personal capacity; (2) the ease with which an 'empty shell' company could be formed. Before the government introduced new regulations in November 1992, it was customary for large developers such as Cheung Kong and Sun Hung Kei to allocate up to 20% of new flats under construction for sales through their management staff as a form of *subsidies* to their salary. They would then resell the flats through their personal networks on a commission basis. The amount of commission would depend on their own network and salesmanship. Incidentally this additional income was 'black money' which was not recorded anywhere and was therefore not subjected to tax. Such marketing methods bear similarity to those marketing strategies called *direct selling* originated largely in North American consumer markets. The only difference lies in the high degree of inflexibility in housing demand and therefore buyers have to bear the responsibility of paying commission rather than the sellers. The second element is that an 'empty shell' company could be established or bought from an accountancy firm for a small sum of money so that home buying could be made entirely through the company with much more tax advantages compared to purchase by an individual. Chan (a)'s case might illustrate this point aptly.

Our chance came in the summer of 1988 when a new development came up in Tsuen Wan - the Riviera Garden. My friend knew somebody working in the developer's firm and he said that something could be arranged that we would be allocated at least four units before they came on the market. We acted very quickly. Using a dummy limited company, we bought four 600 square feet units at $800,000 each. We paid a sum of $320,000 as deposit and about 10% of that as *tips* for the friend in the developer's firm. We also paid about $80,000 for legal fees and stamp duties. We sought mortgages from four different banks, mainly small banks who didn't really care about our credibility. We started to have mortgage repayments in June. It's almost $30,000 each month. It's really a bit scary because our capital outlay could only afford us to pay about three months' mortgage. We planned to resell them all in September. We figured we could get at least $700,000 if there's going to be 30% appreciation. It was unbelievable. You know how long we waited to sell all four. We did all that within just one week in September. Four of them were completely snapped up by a local estate agent. We did not get 30% appreciation. We only got about 25% at most. So just within the summer of 1988, each of us made $300,000, more than double of our initial capital, which was about $250,000 (Mr. Chan (a)).

The action of Mr. Chan (a) reflects both an element of rationality and irrationality. In the 1980s, such kind of investment behaviour was extremely prevalent in the housing market. But the propensity to gamble and high risking-taking behaviour in the 1980s could be regarded as unprecedented. One of the reasons is attributed to the presence of political uncertainties and therefore people wanted to make the most out of what they had and to hold on to their wealth for future security.

The Pragmatic Homeowners

Not all homeowners are entrepreneurial. In fact, many of them in my study have indicated very practical reasons for home owning. They are not as interested in the ups and downs of the property market as Mr. Cheung (b) or Mr. Chan (a), the *stir-fryers*. They have chosen to buy or to rent at different stages of their lives for very pragmatic reasons. Although they are pleased with the appreciation of their property and, to a certain extent, get some psychological comfort from realizing the rising value of their houses, investment and capital appreciation are not their primary intention. They are inclined to think that these are only gains on paper. They would not be able to realize any gains as long as they need a flat to live. The primacy of buying a house, after all, is to meet their genuine housing needs. As a majority group amongst homeowners, they share few commonalties. Some of them are often mistaken to be *stir-fryers* because they also take on a very business-like attitude when coming to buying and selling of properties: getting as much market information as possible, and consulting lawyers and friends familiar with the housing market. In general, they took a much more cautious attitude towards home buying than the *stir-fryers*. If there is one thing common amongst them: it is their distaste for estate agents who are notorious for *price-manipulation*. In particular, agents would try to lure sellers into agreeing to sell at a below-market price while persuading buyer to buy at an above-average price. Since property transactions are done largely through conveyancing solicitors, prospective sellers and buyers could be successfully prevented from meeting with each other, hence, the discrepancies in the selling and buying prices become the profits of unscrupulous estate agents. The pragmatic middle class homeowners would tend to be extremely cautious in dealing with estate agents who are commonly known as 'ferocious crocodiles', or try to avoid them altogether. If they could afford the time and effort, they would rather resort to their own personal network in buying and selling. They would put up their own advertisement for sale and meet with prospective buyers themselves. They believe that *knowledge* and *shingmuk* are two important elements to prevent them from being outwitted by estate agents. Mr. and Mrs. Kwok were both graduates of the Chinese University in 1984 and while Mr. Kwok had been a chemistry teacher since graduation, Mrs. Kwok has switched a few times as an administration officer with commercial firms. They have a 6-year-old son and a 2-year-old daughter. Since marriage, they have moved a few times. They were living in Hang Fa Chuen, a new middle class private housing estate in Hong Kong Island East when I interviewed them.

> Among our contemporaries, we married at quite an early stage, only one year after graduation. That was 1985. The Sino-British negotiation, I can remember, has just begun. Many of our friends were keenly talking about emigration, mostly to Canada and Australia. But since Maggie and I didn't happen to fall into the right occupation group wanted by these countries, we gave up hope of it at an early date. In fact, we were quite put off by not being able to emigrate at first and you know the pressure from our friends was so great. For a moment we even avoided seeing our friends who were about to emigrate because we thought we would look a bit stuck when asked about our plan. It really drove us mad sometimes (Mr. Kwok).

There was enormous pressure during the 1980s for the middle class to seek an 'insurance policy' through emigration. In this respect, the professional and managerial groups gained the best edge because countries such as Canada, Australia and New Zealand had all favoured applicants with qualifications and a certain level of capital assets. The intermediate class of non-manual workers, junior technicians and artisans were in general less welcomed by these countries. This general feeling of *immobility* of the intermediate class had indirect consequences for property ownership. For those who knew that they could not leave Hong Kong, they were much more determined to put their savings into home purchase. For those who planned to emigrate, they would also want to put their money into property so that within a few years time they would be able to amass enough capital for overseas settlement. The final effect of Hong Kong's political uncertainties, especially in the late 1980s, had resulted in an unprecedented upsurge in the demand for property, setting the right climate for speculators from all walks of life to enter the housing market.

> The housing market at that time was rather stagnant because of the slow progress of the Sino-British talks so it was not too expensive to buy. Both our parents were living in public housing estates, mine in Chai Wan and Maggie's in Shau Kei Wan. Both were very early public housing estates on

Island East. For a while, we thought of pulling together some money from our parents and looked for a small flat in North Point, particularly those 10-year-old buildings, which should be cheaper. However, a quick survey told us that we had to have at least $100,000 for the down payment and legal fees etc. for a small flat of $400,000. Our wedding banquet and the honeymoon had already consumed all our savings and we figured we really didn't want to bother our family too much because both of us come from big families with many brothers and sisters. We really liked to have a HOS flat, like what Maggie's brother is having. However, our family income at that time had exceeded the limit by almost $2,000, so we also got to give up hope on that side as well (Mr. Kwok).

Like many other middle class families, the Kwoks were very much disturbed by political uncertainties during the 1980s and were faced with very limited housing options. Getting into home ownership and mortgage was the only alternative they had in terms of meeting their housing needs. Therefore coming to grips with all the nitty-gritty of home buying and selling formed a very important part of their life.

We first rented a small rooftop flat near Maggie's parent home which was about 300 square feet. It was basically a converted studio flat. The rent was only $1,500 per month, which was considered a good deal at that time. Probably because quite a lot needed to be done and therefore the landlord couldn't ask for too much. We lived there until 1989 when Maggie got pregnant. In order to prepare for Joe's arrival, we had to have a bigger place. We were figuring at that time whether we should think seriously about buying. We began to look around. At that time Tai Koo Shing was still not as expensive and heavily inhabited like today. We went to look for a few, mostly by going through newspapers for independent offers. We didn't want to do it through agents because Maggie's brother once got into serious troubles with a real estate agent, not a small one though. The bigger the company, the worse their professional conduct. All agents are thugs, merciless thugs! Anyway, we were not too satisfied with our search. It was either too small or too expensive for us. We were looking for something at least 650 square feet with 3 rooms. But that would fetch up to at least $1.2 million-$1.4million (Mr. Kwok).

Many young couples find great difficulties in satisfying their housing needs as their family life-cycle progresses towards the child-rearing age. Because most middle class families in Hong Kong involve the couples working. Therefore a young family with one kid usually means two extra persons - a baby and a Filipino domestic helper. This means a jump from a family of two to a family of four, hence requiring at least a 3-bedroom flat of about 650 square feet. The post-war baby boom of the 1950s implies that most married couples are now into their child-bearing age, partially accounting for the reason why there is a boom for demand for larger flats in the 1980s. Hong Kong people are known for adaptability and flexibility in their work attitude (Bond, 1991). Evidence could also be found in their approach towards meeting their housing needs.

> Just at that time I met my university roommate Chung. We were good friends. Chung had just sold his flat and was thinking about moving to Canada. It was May 1989. There were already signs of student discontents in Beijing. Chung persuaded us not to make any decision to buy because we really should be thinking ahead. We located a flat of about 1,000 square feet and wanted to co-rent it so that we could share one Filipino maid and reduce our costs. Maggie and I thought that a good idea. Incidentally, it was on June 4th that we were ready to sign a temporary rental agreement with the landlord when the horrible thing happened in Beijing. And things were paralyzing for the next four months. We finally gave up the idea of joint renting altogether (Mr. Kwok).

It is evident here how socio-political change shape the life of the people. Of all those changes in the 1980s, the 'June 4th Event' in China had the deepest effect on life in Hong Kong.

> In November 1989, Chung decided not to emigrate, for similar reasons like us, because we thought it rather unethical to leave Hong Kong at that moment and besides, we wanted to see how China would be affected by the 'June 4th Event'. Because the property market had gone down quite a bit and Chung figured that it would be high time that we bought a big flat together instead of renting one. He was very positive about the market getting robust again in one or two years' time. For us, it seemed we had not much of an alternative. Our money was not enough to buy a big enough place and besides the idea of sharing a Filipino maid sounded very economical. We finally nailed our deal. It's a 850 square feet flat in Tai Koo Shing at a real bargain, only $1.2 million. It should have been $1.7 million or something before June 4th. Each family eventually ended up paying about $100,000, and we paid a monthly mortgage of about $10,000. Splitting it up, it was about $5000 per family, which was just about $1,000 more than our previous rent (Mr. Kwok).

The two families later sold their flat at the end of 1991 when the Chung family got their first baby. After all, it would be too much for the domestic helper to handle the housework as well as the babies. They managed to sell their flat quite quickly because the market was beginning to pick up after the Gulf War. Both families got about half a million in cash, their first real taste of capital gains from home ownership.

> We have never had so much money before in our life. After 7 years of work, we practically spent all our money on the house and the family. It proved money well spent. For a while we didn't know what to do with the money. We thought of renting something immediately and spent some of the money on a trip to Europe and North America. However, both Chung and I agreed that because the market was picking up again and if we didn't buy and be contented with what we had then we would be sorry for ourselves. We would never be able to go back to the homeowner market any more. We have proved our judgement to be correct, haven't we? (Mr. Kwok)

One month after the Kwok family sold their flat, they bought another 700 square feet flat in Hang Fa Chuen, a slightly down market new estate to the east of Tai Koo Shing. They bought it for $1.8 million and paid about $250,000 for down payment and other expenses. They also set aside another $150,000 as contingency. One interesting characteristic to note about middle class homeowners in Hong Kong is that they would not leave the market after they have realized their gains. In general, they would re-enter the market in order to protect their future interest, both in terms of use-value and exchange-value. The difference lies in how much they would re-invest their money in the property market. In the case of the Kwok family, they re-invested three quarters of their capital gains into the housing market again. Only a small amount of capital gains were left for life-enhancing purposes.

> There was some money left and we went for a trip to Toronto during the spring of 1992. We thought we were very lucky indeed to have decided to go back to the market. Look at the price now - $4,000 per square foot, our flat is now what? $2.8 million! I won't buy it if I don't have a flat now. It's just gone crazy! (Mr. Kwok)

As mentioned earlier, people from the intermediate class tend to seek an outlet through engaging themselves in the property market. They would try to create more life opportunities through home buying and selling. This could be seen in the case of the Lee (b) family.

> I think like many other families in Hong Kong, we are quite hopeless about the 1997 question. When some of our friends went to Canada in 1985, we

thought about emigration. But because all these countries, Canada, Australia and New Zealand, they just wanted professional people or people with money to do business and invest. For a while we thought we were going to be stuck in Hong Kong. On the other hand, even if we could go to some less demanding places like Singapore, we were going to need money to settle down. We needed some money to buy a house and some money to tide over the initial period. We felt rather depressed about all these. After all, John is a low-grade technician in the government. We have put in our application for HOS for the last five years using the White Form (application from non-public housing residents) and were so disappointed every time they announced the result (Mrs. Lee (b)).

In 1987, the Lee family made a crucial decision. They bought their first flat.

I think John is more or less influenced by me on home purchase. He never thought about it himself. He's just kind of enjoying what he has now and just doesn't bother what's going to happen tomorrow. We decided since we are not going anywhere we might put our money into buying a flat. We had been renting a place in a Hung Hom old tenement block for very cheap rent. We bought a 600 square feet flat in Whampoa Garden Phase I. It was just $600,000. We pulled together $100,000 and went for it. It's a small flat and we have to shoulder a monthly mortgage of about $5,000, much more than our $2,000 per month rent. John was nagging me all the time and said that I had put the family budget into chaos. But now he knows I was damn right. Our flat is now worth about $2.5 million. If I didn't make all that fuss, we would be in a much more awkward position now. I think now I can think of emigration. Because if we sell the flat, we'll be able to get at least $2 million. Of course, we have to deduct the mortgage paid in the last 6 years. But still how can I expect John to save up all that money! If we were to join my sister in Calgary, we could easily buy two houses, rent one of them and still have $1 million to spend. We can even think about setting up some small business there. Of course we might not be qualified for emigration after all, but before, we couldn't even dare to think about it. There is a real difference here, all because of the flat! (Mrs. Lee (b))

The Catching-Up Homeowners: The Point-34 Civil Servant

For a long time, the civil service in Hong Kong has been regarded the 'golden rice bowl', meaning that there is an extremely high degree of job security and attractive fringe benefits once you get into the service. Burns (1988) has suggested that while the civil service of Hong Kong is modeled after the British system, it carries a distinctive benefit system that the UK system finds it unparalleled. For mid-level civil servants who have reached point-34 of the Master Pay Scale, their pay package includes salary, educational allowances for dependent children, medical and dental care and, most important of all, a housing subsidy or the so-called *Private Tenancy Allowance*. Private Tenancy Allowance comes in a fixed rate and varies slightly between single, married and married with children. Hence, in order to reap the benefit of this allowance, many civil servants would choose to abstain from home ownership. The allowance only permits one to rent. Nonetheless, as house prices skyrocketed in the late 1980s, many civil servants began to find it difficult to use the allowance to rent a decent place, although from time to time the level of allowance was adjusted. They also felt extremely uneasy about their counterparts in the private sector, who obviously went into the housing market much earlier and were able to reap substantially gains from property appreciation and transactions. Pressure from trade unions at various levels of civil servants began to emerge soon after 1991. This also coincided with the other worries of the government - the brain-drain problem as a result of persistent emigration of mid-career civil servants as well as keen competition from the private sector for mid-level management executives. After a number of salary and benefit reviews between the public and the private sectors, the government finally came up with a new scheme at the end of 1991. The new Home Financing Scheme was introduced, which allows civil servants to opt for an interest-free loan as well as a monthly cash allowance for mortgage repayment. The amount of the mortgage allowance was set at about 70% of the Private Tenancy Allowance, to be provided for a maximum of 10 years. This new scheme had an enormous impact on both individual civil servants and the housing market. Concomitant with this was a buoyant economy at the end of the Gulf War. Seizing this golden opportunity to revive the sluggish property market after the 'June 4th Event', real estate companies began to mobilize a massive publicity campaign, aiming to encourage these civil servants to change their tenure. Mr. Chu, who had worked in the Lands and Works Department as a mid-level land surveyor, was caught in exactly the same situation.

I have been working in the government since 1978 and I waited 6 years in order to get to the Private Tenancy Allowance (PTA). It was such a long wait. At one point I almost got fed up with the whole thing and wanted to move to the private sector, if not because Liz was still pursuing her law degree. I got my PTA in 1984 and rented quite a nice flat in Kowloon Tong (a rather expensive upper middle class low-rise residential area in Central

Kowloon). It's about 1,000 square feet. There were 3 very good size rooms and 1 small room for the maid. We liked the neighbourhood. They all seemed to be driving BMW and Mercedes and looked extremely well established. We felt a bit out-of-place sometimes with our second-hand Accord, but who cares! There're also quite a number of my colleagues living nearby. Quite a number of my friends persuaded me to use my PTA as mortgage to buy a flat. Mind you it's illegal! The way to go about is simple. Just ask a friend - a good friend of course, to buy a flat on your behalf and rent it to you or simply to swap with another civil servant who is also at point 34, or even to set up a dummy firm with your friends as directors and rent from it. I know some people in the government do have this secret practice. After all this PTA business is really ridiculous and these seems to be a way out. However, we didn't really consider that seriously. Why? I think basically Liz and I don't like anything that involved cheating and illegal act. It's too much a burden. Besides, I really thought doing that would be too greedy. After all, it's already a 'golden rice bowl'. What really worried us was the housing market. Because I began to realize that if one day I decided to quit the government, then I probably wouldn't be able to afford buying anything any more because flats are becoming so outrageously expensive. Our meagre savings could probably only afford us to buy a 500 square feet and then we would be much worse than our present standard of living (Mr. Chu).

A golden rice bowl! What is striking here is the extent to which the changes in the property market have affected the middle class civil service as a sector. Relative to those working in the private sector, mid-career civil servants (assuming they reach salary point 34 and have switched their tenure to renting) would all suffer to some extent from house price inflation. Hence, the Private Tenant Allowance scheme has basically limited the opportunities of mid-career civil servants. When the new Home Financing Scheme arrived in early 1991, it was too late and too little.

When the new scheme was finally announced in 1991 we were so ambivalent. On the one hand we didn't want to leave our rented flat because it was so nice. On the other hand, we didn't want to be failed by the system. After two months of struggle, we finally decided that we should go for it. We didn't want to be the victim of the system. We began to drive around town to look for our new home. Because if the government was willing to provide an interest-free loan down payment it would make all the difference. We finally bought this new flat by the seaside near Tuen Mun. It's a bit far away from town but the sea view is amazing. Besides it was developed by Sung Hung Kei (SHK). Anything by SHK is reliable and should be guaranteed for value. We bought it for $1.5 million, 900 square feet, very good size and the government is paying 20% down payment for us. We are just paying about $12,000 a month for mortgage, just meeting our level of allowance provision. Our flat now fetches $3 million in the market I think, but we really don't bother. Liz just loves it! (Mr. Chu)

For many senior civil servants, who had been on the Private Tenant Allowance scheme for a long time, the new scheme proves less attractive for various reasons. First, as you move up the salary ladder, the actual amount of the Private Tenant Allowance will increase as well. This would enable some civil servants to enjoy a very high standard of rental accommodation. In some cases, rental flats as large as 2,500 square feet could be afforded by the scheme. Second, a rental agreement is usually fixed for a period of two years. Because rental increases are subject to regulations, old renters would be able to benefit from comparatively cheaper rent. Third, having lived in a certain place for a period of time would mean a more settled family environment, with children going to nearby schools, friends and neighbours all around the same district. Hence, it would be quite difficult for senior civil servants to opt for the new scheme that in most cases involve moving to a new area with the allowance affording them a comparatively smaller accommodation. Mr Tse, a senior administrative officer with the government does carry these grievances:

I think this whole system of Private Tenancy Allowance (PTA) is basically one of the most stupid Hong Kong Government policies. I think it is archaic, colonial and stupid. It should have been scrapped altogether ages ago. I don't blame people leaving the government for the private sector. You see it actually doesn't cost the government a cent more to just pay PTA as part of the salary package, and don't have to care a shit about whether people are going to use the money for renting or mortgage. The government even saves money in the administration of the scheme. Look, this scheme has been in force for about 30 years and because of this, a lot of civil servants are stuck where they are. And now you see, most of them are becoming propertyless. My wife and I have been trying so hard since last year to buy a flat comparable to our rental flat in the Mid-level but in vain. And look, we finally have to come to terms with this tiny flat in Kornhill. Both my son and my daughter hate this so much because now they have to take a 45-minute bus ride to school. Just imagine if this scheme came to us 10 years ago. We would be in a much better position. With that money we might even be able to get something from Repulse Bay (an upper class/upper middle class area in Island South). Now we are living in half the size of what we used to have in the Mid-level. This scheme doesn't help at all, it just make us more frustrated (Mr. Tse).

Although the Home Financing Scheme was not welcomed in the initial stage, in fact, after years of revision in the amount of allowance, it is now more comparable with the level of payment under the Private Tenancy Allowance. In 1998, the Home Financing Scheme was extended to staff of the universities under the University Grants Council funding system. Since the 1998 economic downturn, jobs in the civil service have proved to be extremely popular amongst university graduates as they provide better prospect in housing benefits. The civil servants, as a social group, will continue to be a potent force in the demand for home ownership.

The Old Tenement Homeowners: Disillusionment in Capital Gains

When people talk about homeowners in Hong Kong, they generally take that to mean those living in modern high rise condominium blocks such as those found in Tai Koo Shing or Mei Foo. What they have often overlooked is that about 10% of homeowners still live in inner-city old tenements which, as mentioned in Chapter five, were built either before the First World War or between the two wars. They are usually 4-8 storeys high with no lift and are poorly built and equipped. However, the advantages of these old tenements lie in their spacious layout and in general a high ceiling for ventilation. Some homeowners develop a special fondness for these old tenements because of their good location and layout. For those buildings that remain standing today and have passed periodic inspection tests of the Buildings Department, they are normally of very good built quality. A majority of them are now found in Wan Chai and the Western District of Hong Kong, in Mongkok and Yau Ma Tei of the Kowloon Peninsula, and in Sham Shui Po and Lai Chi Kok of West Kowloon. As a result of the age of these buildings, the rate of capital appreciation over the last two decades has been well below average. Banks are normally reluctant to provide a high percentage of loans.

Mr. Wong, a laboratory technician with a welfare organization, has spent a great part of his life in these old tenement buildings and is still paying a mortgage for his own flat.

> You can say I was born and raised in these tenements. When I was born, my mother refused to go to a hospital. She simply allowed one of those indigenous midwives to come to our flat to do the delivery. As soon as my father arrived from Guangzhou in 1945, he bought our first flat at $2,000. Mortgage from a bank was still something very alien in those days. If people wanted to borrow money, they would either go to a *Kwei Lei* man (a loan shark) or to *Biu Hui* (draw money from an illegal mutual fund society),

186

both involving very high interest rates. I thought my father used the latter way. I spent my childhood in that flat in Wan Chai.

When I was 23, I bought my first tenement flat in old North Point, which was near to my father's furniture shop. It was in fact my uncle's flat. I liked it because it's big. It was almost 1,000 square feet, with 3 huge rooms. I got married later in 1971 and became a salesman of electrical appliances, things like hi-fi and fridge. But because the economy went into recession in 1975, so I left home to visit my relatives in the States, hoping to set up some restaurant business in Detroit. I stayed for a year or so without any success of job opportunity so I returned to Hong Kong the following year. But unfortunately my marriage had problems and my wife left me the following year; at the same time not allowing me to return to my flat. The flat in fact was in her name. I got a job as a junior audio-visual technician in a welfare agency and later on I rented another old tenement in Wan Chai near where I worked. I thought it must be built in the pre-war years. It looked a bit old but that's what I like as long as it is well built. Later the landlord offered to sell it to me because of emigration. The price was $350,000, which was a really good price. He said he just didn't bother to go to the agent because it was too troublesome. But I guessed also there weren't too many prospective buyers around for old tenement flats anyway. At that time I also looked around for flats in other modern estates, such as Whampoa Garden. I went to see a few but finally decided on this one because I liked the spaciousness and the feel. The building is not colossal like the big estates. In fact I sometimes feel a bit sorry for not being able to buy one of those new flats, because if I could afford to do so, my assets would be 7-fold today. In those days Whampoa was just about 20% more expensive than my tenement flat. My flat now is worth only about $600,000 at most. Well, these were just afterthoughts. I am never sorry for what I did. Life is not all for money, eh! I have lived in this flat ever since and I like it very much, it likes me as well! (Mr. Wong)

Mr. Wong differs from other Hong Kong owners in two aspects. First, in his housing trajectory, use-value was his primary concern. He was most concerned with getting a place to live. Throughout most of his housing transactions, asset appreciation for those old tenement blocks where he lived seldom went beyond inflation. It is practically impossible for owners of old tenement block to make a profit out of home buying, except in cases where the tenement is sought after by developers for redevelopment. Second, in Mr. Wong's housing path he kept returning to old tenement block. It was partly attributed to the fact that at his income level, his affordability for other housing type is limited. It was also partly the result of an *old tenement culture*, where owners find their neighbourhood much more congenial than those of the modern high-rise.

The Homeowners in Government Home Ownership Scheme (HOS): The Last to Benefit from Capital Gains

Not all homeowners enjoy capital gains. About 25% of all owner-occupiers do not benefit from capital appreciation in the normal sense of the word. They live in a prestigious segment of public housing called HOS. Started in 1974, the government produces about 3,000-10,000 HOS units per year for sale. They are usually flats of 400-750 square feet with a price deliberately set at 50%-60% below the market price to make them affordable for marginal groups. Residents of these HOS flats are primarily former tenants of public rental housing because they were given priority in application and allocation as long as they are willing to give up their rental units. People outside the public housing sector can apply if they meet the income criteria, but the chance of success is usually lower than that of public housing tenants. The important element which affects HOS flats in relation to capital gains is that these HOS owners cannot exchange their flats within the first 10 years of ownership. If they want to give up their flats within 10 years, they can only sell it back to the Housing Authority. Hence only those HOS properties which have reached the 10-year maturity period are available now in the housing market. In fact, because of the smallness and exclusivity of the market, only a few real estate agents are interested in specializing in HOS properties. Due to their relative low rate of appreciation, owners have a natural tendency to stay put rather than sell because of the meagre gains they get. It is not possible for them to afford anything else in the private market. Mrs. Chow, a government nurse, has been living in Chun Man Yuen, the first HOS estate, for the last 15 years. She has been trying in vain to move to the private sector for the last two years and is extremely frustrated at not being able to do so.

> We moved to Chun Man Yuen in 1976. It was really wonderful for the first 10 years. I remember we felt so proud moving from the 'hole' in Wong Tai Sin Estate to this beautiful place. We thought it was so well designed with all the landscaped gardening etc. We thought we were so lucky to be able to become the first batch of HOS owners. Now all this has more or less gone. There were enormous problems with the plumbing. There's leakage everywhere. We don't know what causes it? May be the typhoons or may be not? Anyway things began to get worse once it got to an age of 10 years or more. We bought the flat for $150,000 in 1976. Now it could at most fetch $400,000. Although I have already paid up my mortgage but with that money I am not going to get anywhere in the private market. Besides, I don't want to pay a large mortgage again. You know, I do sometimes miss

Wong Tai Sin public housing estate, because back there I don't have to worry about anything. The Housing Authority was responsible for all the repairs and they were quite efficient in doing that (Mrs. Chow).

Other HOS homeowners are much more concerned with the social environment of these flats. Mr. Mok, a social worker who has been living with his parental family in Sui Woo Yuen (a prize winning HOS estate on architectural merits) for the last 13 years and eventually ended up buying one of the second-hand HOS flats in the same estate. His comments encapsulated one of the dilemmas of modern home ownership in Hong Kong:

> Well. I can't say I am not grateful to be able to live in one of these new HOS flats. I mean they are nicely built, good price, quite convenient for shopping and schools and all that. But I don't know really. It's just not comparable to those private developments like Tai Koo Shing and Kornhill. Not that they are not good as far as living environment is concerned. It's the *class* or the *style* that makes the different. You know all HOS flats are as a rule situated right next to public rental estates. And obviously you are sharing all facilities with the public housing people. So you can imagine what kind of shops and restaurants could be found there (Mr. Mok).

Residents of HOS flats do carry a great deal of ambivalence about their position. On the one hand, they regard HOS flats much better than public rental flats. On the other hand, they think HOS flats are not comparable to private flats, particularly in two respects: first, their built quality and second, the facilities within the estate. Mrs. Ho, a government nurse had the following views:

> I'm not trying to be snobbish. But you know sometimes you do want to spend money in a more pleasant way, like going to a better hair stylist or to do some better shopping. That also partly explains why all HOS flats don't fetch a high price, even in the best part of the boom period. Not to mention that you can't actually sell it in the first 10 years. If not for the reason that I have to depend on my mother to take care of our son, I wouldn't have decided to buy a flat here. I would save enough money to buy a flat somewhere in the private sector. But now I can't do this. I am stuck because of my family. I don't have many choices. When my child becomes a little older, I'll definitely move away (Mrs. Ho).

Mr. Fung (a), though fell into the income range of HOS, had chosen to buy a flat in the private market. He held a more constructive view about HOS:

> You know I think what the government should do is to build some up market HOS flats in better locations. I think even if it is a little more expensive people would still go for it. Besides they should really shorten the 10-year period so that people can put their flats in the market sooner. How can people wait for that long to sell their flats? (Mr. Fung (a))

Mr. Wan was more positive about HOS. He had been living in Tung Tau Estate (one of the oldest Mark II resettlement estates in Kowloon East) until he got married. His success in getting on to HOS in the early 1980s meant a great improvement on living environment for him when he was allocated a unit in a new HOS estate in Tsing Yi Island (New Territories West). He bought the flat for only $400,000 in 1987 and over the years has managed to pay back three-quarters of the mortgage loan of $360,000. He is now very much into a period of mortgage maturity.

> I basically think it is great to be able to live in one of the HOS flats. I think we are just grateful. The environment is good. The shopping centre is so near and my kid goes to a very good school. I don't know why some people feel dissatisfied. I mean, look, we've been in this estate for how long? Six years already and it's great. I mean except for one or two typhoons where our windows were leaking quite heavily but you know, my friends in Kornhill always had the same problem. It depends on luck sometimes. Lots of people complained about pollution and traffic in Tsing Yi. Yes, I think there are major environmental problems. But where else in Hong Kong you don't find these problems (Mr. Wan).

Tsing Yi is one of the more socially progressive districts (out of 19 districts) where the district board is basically dominated by liberals from the Democratic Party. The district has a long history of well-organized social actions. Mr. Wan happened to be a volunteer of a District Member's ward office in Tsing Yi.

> I go to attend district board meetings whenever I can and channel these problems through the Board. That's got to be a way of moving things here. You know shouting and bragging are no use, you got to know the right way. Well I know my flat isn't worth much. But who cares! I mean what's the use of having a $2 million flat in Tai Koo Shing if you must live in one. This is just vanity! Unless you have two flats, otherwise it is just money on

paper! When the market comes down after 1997 there really won't be a great deal of difference by then (Mr. Wan).

Conclusion

Certain themes emerge from the above discussions of modes of home ownership and capital gains. They provide some important clues to the type of social processes that underlie tenure. I shall draw out three of these themes, each of which serves to raise further questions about the relationship between home ownership, wealth and contemporary societies.

The Pervasiveness of Capital Gains

The first of these concerns the spread of capital gains amongst various modes of home ownership. It has been shown that capital gains from home ownership in Hong Kong over the last two decades have been derived from a variety of sources, for instance, a sustained level of house price inflation, the right time of entry into the market, location of property, frequency of home changes and the presence of speculative activities. All these contribute to a homeowner's gain. In addition, two extremely important socio-economic factors have been cited as providing the impetus for a high motivation to buy, namely, political uncertainty and a robust economy. For those who planned to emigrate before 1997, they saw the property market as an investment leading to quick profits. For those who planned to stay put, they saw home ownership as a means to protect themselves against inflation. This explains why under conditions of political uncertainties there was still a high motivation to own. However, one must note that continual capital gains in home ownership was only possible in Hong Kong largely because the property market had never really experienced any real decline in price and demand. The 1997 Asian economic crisis has actually turned around the home ownership culture. With a depreciation of more than 50% in property price in 1997-98, house prices have come down to the 1992 level. This is still considered expensive on a world standard. Nonetheless it has successfully proved the risks involved in home ownership. People who bought in the high point of the 1997 market suffered tremendously. Some of them blamed the government's housing policy and went on demonstration. A new chapter in home ownership has quietly begun.

Chapter two raised the issues of extreme over-crowdedness and spatial constraint in housing development as two unique factors which shaped an upwardly mobile housing market and provided additional pressure on house prices. Nonetheless, these factors only provide a partial explanation. There are other institutional factors such as the role of the government, family values and consumption culture as discussed earlier which also impact on the growth of home ownership. Two theoretical questions concerning capital gains and social change are raised here. First, given the fact that capital gains for homeowners are quite pervasive, to what extent can the money tied up in the housing market be used by households for other life chances? Second, how are capital gains distributed among homeowners? From the evidence of this study, the answer to the first question depends on the frequency of buying and selling. Those homeowners who involved themselves heavily in property transactions have apparently gained a lot more, although the right timing of entry to and exit from the market remains a key determinant of the level of gains. The findings suggest a different aspect of research on capital gains since in Western literature the emphasis is always inclined to focus on long-term gains and inheritance. In the case of Hong Kong, this is still the first generation of home ownership with relatively mild spatial variation when compared to Western societies. My findings do not reflect the issue of inheritance and regional variations in house prices.

To answer the second question, a rough map of stratification of homeowners according to the level of gains could be drawn on the basis of the cases studied. The highest gains accrued to those who entered the private market in the 1970s and continued to move around the best sector of middle class housing estates, such as Tai Koo Shing. Modest gains accrued to those who entered the market early, stayed put, and moved only when necessary. The least gains were made by those people in the government Home Ownership Scheme flats and old inner-city tenements. What is apparent here is a picture of stratified gains and hence a different impact on life opportunities. The pattern of capital gains in Hong Kong is somewhat biased towards those who bought their properties in the private market. The generalization drawn from this home ownership picture is consistent with what Western housing scholars (Forrest, Murie & Williams, 1990; Thorns, 1992; Hamnett & Randolph, 1988) have fought hard to demonstrate: that while capital gains exist, the spread is uneven and the home ownership sector is both segmented and fragmented.

An important theoretical question remains unanswered. Given a segmented home ownership sector with divergent and yet pervasive gains, what is the net effect on the society within the context of a rapidly changing environment? The answer is: if Hong Kong is already a divided society through years of ruthless capitalism, then what happened in the housing market in the last two decades had not just widened existing social inequalities, but further subdivided the existing middle class.

Entrepreneurship in Home Buying

Do middle class homeowners in Hong Kong utilize the process of home buying and selling as a way of developing a *housing career* or *entrepreneurship*? Do individual homeowners view the exchange-value of housing more important than its use-value and hence seek every means to maximize the exchange-value of their home? The current debate about this is fragmented and sketchy. Farmer and Barrel (1981) have suggested that during the home ownership boom period in 1965-79 in England, there was evidence that homeowners sought to maximize their capital gains from home ownership for a number of reasons. First, there was a clear government policy favouring home ownership. Second, there was a system of housing subsidy which included tax relief and low interest rate, and home purchase had become a comparatively more profitable form of investment. Farmer and Barrel have further argued that these favourable conditions for homeowners fostered speculation within the housing market as the volume of capital gains far outweighed other forms of investment. However, Farmer and Barel's study was based on indirect indicators such as redemption rate for mortgages and the distance and frequency of moving, and therefore could be criticized on the ground that it did not deal directly with the homeowners as entrepreneurs. Forrest and Murie (1989) have argued that there is the possibility of such an entrepreneurial group of homeowners, but they are likely to be people for whom mobility and occupational career are not paramount. Saunders (1990) has further suggested that since homeowners now move house so frequently and often without employment related motivation, they thus demonstrate a deliberate and coherent investment strategy through property exchange. However, Savage et al. (1992) have argued that there is no necessary relationship between home-moving and investment motive because a host of demographic and familial factors could also have the same influence in home-moving. Hence the argument is largely inconclusive. As shown in my case studies, the *stir-fryers* and the *pragmatic homeowners* do indicate to some extent the existence of a gradual interactive development of an entrepreneurial endeavour in home-purchase. In many cases, they started with a clear housing need, then moved on to fulfilling more needs (such as a bigger flat to accommodate the development of family life cycle), and then they became much more entrepreneurial, and eventually developed a housing trajectory closely connected with property transactions. Unlike the UK, Hong Kong homebuyers are not subsidized (except Home Ownership Scheme owners) in any manner. Before 1998, there was no tax relief and mortgage interest rate was fixed by the market. If there is entrepreneurial development in Hong Kong for home buying in the private housing market, it is certainly least influenced by government housing subsidies.

The question here is, to what extent, entrepreneurial activities are present amongst homeowners in Hong Kong? This is a difficult question to answer. More than half of the cases studied appeared to have motives beyond the realm of simple housing needs. This is not to suggest that there is an innate entrepreneurial inclination amongst the middle class homeowners in Hong Kong. However, if we adopt a more interactive framework, it can be argued that during the latter part of the 1980s, such an entrepreneurial spirit within home ownership became quite pervasive. In one case it was stated:

> I really can't explain fully to you why I got so involved in the housing market. There was enormous pressure, I guess, from my family, friends, colleagues and the society in general, that I must buy, or I'll lose, especially when you have already benefited from a booming market by selling your first home. It's so real and tangible. How can you resist the temptation? You see real examples around, your friends, your colleagues gained enormously by trading-up. I mean people just talk about it and do it every day. How can you stay calm and stay put? (Mr. Cheung (b))

Since 1990, there has undoubtedly been a very strong social ethos for people to become homeowners. The state of the market could best be encapsulated in the editorial of the South China Morning Post on 19 August 1991: 'Housing for the greedy instead of the needy?', which condemned the insatiable greed of home speculators. However, the theoretical question remains: how far does this 'collective greed', assuming it does exist, affects middle class formation?

Middle Class Formation

To answer the above question, three reasons could be adduced here. First, as described in Chapter five, it is apparent that those groups who live in the modern private estates built in the 1970s and 1980s have managed to harvest the highest gains from home owning and that they share a common consumption pattern (the so-called 'Tai Koo Shing syndrome'). It is impossible to say that being a homeowner of Tai Koo Shing one would be necessarily accorded a class membership, but as a collective, it certainly reinforces the middle class identity of people residing there.

Second, during the two District Board elections in 1988 and 1991, local political parties such as the Association for Democracy and People's Livelihood and the Democratic Party targeted Tai Koo Shing and Kornhill estates as distinct middle class communities. Political platforms with a clear middle class flavour, for example, more university places and the introduction of a mortgage tax allowance, were raised specially for such middle class communities. This points to the second reason. The middle class in Hong Kong is beginning to form distinct group interests amongst themselves according to their mode of home ownership. First, at the top of the hierarchy, there are modern estates such as Tai Koo Shing and Kornhill for the professional and managerial class; then there are the luxurious condominiums in the Mid-level for the upper service class, followed by Spanish-style low rise estates in Island South and New Territories East, which are for the upper class. The lower end of the middle class will either be in the Home Ownership Scheme flats or in distant modern estates in the New Territories, which although lower in price, provide facilities comparable to Tai Koo Shing. If Savage et al. (1992) and Bridge (1990) are right in suggesting that gentrification in London and other areas essentially indicate a new social class in the making, then the same could be applied in Hong Kong through home ownership. Since most of the land on which Tai Koo Shing, Kornhill and Whampoa Garden estates are now built were sites of old city tenements and derelict dockyards. Some parts of Wan Chai (used to be a red light district in Hong Kong Island near Central District) are now gentrified to become middle class residential areas.

Third, from a cultural perspective as argued in Chapter four, the pursuit for cultural capital through home ownership by the lower service class and the intermediate class is seen as providing one of the prime reasons for the growth of owner-occupation. In addition, differential capital accumulation through property exchange is considered an important force in strengthening middle class formation as well as aggravating segmentation within the middle class.

The home ownership picture being portrayed thus far is undeniably a picture of middle class in the making. Within a family income bracket of $20,000-$40,000 per month, a significant percentage of the cases being studied reaped substantial capital gains through home ownership, provided that they bought their first house before 1993. Financial gains from property transaction and home ownership have afforded them extra purchasing power and set in motion a 'home-chasing' process going beyond mere housing needs. For many people, home ownership, now represents both an *economic* and a *cultural capital*, providing them an opportunity for class advancement and general well being. Using Bourdieu's conception of *habitus*, Hong Kong, in the last two decades, saw extremely active production and reproduction of social conditions that led to a dynamic change in class structure. The engagement by routine non-manual worker, petite-bourgeoisie and lower-grade technicians in *home chasing* has triggered an intense process of social re-structuration. In Bourdieu's sense, capitals, both symbolic and economic, are essentially capacity to control one's own future and that of others. Capital is a form of power. While many Hong Kong Chinese place great emphasis on education for their offspring, many middle class people still possess little symbolic capital. The engagement in home ownership in places like Tai Koo Shing enables these aspiring groups to seek access to the middle class. On an individual level, clerks and other white-collar non-manual workers are seen as maximizing their capital through home ownership, while on a societal level, differential distribution of capital is seen as leading towards social change. In this way, home ownership in Hong Kong is seen as a situation whereby economic capital can be efficiently converted into symbolic capital and vice versa, through the active interplay of the habitus, capital and field.

Note

1. 'Middle class' is both a simple and a complex concept. Contemporary sociology has been fraught with conceptual and measurement problems for the middle class. The difficulties lie in drawing a clear boundary between the working and the middle classes. Traditionally, the separation of manual and non-manual workers seemed a plausible distinction between them. However, it has been suggested that such distinction is futile (Polantzas, 1975). For the purpose of this book, a broad definition of middle class is adopted, seeing it as largely composed of the service class and the intermediate class.

Part Three

CONCLUSION AND DISCUSSION

8 Economic Downturn and the Crisis of Home Ownership

This book began with the following scenario: a booming property market with rampant house price inflation as a result of enormous housing demand and house price speculations, a robust and restructuring economy, a government of declining legitimacy and a society with a strong desire for home ownership. The society was on the brink of a housing crisis for the middle class as house prices had gone far beyond affordability. This was the picture just before the handover of sovereignty in July 1997. The Asian economic crisis and the stock market crash in October 1997 have changed the entire picture. The unexpected economic crisis has triggered off a recession and a property slump. House prices depreciated more than 50%. Companies went bankrupt. Unemployment rate reached 6.1% in mid-1999. Many middle class professionals became jobless. Although the housing market has been somewhat stabilized in the first quarter of 1999, many think that it would go further down if the banking sector could not recover their bad debts from property-related loans. The worse scenario for the housing market is yet to come if the US economy cannot sustain its current vibrancy.

Against these backgrounds, this study poses two simple questions: (1) why did all these happen in the housing market? (2) What lessons could we learn from this? This final chapter will address these two questions in the light of what have been discussed so far. I shall first recapitulate what has been said about home ownership and social change.

Home Ownership and Social Change: A Recapitulation

De-constructing Rationality

One of the key critiques of this book is that the assumption of economic rationality in Hong Kong's housing discourse is essentially flawed and inadequate. A rational model only accounts for the more immediate circumstantial factors (such as the demand and supply of housing, interest rates, access to mortgage and housing finance, or the band-wagon effects of mass consumption psychology) of home ownership, and fails to take full account of the social side of home ownership. The theoretical underpinning of this point lies in the debate by Granovetter (1985) and Swedberg (1990) on the nature and limitation of neo-classical economics. The major argument is that economic decisions are deeply *embedded* in social relationships and therefore a rationalistic explanation for a high motivation for home ownership in Hong Kong should always be taken with caution. Moreover, it has also been pointed out that the hegemony of the rational model in explaining home ownership, not only distorts the housing picture, but also conceals serious unintended policy consequences. Another criticism of the rational model lies in the process of housing commodification. Once housing is treated as purely a commodity for exchange, the rationality model would naturally be further reinforced. Each actor within the housing system is deemed to be acting entirely on the assumption of utility and profit maximization, to the extent that the individual is treated as independent, isolated, and completely rational in choice. As a consequence, the variations and diversities of the social and family background of an individual is either trivialized or taken to be homogenous. Nonetheless, a word of caution should be made clear here. Individuals could be both rational and irrational. The distinction between rational behaviour and irrational behaviour is often difficult to draw. People flocking to buy properties in Hong Kong irrespective of high prices and market instability could be considered quite rational, because people expect prices to go further up. However, there is also a degree of irrationality here because people tend to stretch their mortgage burden to an extent beyond their consumption power and living standard.

Chapter two mapped out the major economic and political reasons for the growth of home ownership in the last two decades. Economically, it was argued that since Hong Kong was constantly besieged by the problem of shortage of affordable housing, coupled with a high level of economic growth, people were generally perceived as exercising their rational choice between the use-value and exchange-value of home ownership. A low interest rate regime, a highly resilient economic environment, easy access to mortgage facilities and, most important of all, extremely high yield potentials for real estates were argued to be the main rational reasons why the housing market became exceptionally buoyant and vulnerable to house price speculation. Politically, it was suggested that since the signing of the Sino-British Agreement in 1984, the Hong Kong government had been dragged into a dual process of confidence crisis and legitimacy decline. To maintain legitimacy and confidence in the run-up to 1997, the government reluctantly launched a series of social policies to woo the middle class to remain in Hong Kong. One of these polices was to promote home ownership through encouraging more capital investments by private developers in housing development.

This line of explanation stems from an assumption of economic rationality for both the state and the individual. On the individual level, the decision to move into home ownership is seen as the result of individuals seeking to maximize housing utility and investment returns. Owing to the extreme scarcity of land and housing, coupled with the potential for capital gains in property ownership, people opted rationally for home ownership. However, a careful examination of the housing histories of homeowners reveals that the assumption of individual rationality is to some extent over-generalized. While utility and profit maximization form part of an individual's goal in home purchase, the actual process of making up one's mind is much more complex, and at times even irrational. It is invariably influenced by other less rational elements, such as, family values, life cycle needs, social predispositions and even the pursuit of status. From the empirical evidence of the homeowners under study, there are strong indications that family values and relationship constitute significant factors that shape an individual's housing trajectory. While not denouncing the analytic value of the rational model, this book seeks a more balanced framework: one that attempts to institute housing histories, family values and consumption culture as a vital part of the debate on home ownership.

Re-constructing Home Ownership

Having revealed the limitations of the rational model, I then moved on to construct a more rounded framework. I started to re-examine the inherent physical constraints of this small international city and the historical factors that led to the growth of home ownership. In the process, the influence of the family on home ownership as well as the question of capital gains were examined. To summarize, the following four themes became the main tenets of my argument:

1. Extreme geographical constraints;
2. Housing history and social change;
3. The Chinese family and culture; and
4. Capital gains and middle class formation.

These themes, while essentially seek to account for the growth and development of home ownership in a particular society, also carry broad implications for the theorization of home ownership.

Extreme Geographical Constraints: Absolute Versus Relative Scarcity

Each society's housing system is invariably subject to a number of constraints. These include (1) the size and the growth of population, (2) the overall land supply, (3) the rate of new household formation, (4) the health of the economy, (5) the level of capital investment in housing, and (6) the state of building technology. The size and growth of population and the rate of new household formation essentially determine the demand for housing, while land supply and capital investments determine the supply. The full impact of these geographical variables together forms a *constraint picture* that sets the limit for the range of feasible housing policy choices. In most Western societies, the combined effects of overall land supply and population are such that they create relative scarcity of housing. Thus for international cities such as London, Paris and New York, where industrial, commercial activities and the urban working population merge, there is always relative scarcity in housing supply for various regions. House prices variations reflect this relative scarcity and homeowners who cannot afford expensive city life have the option to move to the cheaper *city fringe*. In the case of Hong Kong where there is only a very small suburban area outside the city, the distinction between the centre and periphery is effectively blurred. Both the size of the population and the land available for residential use (approximately 52 sq. km) have set a severe limit to the range of policy choices for the state. The effect of geographical extremities actually governs and structures the social relationships of housing. If the state is considered powerful and influential in housing policy, it is probably most powerful in Hong Kong. Why? Because the Hong Kong government controls two trump cards: land supply and public housing policy. If property developers are influential in the economy of other parts of the world, they probably have the most powerful manifestation in Hong Kong. The economic power of the K.S. Li family and the Cheung Kong Group needs no introduction. The power and infleuence of the Li family to influence policy outcome is seldom disputed. The major source of wealth of the Li family before the 1990s, came mainly from property development in Hong Kong. Extreme scarcity of land and housing resources have successfully constructed a pattern of social relationship in the housing market that clearly favoured domination by the developers in Hong Kong.

Implied in this logic is of course, the relative power position of the main agents within the housing system having a responsibility for production, distribution and exchange of housing goods and services. They are the Housing Authority, the Housing Bureau, the major developers, (e.g. the Cheung Kong and Sun Hung Kei Groups), the major banks, (e.g. the Hong Kong and Shanghai Bank and the Hang Seng Bank Groups) and the major real estate agencies (e.g. the Centerline and the Midland Realty). If the provision-thesis proposed by Ball and Harloe (1992) has rightly pointed out the importance, inter alia, of the way in which housing production structures social relationships, the housing situation in Hong Kong is such that the geographical factor (extreme land shortage relative to population) has facilitated the domination of housing producers to a level unraveled by any other capitalist societies. Any meaningful discourse concerning housing in Hong Kong, therefore, must properly address the question of geographical extremity as this is the only way to set the context of the housing question right.

Housing History and Social Change

Chapter five sought to examine the relationship between housing history and the society. The assumption is that the housing choice of an individual is intimately related to social predisposition in housing. The choice of home ownership thus reflects a long process of interaction between the individual, his family and the social environment. Arguing from a constructivist perspective, the production and reproduction of the living environment represents a long process of reflexivity leading towards the construction of an individual's housing trajectory. An individual does not just jump into certain tenure, although a rational explanation can provide some clues as to why such a decision is made within immediate circumstances. I have argued that extreme housing and spatial deprivation in the early life experiences of many people in post-war Hong Kong predispose the individual to a keen search for improvement in housing conditions in later life. Likewise, early deprivation in living standards also contributes to the formation of a culture of endurance, shrewdness and risk-taking as represented by the three core Hong Kong Chinese values introduced: *ngei, shingmuk* and *pok*. Such core values constitute a major part of the habitus of social change in Bordieu's terms. It is with these values that Hong Kong advanced into a culture of home ownership. By studying individual housing trajectories, we are able to witness social change in action. We are able to see how the impact of deprivation in housing solidified itself into cultural values providing the drive for Hong Kong's success. People's early housing trajectories, thus, provide the historical basis for the growth of home ownership. From the empirical evidence, all middle class homeowners coming under this study have demonstrated a history of extremely poor housing in childhood. One of the strongest life aspirations amongst these homeowners is to improve their housing conditions through home ownership.

The Chinese Family and Culture

The Chinese are well known for their close family ties. It became stronger when more than half of the families established their homes in Hong Kong after fleeing China in 1949. Local sociologists have suggested that a *refugee mentality* has contributed towards even stronger family relationships because it required extra bondage to cope with an extremely tough environment in post-war Hong Kong (Lau, 1984; Lau & Kuan, 1988). However, in recent years one of the new foci of research concerns the structure and intensity of *inter-generation help* between close relatives of the family network (Lee, 1991). One finding was that there existed an extensive transfer of both material and non-material help within the family network. Chapter six explored three aspects of this theme. First, it was identified that during the early years of home ownership formation, group ownership through mutual family financial arrangement prevailed. Home ownership was seen more as a family project to cope with the problem of affordability and housing scarcity. Second, the findings also revealed that there existed a matrix of intra-familial financial arrangements to facilitate down payment for home purchase as well as mortgage repayment. Financial transfers to assist home purchase were found to be going from the older generation to the younger generation. Such activities were practiced with clear assumptions of family bondage and obligations. In many ways, this could be seen as a form of *domestic banking*, seeking to maximize family financial resources before soliciting external aid. The paying of interest to family members is seen as circulating benefits within the family network. It is also seen as a form of *collective coping strategies* for the whole family network so as to strengthen individual coping power. The financial services provided are much more personal, made-to-fit and with highly flexible terms of repayment. Third, mutual aids were also found to be structured according to clear *priority of values*, with *family bondage and responsibility* as the primary motive, followed by the consideration of *reciprocity* and with *mutual advantage* as the last concern. One theoretical implication is that family mutual support in home financing in fact serves as an effective means to foster a culture of home ownership: the stronger the family mutual supports in home financing, the higher the chance of home ownership. Given the pervasiveness of a strong bondage within Chinese families in Hong Kong, its impact on home buying is enormous. The question is how such culture affects the society at large. This leads us to the last theme of the book - the relationship between home ownership, capital gains and middle class formation.

Capital Gains and Middle Class Formation

This book began with an observation of a housing problem for some middle class people - those households who are excluded from the public housing system and at the same time find private housing unaffordable. The 30 case studies of homeowners do not belong to this group since all of them have managed at some stage to purchase their first home. But these cases have revealed one important thing. When people are deprived of something they go all out for it later in life. They would summon all their resources and strive to become a member of the 'home ownership club'. While Chapter seven suggested that homeowners gained differently from home purchase, on the whole, homeowners have gained through home ownership as long as they bought their house before 1997. Many of them, who bought their home in the 1980s, now find themselves deriving better financial security and other life chances from their home rather than their job. The are the more fortunate ones in the current recession. This is a strange situation that even Western housing analysts find difficulties to fully comprehend since few housing markets in the world have enjoyed such a long period of price inflation without substantial adjustment. The Asian economic crisis is probably the only period in the history of Hong Kong's housing market that encountered depreciation in real terms.

The theoretical question being examined here is thus how such housing consumption culture and its resultant capital gains impact on the society. In particular, through what processes can home ownership affects class formation? Traditionally, sociologists in Hong Kong tend to relegate the class issue to the backstage. Some even argued that Hong Kong is essentially a classless society with only atomistic social groups. The family is the only thing that binds people together (Lau & Kuan, 1988). In recent years, local sociologists have begun to explore the process of middle class formation (Wong & Lui, 1992b). Using Bourdieu's (1984) conception of culture and Eder's (1993) exposition of the relationship between class and culture, Chapters six and seven argued that the growth process of the middle class in Hong Kong is related to the growth of home ownership through the concept of *cultural capital*. Class formation is seen as the consequence of constant struggles between various groups wielding different *cultural* and *economic capitals*. Findings from the case studies have demonstrated that both the lower service class and routine non-manual employees in commercial and administration jobs have a tendency to use home ownership as both an economic and a cultural capital to gain advance in class position. The aspirations of many routine non-manual employers (such as clerks and other non-manual white collars workers) to buy homes in Tai Koo Shing reflect *a degree of substitution* between economic and cultural capitals. Places like Tai Koo Shing and Kornhill which started as residential areas for the lower service class have now been gentrified to become strong fortresses of the middle class. While the traditional middle class still sees education as an important vehicle for mobility, many white-collar groups see home ownership as providing an *accelerated access* to the middle class. If traditional production-based class analysis is criticized as not entirely applicable to the case of Hong Kong, where historically there was an absence of organized labour and class consciousness, *a cultural perspective* offers an alternative dimension to explain the formation of the middle class in Hong Kong.

Henceforth, empirical evidence has pointed to two possible trends in social change. First, family values, entrepreneurial capacity and consumption culture have enabled some families to amass substantial capital gains through home ownership, resulting in an uplifting of social status and life chances. The most vivid example is that middle class families could now sell their homes in places like Tai Koo Shing and emigrate to Canada and Australia with a substantial amount of liquidity. The capitalization should enable a small family to live on interest for the rest of its life without having to work. This relatively privileged financial position acquired through home ownership has certainly augmented the division between those who want to emigrate but lacking the resources and those who could afford it through home ownership. Second, empirical evidence has also suggested that not all homeowners have the same level of capital appreciation. Homeowners in old inner-city tenements and civil servants who spent a greater part of their lives in private renting and who entered the housing market at a rather late stage certainly capitalize very meagrely. The middle class in Hong Kong has traditionally been rather fragmented amongst a number of occupational groups. It is the professional or administrator class who bought homes in premier housing estates such as Tai Koo Shing or Whampoa that benefit most from home buying.

Housing Policy for a Small City-state: Dilemma and Choice

This book has portrayed a picture of burgeoning home ownership stemming from historical, family and cultural factors. Behind this picture, we have seen a contracting public rental housing sector as well as a dwindling private rental sector. It has been argued that the state has deliberately opted for a policy of home ownership in the mid-1980s in order to regain legitimacy and to woo the middle class to stay on in Hong Kong. What has not been analyzed thus far is in what ways one can explain housing policy failures of the 1990s. What exactly is wrong with the state adopting a policy of home ownership with minimal government support? The argument being advanced here is that for a society so much constrained by extremities in physical and geographical factors, the choice of methods to allocate goods and services such as housing is extremely limited. While the commodification of housing is a common feature of many national housing policies, the form and extent of it differ enormously. It would be erroneous to assume that all societies are subject to a similar set of constraints and that identical policies carry the same effects for the housing system. Simply put, absolute scarcity in housing puts producers and providers of housing in an extremely dominant position. This position is rarely attainable in societies with only relative scarcity in housing resources. To do justice to Hong Kong, the full social impact of its sheer over-crowdedness of people and place could only be felt rather than explained. One only needs to walk along the promenade near the Kowloon Star Ferry to realize why house prices could skyrocket here but not in London. Why the market has failed to provide affordable housing for the middle class here and why not even in California?

My analysis thus far has led to two models of home ownership policy: a rational model and a social model. A *rational housing model* assumes that individuals seek to maximize housing utility and profitability. The state, in order to promote home ownership, would minimize intervention and allow the housing market the maximum freedom to exercise its distributive function in meeting housing demand. Housing as such is seen more as a commodity rather than a social goods. The process of commodification defines the social relationships of housing production, distribution and consumption. As a corollary of housing policy, a minimum amount of subsidized public housing would be allocated through non-market criteria. The state would assume that developers and mortgage lenders would exercise their benevolent conscience and take care to price housing at a *reasonable profit margin*. Of course, all these have to be supported by a robust and growing economy. The social consequence of this rational housing model is far from benign. The housing market would be highly susceptible to market fluctuations and irregularities. Government policies aimed at promoting home ownership through the two policy instruments: the *Home Purchase Loan Scheme* and the early 1990s' attempt to sell off part of the public housing stock, have proved this mode of intervention a fiasco. The state was just not powerful enough to exert sufficient influence on the housing market when most home ownership housing were supplied by the private market. In retrospect, given a strong desire for home ownership and market imperfections in the form of monopolistic competition and speculative activities, the state was actually faced with very limited housing policy choices. Should housing allocation be done mainly through the market or should the state intervene more? The answer to this policy question lies in a fundamental socio-political value towards housing.

The Tung Chee-hwa Administration was confronted with such a dilemma in July 1997. In his maiden policy speech in October 1997, he made a bold attempt - a new blueprint in housing policy, marking an important departure from the colonial housing policy. First, the government would make available more land in the following five years. The market would have sufficient information about land supply to minimize speculations. Second, the government promised to build a total of 85,000 new houses each year in the private and the public sector. Unfortunately, soon after this maiden policy was announced, the Asian economic time bomb exploded. The new government had to take on most political blame. The property market slump was socially constructed as the adverse consequence of a shifting housing policy. The political pressure to stall the new housing policy was mounting, particularly as a result of strong lobbying from big developers. In his second policy speech in October 1998, the Tung Chee-hwa Administration had to substantially tune down its original plan. But even the government knew that temporary political yield under bad economic weather is not going to solve Hong Kong's future housing problems. Something on a longer term basis is the only way out.

This leads us to the second model - *a social housing model*. The essence of this model lies in the fact that once a society decides to treat housing as social goods, then the state or state-appointed institutions must be able to assume responsibility for the production and distribution of housing. In a crude formulation, a housing policy allowing the state the competence to exert price influence on the market would mean that the state needs to either directly or indirectly produce more than half of the housing stock. The state would act like a big developer, but with a social responsibility. Housing investment in the public sector forms a vital part of the overall social development programme. Revenues from home sale will go into either housing investment or infrastructure development. This model may appear social democratic in flavor and stand in stark contrast to the current new right ideology where market is seen as the bulwark of efficient allocation. But for some societies suffering from extreme geographical constraints such as Hong Kong, and having gone through a painful and tortuous market housing path, it is now clear that some social goods must be allocated through the state to minimize the adverse effect of market failure. The distinction between the market and state in this way is thus unnecessary. The central housing issue for these highly constrained societies is hence not simply a matter of tenure choice. It is more a question of what mode of state intervention. A *social housing model* does not mean reversing to welfare state housing or giving up the market as a major distribution mechanism. What is being proposed is that, given the vulnerability of the housing market in some societies, and given the particular socio-political importance of adequate housing provision for an overcrowded mass, the state has no choice but to take a more active role since it is the only institution that has the power and capacity to regulate the housing market. The state, under such circumstances, would act like any big corporations, providing a full range of housing productions and meeting various levels of housing needs at *a socially competitive price*. The consequence is that large developers in Hong Kong would become more competitive and diversified, with their economic activities slowly shifting from the real estate sector to other equally productive sector of the economy, such as high technology. Empirically, the proposal by government to establish a cyberport to develop software technology in April 1999 as a joint venture with C.K. Li, son of the property tycoon K.S. Li of the Cheung Kong Group, is seen as an example of the slow re-structuration of the investment portfolio of large developers. Similar diversifications are happening with other developers such as Sung Hung Kei and Chinachem Group.

To further illustrate the relationship between the state and the market, the Singaporean housing model is a unique example to illustrate the happy marriage of extensive state intervention in housing and the use of market criteria in housing allocation. In the 1950s and 1960s, Singapore suffered from similar over-crowded living conditions as well as extreme geographical constraints. The government decided that home ownership was the favoured tenure for various reasons, one being an utmost desire to maintain stability at the beginning period of nation building and the other being the political necessity to maintain the legitimacy of the People's Action Party. Because Chinese people in Singapore place such high value on home ownership, it became apparent that home ownership was the best guarantee for votes (Chua, 1997). Since the late 1960s, the government began monopolistic domination in the housing market by the production of council housing for sale rather than renting. Using proceeds from housing sales, the Singapore Housing Development Board produces and distributes 90% of all housing stock at a competitive and yet affordable price. Housing affordability is guaranteed through a compulsory savings scheme - the Central Provident Fund - where pooled savings from the people are used for social development purposes. Singapore has one of the most stable housing markets and highest home ownership rates (90%) in the world. As a result of state domination in the housing market, private developers only produce luxury homes for an extremely small upper end market. Simply put, in a high-growth economy, the Singaporean government has decided that housing for the mass could not be allocated by the free market because it would easily lead to an income distribution strongly favouring the developers or whoever invests in real estate. Housing policy is fundamentally a political decision, made on the basis of knowledge about how the housing market works in congested and high-growth cities, with a strong aspiration for home ownership. The choice is thus between collective or market provision, knowing the devils of both extremes.

If the government leaves housing allocation to the private housing market, as in the case of Hong Kong, it would surprise no one that the development of monopolistic competition is entirely possible and predictable, given its physical and social constraints. The same applies to house price speculations. In Hong Kong, all these happened in the 1980s and 1990s. Developers went into elaborate pricing strategies to promote sales and speculations as well as forming themselves into secret cartels to influence government land supply. Large developers were, and still are, the most influential interest group in Hong Kong. Banks used mortgage loan ceilings and interest rates to promote or depress home financing. Unscrupulous real estate agents helped mark up house prices through the control of house price information. The housing scene in the last two decades could thus be seen as a 'housing casino' where the key players (winners) were the state, the developers, the banks and the real estate agents. Homeowners were either winners or losers, depending on their coping strategies and entrepreneurial efforts. As long as absolute housing scarcity prevails, all actors and agents within the housing system are confident that the value of housing will continue to rise. This housing logic works pretty well as long as the most fundamental condition prevails - a growth economy.

Epilogue: Economic Downturn and the Crisis of Home Ownership

The economic crisis that swept Asia in the second half of 1997 has succeeded in demystifying three notions about the Hong Kong housing market. First, that house price will only go up and never come down. Second, that housing provides the most secure tenure and the best form of investment. Third, that home ownership is a status-tenure. Many middle class homeowners now find their employment insecure and fear that they cannot afford their mortgage repayment if they begin to lose their jobs. For those who bought their homes shortly before 1997, many of them are on the brink of negative equities. Many young professionals are turning back to private renting as a preferred tenure since it provides more flexibility and choices. For the first time in the history of public housing, the much-preferred *Home Ownership Scheme* is now in very poor demand. Since the release of the Phase 20B of subsidized sale flats in May 1999, the response rate has been less than satisfactory, to the extent that the Housing Authority is planning to consider readjusting its entire policy on subsidized sale flats. The Housing Society (a small public housing agency concentrating on *sandwich class* housing development) has also been under tremendous pressure since a number of middle class housing projects put on sale in 1998 and early 1999 received poor responses. For many who bought flats off the plan in 1997-98, they are having enormous difficulties· in getting a bank loan big enough to cover its original price since, after the economic downturn, most banks have revalued their loans to buyers of sandwich class flats. This has caught many new homeowners in limbo because, if they cannot secure a big enough loan, they will have to give up their down payment and face possible lawsuits in breach of contractual agreement. Since the market slump in 1998, home sales and purchases have mainly concentrated in the new home market. The second-hand housing market has remained stagnant as banks only provide very low mortgage to homebuyers. Once the most cherished tenure in Hong Kong, the middle class now views home ownership with caution and skepticism. Is home ownership in crisis? Or is it just the economy in crisis?

Housing as a symbolic and cultural capital encapsulates the central theme of this book. Following the Asian economic downturn, the government is now seeking to establish legitimacy through a fundamental overhaul of the public sector. The recent proposal to corporatize the Housing Department by means of hiving off the entire housing management function to the private sector is one example. Within the spectrum of change, one of the least analyzed housing policies is home ownership. In a constructive and accidental way, the recent economic crisis has actually succeeded in unravelling the various risks of home ownership as an economic as well as social phenomenon. It is now gradually recognized that a single-tenure policy in the form of home ownership could be financially and economically vulnerable. Home ownership as a tenure is very much tied with the banking sector, the capital market and the construction sector. There is an intriguing relationship between these sectors as well as the labour market. Too little is known about the relationship between home ownership and the economy. Home ownership is not just a risky undertaking for the individuals, but could also be highly risky for the economy. It should not be identified narrowly as part of the broad housing policy. To achieve balance, home ownership policy should situate itself in a wider political, economic and social policy framework. A policy on mass home ownership cannot sustain itself in the long run unless the state is willing to obtain a social consensus on the nature of housing as well as to identify clearly the constraints and choices of housing policy. Unless the state is willing to commit itself to some form of risk-reduction measures, the policy of mass home ownership could be as risky as a mistaken monetary policy. Moreover, home ownership has been so long associated with the concept of security, to the extent that the concept of risk has never been seriously addressed. Although this book primarily focuses on Hong Kong, the findings and discussions should generate at least a beginning interest in a more thorough understanding of modern home ownership and hence a more rounded research agenda of the relationship between home ownership, economy and society.

Appendix A
Interview Guidelines

Name of interviewee:
Date of interview:
Time of interview:
Place of interview

Section One: Introduction

1. When did you move into this flat?

2. Did you rent or buy this flat?

3. How many persons are currently residing in this flat?

4. How many rooms are there and roughly what size?

5. When was this house built?

6. Have you recently renovated the flat? If yes, when?

Section Two: Housing History

7. Could you tell me the houses you have lived before you left your parental home?

8. Now could you tell me the houses you have lived since you left your parental home?

Section Three: Tenure Preference and Mobility

9.   Did you look at other houses before you chose this one? How many and where?

10. Why did you decide not to choose them?

11. Why did you not looking at any other?

12. How did you come to know this flat?

13. How did you come to decide on this flat finally?

14. Given the same sort of options and constraints, would you still opt to buy the same flat?

15. Are you satisfied/happy with the process of buying this house? Have you solicited the help of a real estate agent? If yes, how do you feel about their services?

16. Looking back, what do you think are the major factors that influenced you to buy this house?

17. When you bought this flat, how much did you pay per square foot?

18. Do you have any idea about the current market price of your house?

19. As far as financial gains are concerned, have you regretted buying this flat? If yes, where would you choose to buy and why?

20. Do you have an intention to move out in the near future? If yes, where?

21. Why do you want to move?

22. Are you happy with the state of repair and decoration of the flat as it now stands?

23. What have you done so far with the house? Is it necessary to do the job?

24. How do you feel about the house when you have done all these jobs now?

25. Would you put in the same sort of effort if you only rented this house?

26. Now looking back a bit, what do you think are the most important physical factors (e.g. environment, quality of build and design, reputation of developer, direction and view of the flat, state of furnishing and decoration, etc.) that influence you most when you decide to buy a flat?

27. Have you consider *Fung Shui* a factor when you buy your flat(s)?

28. From your experiences, what do you consider to be the main advantages of buying a flat of your own?

29. Again, from your experiences, what do you consider to be the main disadvantages of buying a home of your own?

30. Do you think owning a home of your own make you feel differently? (If yes, move on to question 31)

31. How different do you feel?

Section Four: Consumption Pattern and Housing Finance

32. What do your family usually do during holidays and weekends?

33. Have there been any changes in these consumption habits since you bought this house?

34. Many people in Hong Kong love to live in modern self-contained estates, what do you think of that?

35. Are you having a mortgage for your present flat? Which bank/financial institution are you using and roughly what percentage of your family income is spent on the mortgage of this flat? How much did you pay for down payment? How long is your mortgage? Does your bank give you a good interest rate?

36. What are the exact terms of the mortgage? (e.g. size of down payment; maximum percentage of mortgage loan, interest rate, penalty charges, insurance, etc.)

37. Do you think this is a manageable mortgage for your family? If not, how are you resolving the problem?

38. Did any of your family members contribute financially to the down payment?

39. Would you help if one of your family members needs money badly for down payment of a new house? Do you think you want to help?

40. Do you envisage any problem of repayment, say for the coming year?

41. If you were really in financial difficulty, what would be your contingency plan?

42. Do you expect to at least get back all you've spent on your flat (down payment, interest, principal repayment, cost of decoration, etc.) when you resell your flat one day?

Section Five: Family and Neighbourhood Relationship

43. Do most of your family members live around this area? (Draw a sociogram of the location of the major family members if possible.)

44. How often do you visit each other?

45. Do you think you belong to this community by now? (e.g. knowing neighbours by names; belonging to neighbourhood associations;

going to meetings and gatherings; chatting with neighbours; helping with groceries, mutual acquaintance amongst kids etc.)

46.   Are you happy with your neighbours? Why?

47.   Have you ever invited your neighbours into your house?

48.   What do you think of this neighbourhood (just the sort of place you expect it to be)?

49.   What about schooling for your kids?

50.   Are your kids enjoying the place and neighbourhood too?

Section Six: Employment

51.   Can you tell me something more about your job?

52.   What do you think about your present job ?

53.   If you are going to have a substantial increase in income, will you consider moving again?

54.   Do you think you want to live somewhere very near to where you work?

55.   Do many of your colleagues live around this community?

Appendix B
Profile of Homeowners

Total: 30 respondents, 19 males and 11 females

Name	Occupation	Ownership Status	Type of Housing (square feet)	Location	Remark
Mr. Chan (a)	Manager (foreign exchange)	early mortgage	flat in private estate (670)	Shatin, N. T. East	3rd time owner
Mr. Chan (b)	Assistant manager	early mortgage	flat in private estate (700)	N. T. North	2nd time owner
Mrs. Chan	Clerk	mid-mortgage	flat in private block (550)	Taikooshing, H. K. East	1st time owner
Mr. Cheng	Manager	early mortgage	flat in private estate (1,000)	Taikooshing, H. K. East	3rd time owner
Mr. Cheung (a)	University administrator	mid-mortgage	flat in private estate (900)	Mei Foo, Kln. West	2nd time owner
Mr. Cheung (b)	Factory owner	mid-mortgage	flat in private estate (900)	Taikooshing, H. K. East	4th time owner
Mrs. Chow	Senior nurse	outright owner	HOS flat (500)	Chun Man Yuen, Kln. Central	1st time owner
Mr. Chu	Surveyor	early mortgage	flat in private estate (900)	Yuen Long, N. T. North	1st time owner
Mr. Chung	Restaurant captain	mid-mortgage	flat in private estate (600)	Mongkok, Kln. Central	1st time owner

Name	Occupation	Ownership Status	Type of Housing (square feet)	Location	Remark
Miss Fok	University lecturer	early mortgage	flat in private estate (800)	Laguna City, Kln. East	1st time owner
Mr. Fung (a)	Insurance salesman	mid-mortgage	flat in private estate (700)	Castle Peak Rd., N. T. West	1st time owner
Mr. Fung (b)	Shop owner	late mortgage	flat in private block (650)	Yuen Long, N. T. North	4th time owner
Mr. Ho	Restaurant assistant manager	outright owner	flat in private estate (600)	Wanchai, H. K. Central	3rd Time owner
Mrs. Ho	Nurse	outright owner	HOS flat (600)	Lai Chi Kok, Kln. West	2nd time owner
Mr. Hui	Clerk	early mortgage	flat in private estate (800)	Taikooshing, H. K. East	2nd time owner
Mr. Kam	Accountant	early mortgage	flat in private estate (450)	Shatin, N. T. East	1st time owner
Mr. Kwok	School teacher	early mortgage	flat in private estate (700)	Hang Fa Chuen, H K East	2nd time owner
Mrs. Kwok	Accountant	early mortgage	flat in private block (950)	Yuen Long, N. T. North	1st time owner
Mr. Lai	Manager	early mortgage	flat in private estate (650)	Kornhill, H. K. East	1st time owner
Mrs. Lee (a)	Secretary	late mortgage	HOS flat (600)	Chai Wan, H. K. East	1st time owner
Mrs. Lee (b)	Senior clerk	early mortgage	flat in inner city estate (500)	Whampoa Garden, Kln. Central	1st time owner
Miss Leung	School Teacher	early mortgage	flat in private estate (750)	Lido Garden, Tsuen Wan, N. T. West	1st time owner

Name	Occupation	Ownership Status	Type of Housing (square feet)	Location	Remark
Mrs. Liu	Clerk	mid-mortgage	flat in private estate (1200)	Happy Valley, H. K. Central	3rd time owner
Mr. Mok	Social Worker	outright owner	HOS flat (500)	Shui Woo Estate Shatin, N. T. East	1st time owner
Mrs. Poon	Clerk	late mortgage	flat in private block (400)	Shaukiwan, H. K. East	1st time owner
Mrs. Sze	Executive Officer	mid-mortgage	flat in private estate (650)	Whampoa Garden, Kln. Central	1st time owner
Mr. Tse	Administra-tive Officer	early mortgage	flat in private block (750)	Kornhill, H. K. East	1st time owner
Mr. Wan	Technician (airport)	late mortgage	HOS flat (650)	Tsing Yi, N. T. West	1st time owner
Mr. Wong	Laboratory Technician	mid-mortgage	flat in inner city block (500)	Wanchai, H. K. Central	2nd time owner
Mr. Yuen	Manager	mid-mortgage	flat in private block (450)	Aberdeen, H. K. South	1st time owner

H.K. Hong Kong Island
Kln. Kowloon Peninsula
N.T. New Territories
HOS Government Home Ownership Scheme flat

Note: The profile data were collected in April 1994. All names of homeowners are fictitious.

Appendix C
Outline Map of Hong Kong

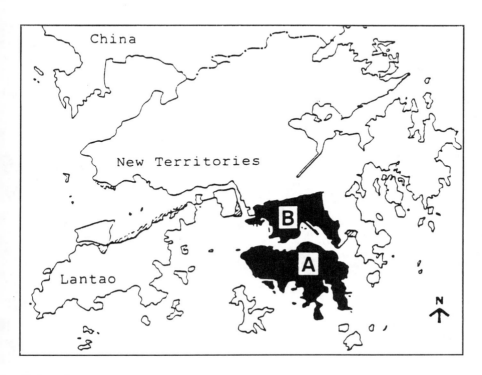

Urban Area

A Hong Kong Island
(major private housing estates are located along Northeast and Southwest coastal areas)
B Kowloon & New Kowloon
(major public housing estates are located in Northeast Kowloon; private housing estates are more scattered)
All new towns and new housing estates (private or public) are located in the New Territories.

Bibliography

Agassi, J. & Jarvie, I. C. (1969), *Hong Kong: A Society in Transition*, London: Routledge & Kegan Paul.

Ambrose, P. (1994), *Urban Process and Power*, London: Routledge.

Anderson, M. (1971), *Family Structure in 19th Century Lancashire*, Cambridge: Cambridge University Press.

Ashworth, G. J. & Voogd, H. (1990), *Selling the City*, London: Belhaven Press.

Auletta, K. (1982), *The Underclass*, New York: Random House.

Ball, M. (1982), 'Housing Provision and the Economic Crisis', *Capital and Class*, Vol. 17, pp. 66-77.

Ball, M. (1983), *Housing Policy and Economic Power: The Political Economy of Owner-Occupation*, London: Methuen .

Ball, M. (1986a), *Home Ownership*, London: RKP.

Ball, M. (1986b), 'Housing Analysis: Time for a Theoretical Refocus?', *Housing Studies*, Vol. 1, pp. 147-165.

Ball, M., Harloe, M. & Martens (1988), *Housing and Social Change in Europe and USA*, London: Routledge.

Ball, M. & Harloe, M. (1992), 'Rhetorical Barriers to Understanding Housing Provision: What the "Provision Thesis" is and is not', *Housing Studies*, Vol. 7(1), pp. 3-15.

Barlow, J. & Duncan, S. (1988), 'The Use and Abuse of Housing Tenure', *Housing Studies*, Vol. 3(4), pp. 219-31.

Bertaux, D. (ed.) (1981), *Biography and Society: The Life History Approach in the Social Sciences*, California: Sage.

Bertaux, D. (1991), 'From Methodological Monopoly to Pluralism in the Sociology of Social Mobility', in Dex, S. (ed), *Life and Work History Analyses: Qualitative and Quantitative Developments*, London: Routledge, pp. 73-92.

Bishop, P. (1971), 'Some Aspects of the Hong Kong Resettlement Program', in Dwyer, D. J. (ed), *Asian Urbanization: A Hong Kong Casebook*, Hong Kong: Hong Kong University Press.

Block, F. (1977), 'The Ruling Class does not Rule: Notes on Marxist Theory of State', *The Socialist Revolution*, Vol. 7, pp. 6-28.

Block, F. (1980), 'Beyond Relative Autonomy', in Miliband, R. & Saville, J. (eds), *Socialist Register*, London: Merlin, pp. 227-242.

Bond, M. (1991), *Beyond the Chinese Face: Insights from Psychology*, Hong Kong: Oxford University Press.

Bourdieu, P. (1984) (English Translation), *Distinction: A Social Critique of the Judgement of Taste*, London: Routledge.

Bratt, Hartman & Meyerson (eds) (1986), *Critical Perspectives on Housing*, Philadelphia: Temple University Press.

Bridge, G. (1990), *Gentrification, Class, and community: A Study of Sands End, London*, Unpublished Doctoral Dissertation, Department of Geography, University of Oxford.

Bristow, R. (1989), *Hong Kong's New Town: A Selective Review*, Hong Kong: Oxford University Press.

Burgess, E. W. (1925), 'The Growth of a City', in Park, R. E. et al. (eds), *The City*, Chicago: University of Chicago Press.

Burns, J. (1988), *The Hong Kong Civil Service and Its Future*, Hong Kong: Oxford University Press.

Burrows, R. & Butler, T. (1989), 'Middle Mass and the Pitt: A Critical Review of Peter Saunders' Sociology of Consumption', *Sociological Review*, Vol. 37(2), pp. 338-364.

Calhoun, LiPuma & Postone (eds) (1993), *Bourdieu: Critical Perspectives*, Chicago: University of Chicago Press.

Castells, M. (1977), *The Urban Question: A Marxist Approach*, London: Arnold.

Castells, M. (1983), *The City and the Grassroots*, California: University of California Press.

Castells, M., Goh, L. & Kwok, R. (1990), *The Shek Kip Mei Syndrome: Economic Development and Public Housing in Hong Kong and Singapore*, London: Pion Limited.

Chai, C. H. (1989), 'Economic Relations with China', in Ho, H. C. Y. and Chau, L. C. (eds), *The Economic System of Hong Kong*, London: Croom Helm, pp.140-152.

Chan, K.W. (1997), *Social Construction of Gender Inequality in the Housing System: Housing Experiences of Women in Hong Kong*, Aldershot: Ashgate.

Chan, R. (1982), *An Analysis of the Failure of the Ten Year Public Housing Programme in Hong Kong*, Hong Kong: Research and Resource Service.

Chan, S. (1985), *Social Conflicts and the Housing Question in Hong Kong*, Unpublished M.SocSc. Dissertation, Centre of Urban Studies and Urban Planning, University of Hong Kong.

Chan, W. K. (1991), *The Making of Hong Kong Society*, New York: Oxford University Press.

Chen, E. (1979), *Hyper-growth in Asian Economies: A Comparative Study of Hong Kong, Japan, Korea, Singapore and Taiwan*, London: Macmillan.

Chen, E. (1988), 'The Pattern of Economic Growth in Hong Kong 1961-1976: A Quantitative Analysis', in Leung et al. (ed), *Hong Kong: Dilemmas of Growth*, Hong Kong: Centre of Asian Studies, University of Hong Kong.

Cheung, B. L. et al. (1988), *Class Analysis and Hong Kong*, Hong Kong: Ching Man Publisher (in Chinese).

Chiu, R. (1997), 'The Promotion of Home Ownership in Hong Kong: Planning and Policy Issues', *Asian Journal of Business & Information System*, Vol.2(1), pp. 89-110.

Chiu, R. & Fong, K.W.P. (1989), *Urban Development in Hong Kong in the 1990s: The Implications of the Long Term Housing Strategy*, Working Paper No.40, Centre of Urban Studies and Urban Planning, University of Hong Kong.

Choi, C. Y. & Chan, Y. K. (1979), 'Housing Development and Housing Policy in Hong Kong', in Lin, T. B., Lee, R. & Semonis, U.E. (eds), *Hong Kong Economic, Social and Political Studies in Development*, New York: Sharpe.

Chua, B. H. (1977), *Political Legitimacy and Housing: Stakeholding and in Singapore*, London: Routledge.

Consumer Council (1996), *How Competitive is the Private Residential Market?*, Report on the Private Residential Property Industry in Hong Kong, Hong Kong: Consumer Council.

Couper, C. & Brindley, T. (1975), 'Housing classes and housing values', *Sociological Review*, Vol. 23, pp. 563-576.

Crompton, R. (1993), *Class and Stratification*, Cambridge: Polity Press.

Cullingworth, J. B. (1963), *Housing in Transition*, London: George Allen & Unwin.

Cuthbert, A. (1991), 'For a Few Dollars More: Urban Planning and the Legitimation Process in Hong Kong', *International Journal of Urban and Regional Research*, Vol. 15 (4), pp. 575-593.

Daunton, M.J. (1987), *A Property Owning Democracy?*, London: Faber & Faber.

Dex, S. (ed) (1991), *Life and Work History Analyses: Qualitative and Quantitative Developments*, London: Routledge.

Dickens, P. (1989), 'Human Nature, Society and the Home', *Housing Studies*, Vol. 4(4), pp. 227-237.

Dickens, P. (1990), *Urban Sociology*, London: Harvester Press.

Dickens, P., Duncan, S., Goodwin, M. & Gray, F. (1985), *Housing, State and Localities*, London: Methuen.

Director of Audit (1993), *Report on the Planning and Financial Control by the Government on Building the Hong Kong University of Science and Technology*, Hong Kong: Government Printer.

Doling, J. (1999) 'Housing Policies and the Little Tigers: How Do They Compare with Other Industrialized Countries?', *Housing Studies*, Vol. 14 (2), pp.229-250.

Donnison, D. (1967), *The Government of Housing*, Harmondsworth: Penguin.

Drakakis-Smith, D. W. (1971), 'Housing Needs and Planing Policies for the Asian City - The lesson from Hong Kong', *International Journal of Environmental Studies*, Vol. 1, pp. 115-128.

Drakakis-Smith, D. W. (1973), *Housing Provision in Metropolitan Hong Kong*, Hong Kong: Hong Kong University Press.

Drakakis-Smith, D. W. (1979), *High Society: Housing Provision in Metropolitan Hong Kong 1954 - 1979: A Jubilee Critique*, Hong Kong: Hong Kong University Press.

Dunleavy, P. (1979), 'The Urban Basis of Political Alignment: Social Class, British Domestic Property Ownership and State Intervention in Consumption Process', *Journal of Political Science*, Vol. 9, pp. 409-443.

Dwyer, D. J. (1970), 'Urban Squatters: The Relevance of the Hong Kong Experience', *Asian Survey*, Vol. 10(7), pp. 607-613.

Dwyer, D. J. (1971), *People and Housing in the Third World*, London: Longman.

Edel, M., Sclar, E. & Luria, D. (1984), *Shaky Palaces*, New York: Columbia University Press.

Eder, K. (1993), *The New Politics of Class: Social Movements and Cultural Dynamics in Advanced Societies*, London: Sage.

Etzioni, A. (1988), *The Moral Dimension: Towards a New Economics*, New York: Free Press.

Evans, P. (1987), *Bring the State Back In*, Cambridge: Cambridge University Press.

Farmer, M. K. & Barrel, R. (1981), 'Entrepreneurship and Government Policy: The Case of the Housing Market', *Journal of Public Policy*, Vol. 1, pp. 307-332.

Fetterman, D. (1989), *Ethnography Step by Step*, London: Sage.

Finch, J. (1989), *Family Obligations and Social Change*, London: Polity Press.

Finch, J. & Mason, J. (1993), *Negotiating Family Responsibilities*, London: Routledge.

Fong, K. W. (1986), *Housing Policy and the Public Housing Programme in Hong Kong*, Working Paper, Centre of Urban Studies and Urban Planning, University of Hong Kong.

Fong, K. W. & Yeh, A. (1984), 'Public Housing Programme in Hong Kong', *Earoph Journal*, Vol. 1, February 1984.

Fong, P. K. W. (1986), 'Public Housing Policies and Programmes in Hong Kong: Past, Present and Future Developments', in Choi, Fong and Kwok (eds), *Planning and Development of Coastal Open Cities: Part II Hong Kong Section*, Centre of Urban Studies and Urban Planning, University of Hong Kong, pp. 97-112.

Forrest, R. & Kemeny, J. (1987), 'Middle Class Housing Careers: The Relationship between Furnished Renting and Home Ownership', in Thrift, N. & Williams, P. (eds), *Class and Space: The Making of Urban Society*, London: Routledge, pp. 208-221.

Forrest, R. & Murie, A. (1987), 'The Affluent Home Owners: Labour Market Position and the Shaping of Housing Histories', *Sociological Review*, Vol. 35(2), pp. 370-403.

Forrest, R. & Murie, A. (1988), *Selling the Welfare State*, London: Routledge.

Forrest, R. & Murie, A. (1989), 'Housing Markets, Labour Markets, and Housing Histories', in Hamnett, C. & Allen, J. (eds), *Housing Markets and Labour Markets*, London: Unwin.

Forrest, R. & Murie, A. (eds) (1995), *Housing and Family Wealth in a Comparative Perspective*, London: Routledge.

Forrest, R., Leather, P., & Kennet, T. (1999) *Home Ownership in Crisis*, Aldershot: Ashgate.

Forrest, R., Murie, A., & Williams, P. (eds) (1990), *Home Ownership: Differentiation and Fragmentation*, London: Unwin, Hyman.

Franklin, A. (1986), *Owner-occupation, Privatism and Ontological Security: A Critical Reformulation*, Working Paper 62, School for Advanced Urban Studies, University of Bristol.

Franklin, A. (1989), 'Working Class Privatism: A Historical Case Study of Bedminster, Bristol', *Society and Space*, Vol. 7, pp. 93-113.

Friedman, M. (1981), *Free to Choose*, Harmondsworth: Penguin.

Gans, H. J. (1962), 'Urbanism and Suburbanism as Ways of Life: A Re-evaluation of Definitions', in Rose, A. (ed), *Human Behaviour and Social Process*, Boston: Houghton Mifflin, pp. 625-648.

Gans, H. (1990), 'Deconstructing the Underclass', *APA Journal*, Vol. 52, pp. 271-277.

Giddens, A. (1984), *The Constitution of Society*, Cambridge: Polity Press.

Giddens, A. (1991), *Self and Modernity*, Cambridge: Polity Press.

Goldthrope, J. et al. (1969), *The Affluent Worker in the Class Structure*, Cambridge: Cambridge University Press.

Goldthrope, J. H. (1987), *Social Mobility and Class Structure in Modern Britain (2nd ed)*, Oxford: Claredon Press.

Granovetter, M. (1985), 'Economic Action and Social Structure: The Problem of Embeddedness', *American Journal of Sociology*, Vol. 91, Nov. 1985, pp. 481-510.

Gugler, J. (1988), *The Urbanization of the Third World*, London: Oxford University Press.

Haddon, R. (1970), 'A Minority in a Welfare State Society', *New Altantis*, Vol. 2, pp. 80-133.

Hall, J. R. & Neitz, M. J. (1993), *Culture: Sociological Perspectives*, New York: Prentice Hall.

Hammersley, M. (1992), *What's Wrong with Ethnography?*, London: Routledge.

Hamnett, C. & Randolph, B. (1988), *Cities Housing and Profits: Flat Break-up and the Decline of Private Renting*, London: Hutchinson.

Harloe, M. (1984), 'Sector and Class: A Critical Comment', *International Journal of Urban and Regional Research*, Vol.8, pp. 228-37.

Harvey, D. (1982), *The Limits to Capital*, Oxford: Blackwell.

Harvey, D. (1989), *The Conditions of Post-Modernity*, Oxford: Blackwell.

Henderson, J. (1991), 'Urbanization in the Hong Kong - South China Region: an Introduction to Dynamics and Dilemmas', *International Journal of Urban and Regional Research*, Vol. 15(2), pp. 169-179.

Henrietta, J. C. (1984), 'Parental Status and Child's Home Ownership', *American Sociological Review*, Vol. 49, pp. 131-140.

Ho, K. L. (1990), *The Political Economy of Hong Kong Housing Policy*, Unpublished M Phil Dissertation, Department of Sociology, University of Hong Kong.

Ho, S. Y. (1986), 'Public Housing', in Cheng, J. Y. S. (ed), *Hong Kong in Transition*, Hong Kong: Chinese University of Hong Kong Press, pp. 331-353.

Hodge, P. (1974), 'The Poor and the People of Quality: An Inaugural Lecture from the Chair of Social Work', *University of Hong Kong Gazette*, November, 1974.

Hong Kong Government, *Hong Kong Annual Report(s) 1979 - 1997 (various issues)* Hong Kong: Government Printer.

Hong Kong Government (1967), *Kowloon Disturbances 1966: Report of Commission of Inquiry*, Hong Kong: Government Printer.

Hong Kong Government (1987), *Long Term Housing Strategy*, Hong Kong: Government Printer.

Hong Kong Government (1994), *Financial Arrangements between Government and the Housing authority*, Hong Kong: Government Printer.

Hong Kong Government (1997), *Long Term Housing Strategy Review: A Consultation Document,* Hong Kong: Government Printer.

Hong Kong Government (1999), *Hong Kong in Figures*, Census and Statistics Department, Hong Kong: Government Printer.

Hong Kong Housing Authority (1985), *Green Paper: Housing Subsidy to tenants of Public Housing*, Hong Kong: Housing Authority.

Hong Kong Housing Authority (1989), *Report of the Ad Hoc Committee on Sale of Flats to Sitting Tenants*, Hong Kong: Housing Authority.

Hong Kong Housing Authority (1990), *Report of the Ad Hoc Committee to Review Domestic Rent Policy and Allocation Standards*, Hong Kong: Housing Authority.

Hong Kong Housing Authority (1992), *Report on the Review of Schemes to Promote Home Ownership,* Hong Kong: Housing Authority.

Hong Kong Housing Authority (1994*), Long Term Housing Strategy - A Policy Statement, A Report on the Mid-term Review, Final Report on the Mid-term Review*, Hong Kong: Housing Authority.

Hong Kong Housing Authority (1995), *Safeguarding Rational Allocation of Public Housing Resources: Consultation Document*, Hong Kong: Housing Authority

Hong Kong Housing Authority (1996a), *Report on the Review of Home Ownership Schemes*, Hong Kong: Housing Authority.

Hong Kong Housing Authority (1996b), *Safeguarding Rational Allocation of Public Housing Resources: Report on Final Recommendations*, Hong Kong: Housing Authority.

Hong Kong Monetary Authority (1996), *Mortgage Corporation Proposal*, Hong Kong: Monetary Authority.

Hong Kong People's Council on Public Housing Policy (1985), *People's Green Paper on Housing Policy*, Hong Kong: Council on Public Housing Policy.

Hopkins, K. (1969), 'Public Housing Policy in Hong Kong: An Inaugural Lecture from the Chair of Sociology', *University of Hong Kong Gazette*, V XV1(5).

Hopkins, K. (1971), *Hong Kong: The Industrial Society*, Hong Kong: Oxford University Press.

Housing Bureau (1998), *Homes for the Hong Kong People into the 21ˢᵗ Century: A White Paper on the Long Term Housing Strategy Review in Hong Kong*, Hong Kong: Government Printer.

Hughes, R. (1968), *Hong Kong: Borrowed Place - Borrowed Time*, London: Andre Deutsch.

Humphries, D. (1977), 'Class Struggle and the Persistence of the Working-class Family', *Cambridge Journal of Economics*, Vol. 1(3), pp. 241-258.

Jao, Y. H. (1990), 'Monetary System and Banking Structure', in Ho, C. Y. & Chau, L. C. (eds), *The Economic System of Hong Kong*, London: Croom Helm, pp. 43-73.

Karn, V. et al. (1985), *Home Ownership in Inner-city - Salvation or Despair?* Aldershot: Gower.

Kehl, F. (1981), *John Stuart Mill's Other Island: Squatters, Real Estate and Hong Kong Government Policy*, Paper presented at the 1981 American Anthropological Association Conference; copy available from Registrar's Office, City University of New York, New York.

Kemeny, J. (1981), *The Myth of Home Ownership*, London: Routledge.

Kemeny, J. (1987), 'Towards a Theorized Housing Studies', *Housing Studies*, Vol. 2, pp. 249-260.

Kemeny, J. (1992), *Housing and Social Theory*, London: Routledge.

Keung, J. (1985), 'Government Intervention and Housing Policy in Hong Kong: A Structural Analysis', *Third World Planning Review*, Vol. 7(1), pp. 23-44.

King, A. (1972), *The Political Culture of Kwun Tong: A Chinese Community in Hong Kong*, Hong Kong: Occasional Paper, Social Research Centre, Chinese University of Hong Kong.

King, A. (1975), 'Administrative Absorption of Politics in Hong Kong: Emphasis on the Grass Roots Level', *Asian Survey*, Vol. 15 (5), pp. 422-439.

La Grange, A. & Lee, J. (1999), 'Housing Policy and the New Hong Kong SAR Government: A Preliminary Investigation of Trends and Implications' *Public Administration and Policy*, Vol.8(1), pp.39-60.

Lau, K .Y. (1984a), 'The Fact and Illusion of Massive-scale Subsidy to Public Housing', *Wang Hsia*, Hong Kong: Hong Kong People's Council on Public Housing Policy, pp. 4-6.

Lau, K. Y. (1984b), 'Public housing policy', in Ngan, R. et al., *Visions of Social Policy*, Hong Kong: Chap Yin Press (in Chinese).

Lau, K. Y. (1991), 'Chapter 18: Housing', in Sung and Lee (eds), *The Other Hong Kong Report*, Hong Kong: Chinese University of Hong Kong Press, pp. 343-388.

Lau, S. K. (1977), *Utilitarianistic Familism: An Inquiry into the Basis of Political Stability in Hong Kong*, Hong Kong: Social Research Centre, Chinese University of Hong Kong.

Lau, S. K. (1984), *Society and Politics in Hong Kong*, Hong Kong: Chinese University of Hong Kong Press.

Lau, S. K. & Kuan, H. C. (1988), *The Ethos of the Hong Kong Chinese*, Hong Kong: Chinese University of Hong Kong Press.

Lau, S. K. et al. (eds) (1991), *Indicators for Social Development 1988*, Hong Kong: Chinese University of Hong Kong Press.

Lau, S. K., Kuan, H. C. & Ho, K. F. (1986), 'Leaders, Officials, and Citizens in Urban Service Delivery: A Comparative Study of Four Localities in Hong Kong', in Yeung and McGee (eds), *Community Participation in Delivering Urban Services in Asia*, Ottawa: International Development Research Centre, pp. 251-258.

Law, W. S. (1988), *Housing Issues and Political Development in Hong Kong: An Application of Claus Offe's Approach*, Unpublished M Phil Dissertation, Chinese University of Hong Kong.

Lee, J. (1990), 'Housing and Social Welfare', in Lau et al. (eds), *Indicators of Social Development Hong Kong 1988*, Hong Kong: Chinese University of Hong Kong Press, pp. 69-82.

Lee, J. (1991), *Housing Studies, Urban Theory, and the Living Environment*, Proceedings of ICSW Asia and Pacific Regional Conference, 1991, Hong Kong: Hong Kong Council of Social Service, pp. 156-168.

Lee, J. (1992), 'Housing and Social Welfare Revisited', in Lau et al. (eds), *Indicators of Social Development Hong Kong 1990*, Hong Kong: Chinese University of Hong Kong Press, pp. 53-78.

Lee, J. (1993), 'Book review on Castells et al.: Shek Kip Mei Syndrome', *Housing Studies*, Vol. 8(2), 1993, p. 150.

Lee, J. (1994), 'Affordability, Home Ownership and the Middle Class Housing Crisis in Hong Kong', *Policy and Politics*, Vol. 22(3), pp. 179-189.

Lee, M. K. (1991), 'Family', in Lau, S. K. et al. (eds), *Indicators of Social Development 1988*, Hong Kong: Chinese University of Hong Kong Press.

Lee, M. K. (1993), 'Community and Identity in Transition in Hong Kong', in Kwok, R., Ames, R., & So, A. (eds), *The Hong Kong - Guangdong Link: Partnership in Flux*, New York: M. E. Sharpe.

Lefebvre, H. (1970), *The Urban Revolution*, Paris: Gallimard.

Lethbridge, D. (ed) (1980), *The Business Environment of Hong Kong*, Hong Kong: Oxford University Press.

Leung, B. (1994), 'Class and Class Formation in Hong Kong Studies', in Lau, Lee, Wan & Wong (eds), *Inequalities and Development: Social Stratification in Chinese Societies*, Hong Kong: Institute of Asia-Pacific Studies, pp. 47-72.

Lewis, J. & Meredith, B. (1988), *Daughters Who Cares*, London: Routledge.

Li, Y. Y. & Yang, K. S. (1976), *The Chinese Personality*, Taipei: Institute of Ethnology, Academia Sinica, Monograph Series B, No. 4 (In Chinese).

Lui, T. L. (1983), *Urban Protests in Hong Kong: A Sociological Study of Housing*, Unpublished Thesis, Department of Sociology, University of Hong Kong.

Lui, T. L. (1995), 'Coping Strategies in a Blooming Market: Family Wealth and Housing in Hong Kong', in Forrest, R. & Murie, A. (eds), *Housing and Family Wealth in Comparative Perspective*, London: Routledge, pp. 108-132.

Lui, T. L. & Kung, J. (1985), *City in Conflict*, Hong Kong: Wide Angle Press (In Chinese).

Madge, J. & Brown, C. (1981), *First Home*, London: Policy Studies Institute.

Malpass, P. (1990), *Reshaping Housing Policy*, London: Routledge.

Marx, K. & Engels, F. (1969), *Selected Works*, London: Lawrence & Wishart.

McGee, T. G. (1971), *The Urbanization Process in the 3rd World*, London: Bell & Son.

McLaverty, P. (1993), 'The Preference for Owner-occupation', *Environment and Planning A*, Vol. 25, pp. 1559-1572.

Merrett & Gray (1982), *Owner Occupation in Britain*, London: RKP.

Miner, N. (1975), 'Hong Kong: A Case Study in Political Stability', *The Journal of Commonwealth and Comparative Politics*, Vol. 13(1), March, pp. 26-39.

Miner, N. (1986), *The Government and politics of Hong Kong* (4th ed.), Hong Kong: Oxford University Press.

Mitchell, C. (1983), 'Case Study and Situational Analysis', *Sociological Review*, Vol. 31(2), pp. 187-211.

Murie, A. (1989), 'Divisions of Home Ownership: Housing Tenure and Social Change', A Conference paper presented at the University of Surrey, April, 1989, later published with the same title at (1991), *Environment and Planning A*, Vol. 23, pp. 349-370.

Nevitt, D. (1968), *The Economic Power of Housing*, London: Macmillan.

Nientied & Linden (1985), 'Approaches to Low Income Housing in the 3rd World', *International Journal of Urban and Regional Research*, Vol. 9(3).

Offe, C. (1984), *Contradictions of the Welfare State*, Mass: Massachusetts Press.

Pahl, R. (1975), *Whose City?* Harmondsworth: Penguin.

Pahl, R. (1991), 'Is the Emperor Naked? A Debate on the Adequacy of Sociological Theory in Urban and Regional Research', *International Journal of Urban and Regional Research*, Vol. 15(1), pp. 107-129.

Park, R. E. (1952), *Human Community: The City and Human Ecology,* New York: Free Press.

Pattern, C. (1998), *East and West*, London: Macmillan.

Planning, Environment & Lands Branch (1994), *Report of the Task Force on Land Supply and Property Prices*, Hong Kong: Government Printer.

Planning, Environment & Lands Branch (1995), *Urban Renewal*, Hong Kong: Government Printer.

Planning, Environment & Lands Branch (1996a), *A Consultative Digest Territorial Development Strategy Review 1996*, Hong Kong: Government Printer.

Planning, Environment & Lands Branch (1996b), *Urban Planning in Hong Kong*, Hong Kong: Government Printer.

Polantzas, N. (1975), *Classes in Contemporary Capitalism*, London: New Left Book

Prescott, J. (1971), 'Hong Kong: the Form and Significance of a High-density Urban Development', in Dwyer, D. J., *Asian Urbanization: A Hong Kong Casebook*, Hong Kong: Hong Kong University Press, pp. 11-19.

Preteceille, E. (1986), 'Collective Consumption, Urban Segregation and Social Classes', *Environment and Planning D, Society and Space*, Vol. 4, pp. 145-154.

Pryor, E. G. (1973), *Housing in Hong Kong*, Hong Kong: Oxford University Press.

Qureshi, H. & Simons, K. (1987), 'Resources within Families: Caring for Elderly People', in Brannen, J. & Wilson, G. (eds), *Give and Take in Families*, London: Allen & Unwin.

Rabushka, A. (1976), *Value for Money,* Stanford: Hoover Institution Press.

Rating and Valuation Department, *Hong Kong Property Review (Various issues)*, Hong Kong: Printing Department.

Renaud, B. (1989), *Affordable Housing and Housing Sector Performance*, Hong Kong: Centre for Urban Planning and Urban Studies Working Paper, University of Hong Kong.

Rex, J., & Moore, R. (1967), *Race, Community and Conflict*, Oxford: Oxford University Press.

Roberts, E. (1984), *A Woman's Place: An Oral History of Working Class Women 1890-1940*, Oxford: Basil Blackwell.

Saunders, P. (1978), 'Domestic Property and Social Class', *International Journal of Urban and Regional Research*, Vol. 2, pp. 233-251.

Saunders, P. (1979), *Urban Politics: A Sociological Interpretation*, London: Hutchison.

Saunders, P. (1984), 'Beyond Housing Classes', *International Journal of Urban and Regional Research*, Vol. 8, pp. 202-227.

Saunders, P. (1986a), 'Comment on Dunleavy and Preteceille', *Environment and Planning D: Society and Space*, Vol. 4, pp. 155-163.

Saunders, P. (1986b), *Social Theory and the Urban Question (2nd ed.)*, London: Unwin.

Saunders, P. (1990), *A Nation of Home Owners*, London: Unwin, Hyman.

Saunders, P. & Williams, P. (1988), 'The Constitution of Home: Towards a Research agenda', *Housing Studies*, Vol. 3(2), pp. 81-93.

Savage, M. et al. (1992) *Property, Bureaucracy and Culture: Middle Class Formation in Contemporary Britain*, London: Routledge.

Schiffer, J. (1983), *Anatomy of a Laissez-faire Government: The Hong Kong Growth Model Reconsidered*, Centre of Urban Studies and Urban Planning Working Paper, University of Hong Kong.

Schiffer, J. (1991), 'State Policy and Economic Growth: A Note on Hong Kong Model', *International Journal of Urban and Regional Research*, Vol. 15(2), June, 1991, pp.

Scott, I. (1989), *Political Change and the Crisis of Legitimacy in Hong Kong*, Hong Kong: Oxford University Press.

Segallen, M. (1984), 'Avoir sa Part: Sibling Relations in Partible Inheritance in Brittany', in Medick & Sabean (eds), *Interest and Emotion- Essays on the Study of Family and Kinship*, Cambridge: Cambridge University Press.

Shea, K. L. (1989), 'Income determination, fluctuation, stabilization and growth', in Ho, H. C. Y. & Chau, L. C. (eds), *The Economic System of Hong Kong*, Hong Kong: Asian Research Service, pp. 6-16.

Siu, H. H. (1993), 'Land, Housing Problems and the Limits of the Non-homeowners Movement in Taiwan', *Hong Kong Journal of Social Sciences*, Vol. 2, pp. 1-20.

Sklair, L. (1991), 'Problems of Socialist Development: The Significance of Shenzhen Special Economic Zone for China's Open Door Development Strategy', *International Journal of Urban and Regional Research*, Vol. 15(2), pp. 197-215.

Skocpol, T. (1985), *States and Social Revolutions: A Comparative Analysis of France, Russia and China*, New York: Cambridge University Press.

Smart, A. (1986), 'From Village to Squatter Area: The Historical Transformation of Diamond Hill', *Asian Journal of Public Administration*, Vol. 8, pp. 24-63.

Smart, A. (1989), 'Forgotten Obstacles, Neglected Forces: Explaining the Origins of Hong Kong Public Housing', *Environment and Planning D: Society and Space*, Vol. 7, pp. 179-196.

Smart, A. (1991), 'Personal Relations and Divergent Economies: A Case Study of Hong Kong Investment in South China', *International Journal of Urban and Regional Research*, Vol. 15(2), pp. 216-232.

Swedberg, R. (1990), *Economics and Sociology*, New Jersey: Princeton University Press.

Thorns, D. (1989), 'The Impact of Home Ownership and Capital Gains upon Class and Consumption Sector', *Environment and Planning D*, Vol. 7, pp. 293-312.

Thorns, D. (1992), *Fragmenting Society? A Comparative Analysis of Regional and Urban Development*, London: Routledge.

Titmuss, R. (1974), *Social Policy: An Introduction*, London: George Allen & Unwin.

Tosi, A. (1995), 'Shifting Paradigms: The Sociology of Housing, the Sociology of the Family, and the Crisis of Modernity', in Forrest & Murie (eds), *Housing and Family Wealth in Comparative Perspective*, London: Routledge, pp. 261-288.

Townsend, P. (1979), *Poverty in the United Kingdom*, Harmondsworth: Penguin.

Tsang, W. K. (1992), *The Class Structure in Hong Kong*, Hong Kong: Occasional Paper No. 17, Hong Kong Institute of Asia-Pacific Studies, Chinese University of Hong Kong.

Ungerson, C. (1987), *Policy is Personal: Sex, Gender and Informal Care*, London: Tavistock.

Van Maanen, J. (1988), *Tales of the Field: On Writing Ethnography*, Chicago: University of Chicago Press.

Van Vliet, W. (ed.) (1990), *International Handbook of Housing Policy and Practices*, New York: Greenwood Press.

Veblen, T. (1970), *The Theory of the Leisure Class*, London: Unwin.

Warde, A. (1990), 'Production, Consumption and Social Change: Reservation regarding Peter Saunders' Sociology of Consumption', *International Journal of Urban and Regional Research*, Vol. 14, p. 233.

Warde, A. (1992), 'Notes on the Relationship between Production and Consumption', in Burrow & March (eds), *Consumption and Class: Division and Change*, London: Macmillan, pp. 15-31.

Williams, P. (1983), *Social Process and the City*, Sydney: George Allen & Unwin.

Williams, P. (1984), 'The Politics of Property: Home Ownership in Australia', in Halligan and Paris (eds), *Australian Urban Politics*, Melbourne: Longman.

Williams, P. (1986), 'Social Relations, Residential Segregation and the Home', in Hoggart and Hofman (eds), *Politics Geography and Social Stratification*, London: Croom Helm.

Williams, P. (1987), 'Constituting Class and Gender: A Social History of the Home 1700-1901', in Thrift and Williams (eds), *Class and Space*, London: Routledge.

Wong, F. M. (1975), 'Industrialization and Family Structure in Hong Kong', *Journal of Marriage and Family*, Vol. 37, pp. 958-1000.

Wong, L. (1971), 'The Aplichau Squatter Area: a Case study', in Dwyer, D. J. (ed), *Asian Urbanization*, Hong Kong: Hong Kong University Press, pp. 89-110.

Wong, L. (1976), *Housing in Hong Kong: A Multi-Disciplinary Study*, Hong Kong: Heinemann Educational Book (Asia).

Wong, T. W. P. & Lui, T. L. (1992a), *From One Brand of Politics to One Brand of Political Culture*, Hong Kong: Occasional Paper No. 10, Institute of Asia-Pacific Studies, Chinese University of Hong Kong.

Wong, T. W. P., & Lui, T. L. (1992b), *Reinstating Class: A Structural and Developmental Study of Hong Kong Society*, Social Science Research Centre Occasional Paper 10, University of Hong Kong, p.30.

Woronoff, J. (1980), *Hong Kong: Capital Paradise*, Hong Kong: Heinemann.

Wright, E. (1985), *Class*, London: Verso.

Yu, F. L. & Li, S. M. (1985), 'The Welfare Costs of Hong Kong's Public Housing Programme', *Urban Studies*, 22, pp. 130-140.

Yu, F. L. & Li, S. M. (1990), 'The Redistributive Effects of Hong Kong's Public Housing Programme 1976-86', *Urban Studies*, Vol. 27(1), pp. 105-118.

Index